GENDER-INCLUSIVE LEGISLATIVE FRAMEWORK AND LAWS TO STRENGTHEN WOMEN'S RESILIENCE TO CLIMATE CHANGE AND DISASTERS

DECEMBER 2021

ADB

ASIAN DEVELOPMENT BANK

© 2021 Asian Development Bank
6 ADB Avenue, Mandaluyong City, 1550 Metro Manila, Philippines
Tel +63 2 8632 4444; Fax +63 2 8636 2444
www.adb.org

Some rights reserved. Published in 2021.

ISBN 978-92-9269-220-9 (print), 978-92-9269-221-6 (electronic), 978-92-9269-222-3 (ebook)
Publication Stock No. TCS210482-2
DOI: http://dx.doi.org/10.22617/TCS210482-2

The views expressed in this publication are those of the authors and do not necessarily reflect the views and policies of the Asian Development Bank (ADB) or its Board of Governors or the governments they represent.

ADB does not guarantee the accuracy of the data included in this publication and accepts no responsibility for any consequence of their use. The mention of specific companies or products of manufacturers does not imply that they are endorsed or recommended by ADB in preference to others of a similar nature that are not mentioned.

By making any designation of or reference to a particular territory or geographic area, or by using the term "country" in this document, ADB does not intend to make any judgments as to the legal or other status of any territory or area.

Please contact pubsmarketing@adb.org if you have questions or comments with respect to content, or if you wish to obtain copyright permission for your intended use that does not fall within these terms, or for permission to use the ADB logo.

Corrigenda to ADB publications may be found at http://www.adb.org/publications/corrigenda.

Notes:
In this publication, "$" refers to United States dollars.
ADB recognizes "China" as the People's Republic of China.

On the cover: A Hmong tribe woman carrying her child on her back in Sa Pa, Viet Nam.

Cover design by SDTC-GEN.

Contents

Figure

Foreword

Climate change is having a profound effect on the economies, environment, and lives of women and men in Asia and the Pacific. The evidence clearly shows it is also having a disproportionate impact on women's and girls' lives, including during and after climate-related disasters. Despite progress in reducing gender inequality in the past decades in the region, persistent gender gaps remain and have been exacerbated by emerging and regional challenges. The coronavirus disease (COVID-19) pandemic has also further exposed deep gender inequalities and gender gaps that remain in the region. It has challenged all stakeholders to work with renewed urgency to ensure women's resilience to shocks, including those related to climate change and disasters. As we collectively aim our efforts toward sustainable and more resilient development, it is clear that addressing gender inequality needs to be central to our work with developing member countries (DMCs).

With a strong institutional mandate on gender equality as one of seven operational priorities outlined in Strategy 2030, the Asian Development Bank (ADB) has been working to mainstream gender and reduce existing gender inequalities in projects that support DMCs in their efforts to become climate resilient, including through technical assistance to strengthen climate change and disaster management laws and policies.

Most ADB DMCs have ratified the United Nations Convention on the Elimination of All Forms of Discrimination against Women and adopted laws and policies to promote and support gender equality and women's empowerment. While there are many factors that affect progress on gender equality in climate change and disaster risk management, legal and institutional frameworks pose a challenge when provisions embedded into laws and policies do not consider women's specific needs, vulnerabilities, and capacity as agents of change. While gender equality is enshrined in the constitution of most countries in the region, much work remains to be done to eliminate barriers and discriminatory practices that inhibit women's rights and limit their resilience and adaptive capacity.

This report is a result of work undertaken by ADB's Gender Equality Thematic Group to promote national legislation that supports women's resilience through gender-inclusive approaches to climate change and disaster risk management. It is part of a regional knowledge and support technical assistance project on Strengthening Women's Resilience to Climate Change and Disaster Risk in Asia and the Pacific. The project specifically aims to increase the capacity of three DMCs: Fiji, the Lao People's Democratic Republic, and Mongolia, to develop and advance gender-responsive national and sector policies and actions on climate change and disaster risk management.

This report contributes to the growing body of work by ADB aimed at addressing gender inequality in relation to disasters and climate change, strengthening approaches to secure women's rights, and creating opportunities for women to participate equally in lawmaking and governance. While the main audience for this report are lawmakers, it can also serve as a tool for women's organizations, development partners, and other key stakeholders in engaging with governments to make laws and policies more gender responsive. The National Good Practice Legislative Framework used in this report can be used as an analytical tool to not only look at legislation relating to disasters and climate change, but also at broader legislative frameworks that have a major impact on women's resilience.

Much progress has been made in setting out a legal and policy framework in line with international commitments on gender equality, climate change, and disasters in the region. However, further efforts are needed to mainstream gender in laws and policies on disasters and climate change. We hope that the good practice examples of various laws presented in this report, while not exhaustive, will serve as starting points for our DMCs as they work to make their legal frameworks and laws more gender responsive.

Bruno Carrasco
Director General concurrently Chief Compliance Officer
Sustainable Development and Climate Change Department
Asian Development Bank

Acknowledgments

This report is based on work undertaken under ADB Technical Assistance (TA) 9348-REG: Strengthening Women's Resilience to Climate Change and Disaster Risk in Asia and the Pacific. The report was prepared under the overall guidance of Malika Shagazatova (social development specialist) and Zonibel Woods (senior social development specialist) in the Sustainable Development and Climate Change Department (SDCC) with support and contributions from Alih Faisal Pimentel Abdul, TA coordinator and Ma. Celia A. Guzon, senior operations assistant. Consultants Robyn Layton (gender and law) and Mary Picard (climate change and disaster risk management/environmental law) undertook research and analysis and drafted the report. The report was edited by Amy Reggers, gender and climate change consultant.

Special thanks to Samantha Hung, chief of gender equality thematic group, SDCC; and Sonomi Tanaka, country director, Lao People's Democratic Republic and former chief of gender equity thematic group, SDCC, for their overall support and guidance in the implementation of the TA.

The report benefited significantly from comments by Arghya Sinha Roy, principal climate change specialist, SDCC; and Takako Morita, senior council, Office of the General Counsel, as peer reviewers. Briony Eales, Victoria Bannon, Rosanna Drew, and Hannah Irving also provided inputs to the report.

Special thanks to the contributions of participants in national workshops in Fiji, the Lao People's Democratic Republic, and Mongolia.

Abbreviations

AADMER	ASEAN Agreement on Disaster Management and Emergency Response
ADB	Asian Development Bank
ASEAN	Association of Southeast Asian Nations
CEACR	Committee of Experts on the Application of Conventions and Recommendations
CEDAW	Convention on the Elimination of All Forms of Discrimination against Women
COP	Conference of the Parties
COVID-19	coronavirus disease
DMC	developing member country
DRM	disaster risk management
DRR	disaster risk reduction
DRRM	disaster risk reduction and management
DRRMC	Disaster Risk Reduction and Management Council
ECHR	European Convention on Human Rights
EIA	environmental impact assessment
FAO	Food and Agriculture Organization of the United Nations
FRDP	Framework for Resilient Development in the Pacific 2017–2030
GBV	gender-based violence
GHG	greenhouse gas
ICCPR	International Covenant on Civil and Political Rights
ICESCR	International Covenant on Economic, Social and Cultural Rights
IFRC	International Federation of Red Cross and Red Crescent Societies
IDP	Internally displaced person
ILO	International Labour Organization
ILO C100	ILO Convention 100 on Equal Remuneration
ILO C111	ILO Convention 111 on Discrimination (Employment and Occupation)
IPCC	Intergovernmental Panel on Climate Change
IPU	Inter-Parliamentary Union
Lao PDR	Lao People's Democratic Republic
LAT	legal assessment tool
LPGE	Law on Promotion of Gender Equality
LSE	London School of Economics and Political Science
MOLISA	Ministry of Labour, Invalids and Social Affairs
MSMEs	micro, small, and medium-sized enterprises
NDC	nationally determined contribution
NGO	nongovernment organization
OECD	Organisation for Economic Co-operation and Development
OHCHR	Office of the High Commissioner for Human Rights
OSCE	Organization for Security and Co-operation in Europe
SAARC	South Asian Association for Regional Cooperation
SDG	Sustainable Development Goal
SGBV	sexual and gender-based violence

SMEs	small and medium-sized enterprises
UDHR	Universal Declaration of Human Rights
UN	United Nations
UNDP	United Nations Development Programme
UNDRR	United Nations Office for Disaster Risk Reduction
UNFCCC	United Nations Framework Convention on Climate Change
UNFPA	United Nations Population Fund
UNICEF	United Nations Children's Fund
UNHCR	United Nations High Commissioner for Refugees
UN OCHA	United Nations Office for the Coordination of Humanitarian Affairs
VAW	violence against women

Executive Summary

Disaster risk management (DRM) and climate change laws are part of a national framework of laws which need to work together to support women's resilience. This report focuses on laws and policies, which are an essential foundations to build equality, prohibit discrimination, and empower women to participate in DRM and action on climate change. While the specific laws relating to disasters and climate change are an important focus area, good laws to support women's resilience need to extend much further. This report develops and applies a National Good Practice Legislative Framework (hereinafter, "the Framework") as an analytical tool to present a range of different laws across constitutional and national laws. It then provides individual country laws as examples.

This report can also be used as a good practice guide on developing laws that support women's resilience to climate change and disaster risk. It draws on international norms, national laws, and research to create a tool for policy makers.

The Framework used in this report builds on research into the differential impacts of disasters and climate change on women. Women suffer disproportionate impacts from disasters, including higher mortality rates, injuries, loss of property, increased gender-based violence, loss of income and limited access to the means for recovery. This is not because women are inherently vulnerable, but because they collectively start from a position of disadvantage relative to men. Disaster impacts also vary greatly between national contexts, types of disasters, and different communities, but gender inequality and differentiated gender roles in work and family are important risk factors. The process of DRM itself can also further women's vulnerability if systems and processes are not gender-sensitive and inclusive of women's differentiated needs and priorities.

Climate change also adds to overall disaster risk through increased weather extremes such as storms, floods, and droughts. Slower-onset effects of global warming are seen in agriculture, forestry, water, and fisheries, through changes in weather patterns and temperatures, sea level rise, and ocean acidification, as well as disease vectors such as malarial mosquitoes and crop pests moving into newly warmer regions. All of these require adaptation responses as they impact livelihoods and well-being, and may force people to move away from high-risk areas or inundated islands and shores. Unless women are empowered as equal participants and decision-makers, government actions to respond to these changes through adaptation and mitigation can also reinforce existing gender inequalities and limit women's access to emerging opportunities.

Too often, laws and policies on climate change and disasters fail to include women, and when they do, they are described as a vulnerable group or recognized only in relation to women's reproductive role such as childbearing. While it is essential to meet women's sexual and reproductive health needs in disasters and prevent and respond to gender-based violence in disaster-affected, climate-stressed, and displaced communities, there is an overarching need to address underlying gender inequalities and the need for women's empowerment.

Countries need to fulfill their economic and social rights obligations and adopt proactive measures to promote gender equality and women's empowerment to address gender inequality in relation to disasters and climate change. These include women's rights to participate equally in lawmaking and governance; be free from violence and sexual harassment; receive equal remuneration for work of equal value; equality in access to inheritance, land, and assets; decent employment and business opportunities; all of which contribute to women's resilience to shocks and climate-related disasters.

The report provides a Framework and is a resource for law and policy makers in developing laws that support women's resilience to climate change and disaster risk. It is structured by topic, each of which:

(i)   explains the context and challenges;

(ii)   identifies the relevant international norms and guidance;

(iii)   defines "key elements" of good law for the topic. These elements are distilled from the international norms and legal research and are effectively a checklist for lawmakers to ensure that each type of law supports women's empowerment and resilience;

(iv)   provides examples of "good laws"* or legal provisions as practical illustrations, drawn from Asia and the Pacific and beyond; and

(v)   includes additional notes for lawmakers tasked with drafting or amending laws.

Part 1 of the report provides an overview of the research documenting the ways in which women are differentially impacted by disasters and climate change. Part 2 provides an overview of women's human rights in international law and their implementation in domestic law through constitutional provisions, national laws on gender equality, and laws that support gender mainstreaming in the lawmaking processes.

Parts 3 and 4 consider the elements of good gender-sensitive laws on disasters and climate change. This includes environmental laws, environmental impacts assessments, and regulation of planned relocations. Using international norms and guidance, the report sets out the key elements needed to make such laws gender-sensitive and identifies some good law examples. Finding that most laws and institutions for disaster, climate, and the environment are not gender sensitive, it also explores how these systems can be strengthened through improved links to constitutional rights and gender equality laws. This also demonstrates that DRM and climate change laws are part of a national framework of laws, which need to work together to support women's resilience. A section on the interpretation of these laws by judges in litigated cases sheds light on likely future directions in enforcement of the positive obligations of governments to protect resident populations from climate change, including attention to the differential impacts on women.

Part 5 of the report focuses on laws that underpin a range of other important rights and opportunities that support women's overall resilience in the face of climate and disaster risk. The selected topics include the essential ingredients for strengthening women's socioeconomic status and opportunities, including the need for good laws to:

(i)   combat violence against women, which is a form of gender discrimination that reduces women's health and well-being, impacts their livelihoods through lost time in work or education, and increases their vulnerability to shocks due to diminished personal and economic resources;

(ii)   protect the right to decent work and income, by prohibiting sexual harassment in the workplace and underpinning equal remuneration for work of equal value, minimum wage setting, and monitoring working conditions; and

(iii)   establish and enforce women's legal rights to assets and resources, including gender equality in access to and control over land, inheritance, and housing. It also includes opportunities to own and manage businesses, especially accessing micro, small, and medium-sized enterprises development.

Part 6 makes concluding observations and highlights the different ways in which the National Good Practice Legislative Framework can be used.

---

*   Good laws are those that include a number of "key elements," which may be contained within individual laws or provisions, or in combination with other laws.

Background

Globally, women are disproportionately affected by the negative impacts of disasters and climate change. This is largely due to the preexisting structural disadvantages in society that leads to inequality, discrimination, and the exclusion of women from decision-making. This affects their ability to withstand disaster and climate shocks and stresses and leads to much poorer outcomes as compared to men. Laws and policies at the national and international levels can play a critical role in addressing this imbalance. However, there still are significant barriers that must be overcome to better support the inclusion of women in laws and policies on disasters and climate change, as well as to ensure equal outcomes of social and economic resilience.

Purpose of This Report

The purpose of this report is to provide a conceptual framework and good practice guide, based on international norms and examples of good national laws, to support governments to develop laws that better support women and ensure their full and effective participation and empowerment in disaster risk management (DRM) and action on climate change.

This report is intended as a resource that will benefit governments, as well as organizations and individuals engaged in supporting governments to implement legislative reform. It provides specific guidance for strengthening gender-inclusive legislative frameworks and implementing gender-sensitive laws to increase women's resilience to climate and disaster risk. It can also support public awareness by offering a basic source of information on rights and legislation related to climate change and disaster risk management, as well as how these measures can support women's resilience.

Some content is targeted specifically to lawmakers. Lawmakers are those who are directly involved in the drafting or revision of legislation, often in various sector ministries, and who may not be as conversant with the broader content of climate change and disaster risk management and gender-related issues. Issues for specific consideration are included in the "Notes for Lawmakers" sections in each topic.

Structure of This Report

The report structure comprises several parts:

Part 1: Understanding gender differences in the context of disaster and climate change provides an overview, based on current research of how women's experience of disasters and climate change can be different from men's experience. It addresses both the impact of these events on women, as well as their participation in mitigation and response systems, emphasizing the critical importance of addressing these issues through legal frameworks.

Part 2: Overview of international norms and national legal frameworks provides a brief summary of the main legal instruments and other persuasive international guidance directly relevant to issues of gender equality and women's empowerment in the context of disasters and climate change. It notes the significance of the United Nations Convention on the Elimination of All Forms of Discrimination against Women (CEDAW) Committee General Recommendation 37 of 2018 (GR37) on climate change and disaster risk, which guides the National Good Practice Legislative Framework and the framework for this report.

Parts 3, 4, and 5 address a range of specific topics arranged thematically as follows:

(i) **Part 3: Good gender-sensitive lawmaking** describes the relationship between national laws and policies and the role of international law in establishing rights, standards, and norms in this area. It outlines the requirements for lawmaking processes that are gender responsive and inclusive of women, which are essential underpinnings for good gender-sensitive laws.

(ii) **Part 4: Gender-sensitive disaster risk management and climate change** addresses legislation specifically developed to support climate change and disaster risk management, as well as environmental laws and regulations related to environmental impacts of development and relocation of communities. It provides key elements and examples of how these could be more inclusive of women. It also analyzes recent case law to show how courts have interpreted laws in this area with regard to gender and inclusion.

(iii) **Part 5: Good lawmaking to improve the overall resilience of women** addresses the wider legal framework on key areas that contribute to the safety of women and support their social and economic empowerment to better withstand and contribute to the mitigation of disasters and the negative impacts of climate change. These include combating violence against women and protecting the right to decent work and income (prohibiting workplace sexual harassment, supporting equal remuneration for work of equal value, minimum wage setting, and monitoring working conditions). It also includes enforcing women's legal rights to assets and resources (gender equality in access to land, inheritance and housing, and to micro, small, and medium-sized enterprises [MSMEs] development).

Each of the preceding parts is structured in the following way:

(i) **Context.** A brief background to contextualize the issues.
(ii) **International norms.** A list of key international norms from which the key elements have been derived and/or adapted.
(iii) **Key elements for good laws.** A summary of the legislative content required to constitute "good laws" on this topic.
(iv) **Examples of good laws.** Extracts or descriptions of legislation from different countries that illustrate aspects of the key elements and why they are examples of good law and relevant to strengthening women's resilience to climate and disaster risk.
(v) **Notes for lawmakers.** Additional observations and commentary on the topic which may be useful for lawmakers are placed in a spotlight box at the beginning of each section.

Part 6: Concluding observations draw together some overall conclusions based on the report as a whole.

Methodology

The research for this report included desk research, and in-country discussions and workshops for three countries (Fiji, the Lao People's Democratic Republic, and Mongolia) that gave valuable specific information and insights on the laws and legislative frameworks. The CEDAW General Recommendation 37 (detailed in the next section) provided guidance on the scope of laws to be assessed and analyzed. The combined research contributed to the development of a National Good Practice Legislative Framework.

Development of the National Good Practice Legislative Framework

The National Good Practice Legislative Framework (hereinafter, "the Framework") was developed primarily through desk-based research on international norms derived from international agreements, covenants, conventions, strategies, and other international standards on gender equality, disaster risk reduction, and climate change, as well as reports from United Nations bodies, academic institutions, and general publications. In particular, the CEDAW Committee's GR37 on "gender-related dimensions of disaster risk reduction in the context of climate change" was used as an anchor for this research as it sets out guidance for States Parties on the implementation of their obligations under the CEDAW in relation to disaster risk reduction and climate change. In particular, GR37:

(i) Highlights the underlying inequalities faced by women and girls that mean they are less able to adapt to the negative impacts of disasters and climate change.

(ii) Urges States Parties to take effective measures to prevent and mitigate the adverse effects of, and respond to, disasters and climate change to ensure that the human rights of women and girls are respected, protected, and fulfilled.

(iii) Emphasizes the importance of taking a "legislative framework" approach to national laws in implementing the CEDAW and supporting women's resilience.

(iv) Requires States Parties to not only address laws and policies specific to climate and disaster risk, but also those that affect the broader socioeconomic position of women including:
    (a) rights to substantive equality and nondiscrimination,
    (b) rights to participation and empowerment,
    (c) rights to accountability and access to justice,
    (d) rights to work and social protection, and
    (e) rights to health and living standards.

(v) Emphasizes the importance of data collection and the monitoring and assessment of laws. These aspects are also supported by the Sustainable Development Goals (SDGs) agreed under *Transforming Our World: The 2030 Agenda for Sustainable Development* (2030 Agenda), in particular SDG5, which provides a supplementary monitoring mechanism through global data collection against SDG indicators.

The content of GR37 provides the overall structure for this report and the Framework (Figure). It was used to identify the legal topics that are most relevant to achieve the purpose of this report, namely:

(i) gender-sensitive laws on climate change;
(ii) gender-sensitive laws on DRM;
(iii) laws to promote equality and prohibit discrimination against women;

(iv)   gender mainstreaming in lawmaking;
(v)   laws prohibiting gender-based violence (GBV) against women;
(vi)   laws on decent work and employment for women:
    (a)   sexual harassment in the workplace,
    (b)   equal remuneration for work of equal value,
    (c)   minimum wage setting, and
    (d)   monitoring decent work conditions, and
(vii) laws to improve women's rights to assets and resources:
    (a)   land,
    (b)   inheritance and housing, and
    (c)   support for women's MSMEs.

Figure: A National Good Practice Legislative Framework for Strengthening Women's Resilience to Climate Change and Disasters

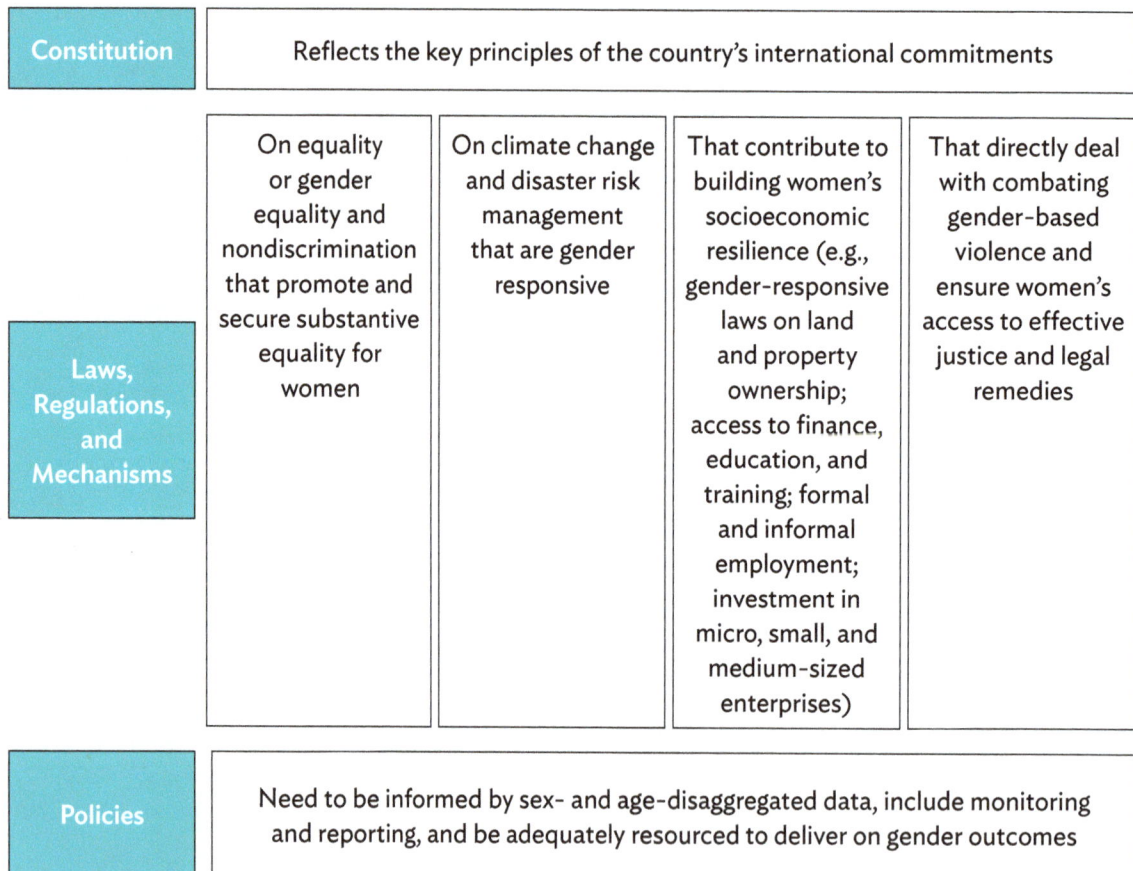

Constitution	Reflects the key principles of the country's international commitments			
Laws, Regulations, and Mechanisms	On equality or gender equality and nondiscrimination that promote and secure substantive equality for women	On climate change and disaster risk management that are gender responsive	That contribute to building women's socioeconomic resilience (e.g., gender-responsive laws on land and property ownership; access to finance, education, and training; formal and informal employment; investment in micro, small, and medium-sized enterprises)	That directly deal with combating gender-based violence and ensure women's access to effective justice and legal remedies
Policies	Need to be informed by sex- and age-disaggregated data, include monitoring and reporting, and be adequately resourced to deliver on gender outcomes			

Source: Developed for this report based on the Convention on the Elimination of All Forms of Discrimination against Women General Recommendation 37.

Many of the topics also include cross-cutting themes on participation and empowerment of women; accountability and access to justice; and data collection, monitoring, and assessment. Not every topic of law relevant to women's resilience was selected for review, notably health, education, and social security. These are complex issues and are often addressed primarily by policies. It was considered beyond the scope of this report to try to address them.

GR37 also mentions the importance of equitable natural resource management. In addition to the overarching national laws on climate change and the environment, natural resource management includes many specific laws on aspects such as forests, land, water, fisheries, and agriculture. While the relevance of these sector laws in addressing climate change is recognized, each of these is a complex area of legal regulation in its own right and is beyond the scope of this study. However, the gender issues raised in this report on access to land, and the challenges for women's participation and equality in disaster, climate, and environmental management, also apply to law reform in sector laws on natural resource management.

Once the Framework was identified, the research specifically focused on individual laws in countries globally and, more particularly, in Asia and the Pacific, to identify the "key elements" for the "good laws" on each of the topics for this report (discussed further in the report). "Key elements" are the characteristics identified from the international norms and the overall research, as well as drawing on the specific knowledge and experience of the consultants on international and comparative law on each topic. These "key elements" individually or collectively contribute to a "good law" on the topic.

Identifying Examples of Good Laws

The examples of good laws provided in this report may be entire laws, specific articles or sections of a law, or combinations of laws, which contain some or all the key elements. There are no perfect or "model" laws. The very nature of law requires continual adjustment and amendment to take account of new circumstances, new knowledge, and unique country contexts. The good law examples provided are not exhaustive, but serve as a sample for illustration purposes.

To qualify as a "good law" for the purposes of this report, it is not essential to know whether or how that law is implemented. This is a common methodology in comparative law research.[1] An analysis of the extent to which each "good law" example is implemented in each country is beyond the scope of the current project, as it requires a greater depth of country knowledge and highly specific quantitative and qualitative sex-disaggregated data sets. However, laws that provide for effective monitoring and assessment mechanisms are important requirements as they identify whether the objectives of the law are implemented effectively in practice and can lead to important modifications and improvements to the law.

---

[1] For example, international monitoring bodies such as the CEDAW Committee and the International Labour Organization (ILO) comment favorably simply on the basis that certain laws have been passed by a country (although they also call for additional information on their implementation). Similarly, the World Bank Group's annual *Women, Business and Law Report* also assesses improvements in the 190 countries reviewed, based on the existence of laws in the country and addressing the eight criteria of laws to assess gender progress.

Part 1
Gender Differences in the Context of Disasters and Climate Change

To appreciate the critical role of legislation in supporting women's resilience, it is important to understand how disasters and the negative impacts of climate change can be experienced differently by women compared to men. These experiences are further influenced by other factors such as poverty, health, ethnicity, and locations in rural or urban environments. While the available statistical data has many gaps, it reveals several common trends and issues that are highly relevant to the development of good law.

Gender Differences in Disaster Situations

Much is understood about the gendered impacts of disasters, largely based on post-disaster needs assessments (PDNAs), evaluations of response efforts, and country case studies. This evidence presents gender differences in survival, access to relief and recovery assistance, sex discrimination, and gender-based violence (GBV), and economic impacts and recovery exist and disproportionately affect women more than men. This section presents evidence on the gender differences in disasters with examples from Asia and the Pacific.

The relative lack of equality between men and women in social, economic, and political spheres influences the differentiated impact of disasters. A meta-analysis of reports on disasters in 141 countries found that higher death rates for women were directly linked to their level of economic and social rights as compared to men.[2] In societies where women and men enjoyed equal rights, there were no significant differences in the number of deaths based on sex (footnote 2). A recent analysis of 85 less developed countries found that improving women's economic standing both directly and indirectly reduced the human cost of disasters.[3]

Many factors affect people's survival in sudden-onset hazards such as cyclones. In terms of disaster preparedness, these include the quality of buildings and infrastructure, the extent of household preparedness, and the effectiveness and reach of early warning systems. Women are often excluded from decision-making on disaster preparedness and information on early warning systems is often shared in ways that are inaccessible to women.[4] In terms of immediate disaster response, people's location in relation to the hazard and their autonomy, capacity, and means to evacuate are important. In Bangladesh, male heads of household are typically responsible for evacuation decisions and the purdah system restricts women's independent movement.[5] If male heads of household are not present during disaster warnings, marginalized women's evacuation may be delayed, putting them at greater risk.[6] The efficiency and scope of initial rescue response and medical

---

[2] E. Neumayer and T. Plumper. 2007. The Gendered Nature of Natural Disasters: The Impact of Catastrophic Events on the Gender Gap in Life Expectancy 1981–2002. *Annals of the American Association of Geographers.* 97 (3). pp. 551–566.

[3] K.F. Austin and K.A. McKinney. 2016. Disaster Devastation in Poor Nations: The Direct and Indirect Effects of Gender Equality, Ecological Losses, and Development. *Social Forces.* 95. pp. 355–380.

[4] UN Women and UN Development Programme (UNDP). 2018. *Gender and Disaster Risk Management in Europe and Central Asia.* Istanbul. pp. 62–64.

[5] E. Alam, and A.E. Collins. 2010. Cyclone Disaster Vulnerability and Response Experiences in Coastal Bangladesh. *Disasters.* 34 (4). pp. 931–954; L. Juran, and J. Trivedi. 2015. Women, Gender Norms, and Natural Disasters in Bangladesh. *Geographical Review.* 105 (4). pp. 601–611.

[6] E. Alam, and A.E. Collins. 2010. Cyclone Disaster Vulnerability and Response Experiences in Coastal Bangladesh. *Disasters.* 34 (4). pp. 931–954.

treatment, and the provision of and access to emergency relief and resources to facilitate quicker recovery are key and also differentiated by gender as this section presents.

Women's limited access and control over resources and the gendered division of labor in families create barriers to women's coping with and recovering from disasters. This is supported by some studies of large-scale sudden-onset disasters in Asia, which have shown that a higher proportion of women and girls died than men and boys. For example, women and girls represented 55% of deaths in the 2015 Nepal earthquakes.[7] This was attributed to a range of factors, including the prior migration of more men than women away from the affected areas to seek work, that women were more likely to be inside their homes at the time due to gender roles in families, and that many women with care responsibilities delayed their escape to rescue children, older family members, and family valuables (footnote 7). Similarly, women died at much higher rates than men in the 2004 Indian Ocean Tsunami. In two regions of Aceh, Indonesia, women represented between 77% and 80% of all deaths. In Cuddalore in India during the same tsunami, women comprised 66% of all deaths.[8] In these cases, men and women were predominantly in different locations at the time the disaster struck due to their different work routines and locations (footnote 8). These examples demonstrate that gender roles and prior inequalities can play a key role in disaster mortality rates.

Differentiated disaster impacts may also be affected by sex discrimination and/or a lack of a gender perspective in humanitarian response and recovery operations. After a disaster, women often face difficulties proving their land and property ownership, which can magnify and exacerbate the preexisting inequalities and disadvantages they face in relation to men. For example, following the 2015 earthquakes in Nepal, women heads of households experienced direct discrimination when local government officials insisted that distribution would be through male heads of household only.[9] Other women experienced indirect discrimination through a lack of access to key documentation. For example, some assistance was conditional on showing a marriage certificate and identity documents, which few women held. Some housing support for women whose husbands had died required proof of title to marital property, which in some regions were only registered in the man's name, making women's ownership difficult to prove (footnote 9). These discriminatory barriers deprived some women of urgent support, and contributed to the loss of some women's homes and property, causing longer-term impoverishment.[10]

Sexual violence and GBV is another significant form of gender discrimination that impacts women in disasters. Evidence from across Asia and the Pacific demonstrates that disasters are associated with increased rates of GBV.[11] A 2015 study by the International Federation of Red Cross and Red Crescent Societies (IFRC) revealed that in some settings, both domestic violence and sexual violence increase following disasters[12] and a 2018 IFRC publication of research in Indonesia, the Lao People's Democratic Republic (Lao PDR), and the Philippines confirmed that risks of sexual and gender-based violence (SGBV) are exacerbated during disaster situations, a trend that is applicable to other disaster contexts in other countries.[13] IFRC also identified several main characteristics of GBV in disasters:

---

[7]   Government of Nepal National Planning Commission. 2015. Nepal Earthquake 2015: *Post Disaster Needs Assessment. Vol. B: Sector Reports*. Kathmandu. p. 227.

[8]   Oxfam International. 2005. *The Tsunami's Impact on Women, Oxfam Briefing Note*. Oxford.

[9]   IFRC and S. Shrestha. 2017. *Nepal Country Case Study—Effective Law and Policy on Gender Equality and Protection from Sexual and Gender-Based Violence in Disasters*. Geneva. pp. 35–38.

[10] IFRC and M. Picard. 2017. *Effective Law and Policy on Gender Equality and Protection from Sexual and Gender-Based Violence in Disasters: Global Report*. Geneva. pp. 49–51.

[11] Global Gender and Climate Alliance (GGCA). 2016. *Gender and Climate Change: A Closer Look at Existing Evidence*. New York, Nairobi and Gland, Switzerland. pp. 30–31.

[12] IFRC and E. Ferris. 2015. *Unseen, Unheard: Gender-Based Violence in Disasters. Global Study*. Geneva; IFRC, Myanmar Red Cross Society and L. Manning. 2016. Case Study 3: An Intersection between Conflict and Disaster: Myanmar. In *Unseen, Unheard Gender-Based Violence in Disasters. Asia-Pacific Case Studies*. Kuala Lumpur. pp. 63–88.

[13] IFRC. 2018. *The Responsibility to Prevent and Respond to Sexual and Gender-Based Violence in Disasters and Crises*. Kuala Lumpur.

(i)   while domestic violence was present in affected communities before the disaster, it increased following sudden-onset disasters and during prolonged disasters, such as droughts;[14]

(ii)   rape and sexual assault were higher in emergency shelters and disaster-affected communities, necessitating an increase in the capacity of specialist support and justice services to meet the needs of victims and survivors;[15] and

(iii) impoverishment due to disaster increased the risk of GBV, including through economic coping strategies such as child or early marriage, transactional sex, and trafficking.[16]

Further research by IFRC in 2017 explored effective legislative frameworks on gender equality and GBV in disasters and concluded that systems for prevention, access to support and justice for GBV victims and survivors tend to be under-resourced in normal times and are not adapted to provide services in emergencies.[17] Another recent in-depth qualitative analysis examines how GBV emerges and impacts women following cyclones and uses a case study of a coastal region in Bangladesh shortly after Cyclone Roanu in 2016. It sheds light on the mechanisms linking GBV to cyclones through the eyes of victims and survivors, which are described as "slow violence and layered disasters."[18] Moreover, emergency shelter that is not designed and organized with local cultural norms and women's safety in mind can expose women to additional risks of harassment and violence.[19]

In terms of economic impacts of disasters on women in comparison to men, much of what is known comes from qualitative and narrative reports, especially PDNAs. However these are not always followed by analysis of longer-term gendered economic impacts. Some approaches to the concept of "building back better" after a disaster apply this principle only to physical reconstruction, leaving out the social dimension and, therefore, also the gender lens. This is unlikely to change unless women's organizations and women play a greater role in reconstruction planning and implementation. A negative example in this respect is the composition of the Nepal Reconstruction Authority, established by a special law following the 2015 earthquake, with a national committee including only two women (the statutory minimum) among 96 members, and no women on the technical or executive committees.[20]

In Fiji, following Tropical Cyclone Winston in 2016, housing and shelter was considered the most affected social sector. For women whose livelihoods were home-based, such as mat and basket weaving, the destruction of their homes and raw materials had a significant economic impact.[21] Women are extensively engaged in the informal sector, in microenterprises that are agricultural-based. In Fiji, for example, these comprise mainly food processing, handicrafts, and weaving. The PDNA notes that these are precarious livelihoods without the protection of insurance or access to finance, resulting in greater disaster losses and increasing women's economic dependence.[22] In the formal productive sector, primarily agriculture, women's overall economic losses were lower due to their lower rates of employment and lower wages. The PDNA notes that "women are poorer, earn less income, are more dependent on subsistence economies, and, therefore, have fewer options to cope with the disaster impact than their male counterparts."[23] This fits with a wider trend in developing economies, where women-owned enterprises often face difficulty accessing disaster risk financing and reconstruction loans,

---

[14]   IFRC and E. Ferris. 2015. *Unseen, Unheard: Gender-Based Violence in Disasters. Global Study*. Geneva. p. 20.

[15]   IFRC et al. 2016. *Unseen, Unheard Gender-Based Violence in Disasters - Asia-Pacific Case Studies*. Kuala Lumpur. p. 27.

[16]   Footnote 14, pp. 22–25.

[17]   Footnote 10, pp. 49–51.

[18]   N. Rezwana and R. Pain. Gender-Based Violence Before, During and After Cyclones: Slow Violence and Layered Disasters. *Disasters*. May 2020.

[19]   IFRC. 2010. *A Practical Guide to Gender-Sensitive Approaches for Disaster Management*. Geneva. pp. 19–20.

[20]   Footnote 10, p. 52.

[21]   Government of Fiji and S. Esler. 2016. *Fiji Post-Disaster Needs Assessment—Tropical Cyclone Winston, 20 February*. Suva. pp. 99–105.

[22]   Footnote 21, p. 99.

[23]   Footnote 21, p. 102.

due to their concentration in micro and small businesses, their operation in the informal sector (especially in agriculture), and direct or indirect discrimination in access to financial services.

This section presents the gendered impacts of disasters. It is notable that hazards such as temperature extremes (hot or cold), drought and water shortages, storms, heavy rains, and floods will become more extreme, prolonged, or frequent due to climate variability caused by climate change. In turn, this will cause more extreme impacts on human lives, health, livelihoods, housing, infrastructure, and natural ecosystems.[24] For example, in the project countries, the Lao PDR has recently experienced drought and major floods and faces the risk of increased intensity of rain, flash floods, landslides and river flooding, dam operation, and safety, as well as longer dry periods. Fiji has recently faced more extreme cyclones and storms, floods, and landslides. Mongolia now has an increased risk of floods, drought, and the harsh winter conditions of blizzards and the weather pattern known as *zud*, which causes the death of many livestock. The magnification of disaster risk due to climate change is likely to also magnify the gendered impacts of these types of hazards—making action on these issues critically important.

Gender Differences in the Context of Climate Change

There are major information and data gaps on the gendered impacts of climate change, due to the limited collection of sex-, age-, and diversity-disaggregated data.[25] However, climate change is a clear cause of environmental and socioeconomic disruption across diverse sectors and activities. Women's relative lack of equality in social, economic, and political spheres all influence the differentiated impacts of climate change. By addressing underlying gender inequalities and sex and gender discrimination, climate change mitigation and adaptation actions can also promote gender equality.

Due to gender inequalities, women are disproportionately impacted by climate change. Worldwide, across all family and household types, women spend significantly more time on household work than men: by United Nations (UN) Women's estimate, two and a half times more.[26] The impacts of climate change have made many of these tasks, such as fuel and water collection, more time-consuming. In both rural and urban environments, climate change-induced drought can increase the daily distance women and girls are expected to travel to collect water by up to 15 kilometers (km), reducing their available time for livelihood activities, education, and leisure.[27] For example, water shortages due to climate change in Nujiang, Yunnan Province, the People's Republic of China (PRC) caused women to spend more time managing water resources, and threatened the sustainability of women's livelihoods more than men's.[28] In many communities, women's livelihoods are also more affected by climate change than men's, as they are more dependent on natural resources. For instance, in Viet Nam, the adverse impacts of climate change affect women farmers most, as they must plant additional crops and replant rice crops to replace lost yields.[29]

[24] Intergovernmental Panel on Climate Change (IPCC). 2012. *Managing the Risks of Extreme Events and Disasters to Advance Climate Change Adaption—Special Report of the Intergovernmental Panel on Climate Change.* Cambridge and New York.

[25] UN Women. 2018. *Gender and Climate Change Under the Gender Action Plan (GAP): Submission by the United Nations Entity for Gender Equality and the Empowerment of Women (UN Women).* New York. p. 2.

[26] UN Women. 2015. *Progress of the World's Women 2015–2016. Transforming Economies, Realizing Rights.* New York; UN Women. 2019. *Progress of the World's Women 2019–2020.* New York; UN Women and International Labour Organization. 2020. *Spotlight on SDG 8: The Impact of Marriage and Children on Labour Market Participation.* New York.

[27] GGCA. 2016. Gender and Climate Change: A Closer Look at Existing Evidence. New York, Nairobi and Gland, Switzerland.

[28] Y. Zhou and X. Sun. 2020. Toward Gender Sensitivity: Women and Climate Change Policies in China. *International Feminist Journal of Politics.* 22 (1). pp. 127–149.

[29] Oxfam Great Britain and United Nations Viet Nam. 2009. *Responding to Climate Change in Viet Nam: Opportunities for Improving Gender Equality.* Oxford.

Climate change is also likely to increase food insecurity in the Global South, which experts expect to disproportionately burden women and girls.[30] For example, during food shortages, women in Viet Nam restrict their eating more than men, causing unequal health impacts, which both men and women legitimize based on the gendered division of labor.[31] In Andhra Pradesh, India, twice as many women as men reported responding to drought by reducing their food consumption.[32]

Women's lack of ownership and access to land compared to that of men, along with women's limited resources, also affect their capacity to respond to the changing climate. While women make up an estimated 43% of the agricultural labor force, they constitute less than 20% of the world's landowners.[33] This is a result of both discriminatory laws and inequitable traditional practices and social norms. While men and women may legally have equal land rights, these rights are not upheld in practice in nearly 60% of countries, according to a 2016 UN Women report.[34] Land rights not only ensure women income security, but also access to credit, as land is commonly used as a financial guarantee.[35] Women farmers also face barriers in accessing tools and supplies,[36] and are less likely to receive information on climate-smart agriculture, partly because training programs tend to target men.[37] These challenges reduce women's capability to invest in land quality and, in turn, to adapt to climate change impacts and sustainably recover from disasters. They also need to take into consideration climate change adaptation policy-making to ensure sustainable and equitable development.

Improving women's access to land and resources can make a significant positive social and environmental impact and support women's resilience to climate change impacts. Providing women with the same access as men to land, technology, financial services, education, and markets could enhance women's farm yields by 20%–30% by 2050,[38] reducing the number of hungry people globally by an estimated 12%–17% (footnote 38). Additionally, providing women smallholder farmers with resources, financing, and training would reduce carbon dioxide emissions by 2.06 gigatons by 2050 (footnote 38), or 5.5% of the total fossil fuel emissions in 2017, according to Project Drawdown.[39] Providing women with equal access to resources and land tenure not only strengthens women's human rights and economic empowerment, but also generates positive food security and climate change outcomes.

Furthermore, women and girls face structural challenges contributing to all levels of climate change decision-making.[40] Women's unequal position in the political sphere means they hold fewer positions of power and decision-making roles. At the start of 2021, women made up only 5.9 % of heads of state or 6.7% of heads of government.[41] Globally, three-quarters of parliamentarians are men, and in Asia, four-fifths are men (footnote 41). Following this trend, women are also underrepresented in decision-making on climate

---

[30] IPCC. 2014. Food Security and Food Production Systems. Climate Change 2014: Impacts, Adaptation, and Vulnerability. In *Part A: Global and Sectoral Aspects. Contribution of Working Group II to the Fifth Assessment Report of the Intergovernmental Panel on Climate Change*. Cambridge and New York. pp. 485–533; UN Women. 2016. *Leveraging Co-Benefits Between Gender Equality and Climate Action for Sustainable Development*. New York.

[31] Footnote 29.

[32] Food and Agriculture Organization of the United Nations (FAO). 2010. *Farmers in a Changing Climate: Does Gender Matter?* Rome.

[33] Inter-Agency Task Force on Rural Women. 2012. *Fact Sheet. Rural Women and the Millennium Development Goals*. Rome.

[34] UN Women. 2016. *Leveraging Co-Benefits Between Gender Equality and Climate Action for Sustainable Development*. New York. p. 20.

[35] D. Fletschner and L. Kenney. 2014. *Rural Women's Access to Financial Services: Credit, Savings, and Insurance. Gender in Agriculture: Closing the Knowledge Gap*. 11. pp. 187–208; P. Antwi-Agyei, A.J. Dougill, and L.C. Stringer. 2015. Impacts of Land Tenure Arrangements on the Adaptive Capacity of Marginalised Groups: The Case of Ghana's Ejura Sekyedumase and Bongo Districts. *Land Use Policy*. 49. pp. 203–212.

[36] Footnote 27.

[37] GGCA. 2016. *Gender and Climate Change: A Closer Look at Existing Evidence*. New York, Nairobi and Gland, Switzerland.

[38] Project Drawdown. Solutions. Project Drawdown is a research organization dedicated to reviewing, analyzing, and identifying the "most viable global climate solutions." See Project Drawdown. About Project Drawdown.

[39] Fossil fuels emitted 36.2 gigatons of CO_2 in 2017. K. Levin. 2018. New Global CO_2 Emissions Numbers Are In. They're Not Good. *World Resources Institute*. 5 December.

[40] Footnote 34.

[41] Inter-Parliamentary Union (IPU) and UN Women. 2021. *Women in Politics: 2021*. Geneva.

change. Across many national laws and policies, women are mostly considered a vulnerable group and not expressly mentioned as active participants and decision-makers. Consequently, women suffer the effects of indirect discrimination and are routinely excluded from leadership roles and decision-making bodies. For example, women comprised 22% of heads of delegation at the United Nations Framework Convention on Climate Change (UNFCCC) Conference of the Parties (COP) in Katowice in 2018.[42] At a local level, women face barriers to their participation in natural resource management, including unequal control over assets and disproportionate burden of household labor. For example, in rural Kenya, despite their responsibility for collecting water, women are largely barred from participating in water management groups. This is due to the challenges they face in attaining land titles, which are a prerequisite for participation.[43] While women are active agents of climate change mitigation and adaptation, they face considerable barriers to contributing to climate change decision-making.

This is a missed opportunity for designing and implementing more effective and gender-sensitive climate change policies. Women decision-makers are more likely to design policies and laws that benefit women and address gender gaps in access to and control over resources. A study of 91 countries found that a higher proportion of women in national politics led to stricter climate change policies, concluding that "Female political representation may be an underutilized tool for addressing climate change."[44] Moreover, the Intergovernmental Panel on Climate Change (IPCC) recommends that the participation of women and other marginalized groups enhances the effectiveness and governance of land-based climate change mitigation and adaptation.[45] Extensive international evidence demonstrates the benefits of women's participation for the effectiveness of household renewable energy adoption,[46] water supply and sanitation,[47] forest regeneration,[48] and climate change adaptation measures.[49] Eliminating the structural barriers women face in contributing to and leading climate action at local, national, and international levels will drive more sustainable and equitable outcomes.

[42] S. Greene. 2019. What Do the Statistics on UNFCCC Women's Participation Tell Us? *Women's Environment and Development Organisation (WEDO)*. 5 December.

[43] L. Onyango et al. 2007. Coping with History and Hydrology: How Kenya's Settlement and Land Tenure Patterns Shape Contemporary Water Rights and Gender Relations in Water. In B. van Koppen, M. Giordano, J. Butterworth, eds. *Community-Based Water Law and Water Resource Management Reform in Developing Countries*. Wallingford: Centre for Agriculture and Bioscience International (CAB International); E. Were, J. Roy and B. Swallow. 2008. Local Organisation and Gender in Water Management: A Case Study from The Kenya Highlands. *Journal of International Development*. 20 (1). pp. 69–81.

[44] A. Mavisakalyan and Y. Tarverdi. 2019. Gender and Climate Change: Do Female Parliamentarians Make a Difference? *European Journal of Political Economy*. 56. p. 151.

[45] IPCC. 2018. Summary for Policymakers. In V. Masson-Delmotte et al., eds. *Global Warming of 1.5°C. An IPCC Special Report on the Impacts of Global Warming of 1.5°C Above Pre-Industrial Levels and Related Global Greenhouse Gas Emission Pathways, in the Context of Strengthening the Global Response to the Threat of Climate Change, Sustainable Development, and Efforts to Eradicate Poverty*. Geneva. pp. 3–24.

[46] EmPower and United Nations Environment Programme (UNEP). 2020. *Powering Equality: Women's Entrepreneurship Transforming Asia's Energy Sector*. Bangkok.

[47] C. Anderson et al. 2017. Promoting Resilience, Rights and Resources: Gender-Responsive Adaptation Across Sectors. In M. Granat, C. Owren, and L. Aguilar, eds. *Roots for the Future: The Landscape and Way Forward on Gender and Climate Change*. International Union on the Conservation of Nature (IUCN) and GGCA. New York, Nairobi, and Gland, Switzerland. pp. 129–202.

[48] B. Agarwal. 2009. Rule Making in Community Forestry Institutions: The Difference Women Make. *Ecological Economics*. 68 (8–9). pp. 2296–2308.

[49] UN Women. 2017. *Understanding Cost-Effectiveness of Gender-Aware Climate Change Adaptation Intervention In Bangladesh*. New York.

Part 2
Overview of International Norms and National Legal Frameworks

Overview of International Norms

This part provides a brief overview of some of the main international laws and other guidance, which form the basis of the international norms analyzed in this report. The meaning of **international law** can be complex and dynamic, but in this report it is referring to international treaties, covenants, conventions, declarations, agreements, and frameworks agreed to by states or countries. **International norms** refer to their content, specifically the principles or standards contained within them.

At the root of most national legal frameworks are concepts of human rights, including the protection of individuals from harm, participation of individuals and groups and society, and provision of opportunities for individual growth and development.[50] These, and other essential principles, are derived from international norms. Of central importance is the "International Bill of Human Rights." This consists of three international instruments and two optional protocols to the Covenants:

(i) Universal Declaration of Human Rights (UDHR) 1948;
(ii) International Covenant on Civil and Political Rights (ICCPR) 1966; and
(iii) International Covenant on Economic, Social and Cultural Rights (ICESCR) 1966[51]

Of particular relevance is the Convention on the Elimination of All Forms of Discrimination against Women (CEDAW), the key international human rights instrument that seeks to ensure the enforcement of the human rights of women on an equal basis with men. CEDAW has often been described as an "international bill of rights" for women. Its preamble and 30 articles set out key principles of equality and an agenda for national action to end discrimination against women.[52] Recognizing the significant impacts on women posed by disasters and climate change, the CEDAW Committee identified the need for international standards to provide a backbone for strengthening the inclusion and resilience of women in these situations. Hence, it adopted GR37 as described in detail in Section D of this report. The content of GR37 is an important source of international norms on climate change and disaster risk in relation to women and is formative in relation to the whole report.

The principles embodied in these instruments are widely applicable, and national laws concerning climate change and disaster risk management and environmental management should, at the very least, expressly refer to these international norms.

---

[50] N. Perrault and C. Lundy. 2008. *Assessing Compliance of National Legislation with International Human Rights Norms and Standards.* UNICEF. New York. p. 1.
[51] United Nations Office of the High Commissioner for Human Rights (OHCHR). 1996. *The International Bill of Human Rights, Fact Sheet No. 2 (Rev1).* Geneva.
[52] Convention on the Elimination of All Forms of Discrimination against Women, United Nations Treaty Series, A/RES/34/180. 18 December 1979.

Post-2015 Agreements on Disaster and Climate Change Risk

The key international agreements related to disaster and climate risk are:

(i)   Sendai Framework for Disaster Risk Reduction 2015–2030 (Sendai Framework);[53]

(ii)   The 2030 Agenda, including the Sustainable Development Goals (SDGs);[54] and

(iii) The mechanisms of the United Nations Framework Convention on Climate Change (UNFCCC),[55] including the Paris Agreement.[56]

Gender equality, as a recognized priority area, has only recently emerged in these agreements and their monitoring. For example, paragraphs 19(g) and 25(a) of the Sendai Framework emphasize the importance of gender inclusion and disaggregated data, but the indicators agreed by State Parties for reporting so far require only numbers of persons, and sex-disaggregated data is optional.[57] On the other hand, SDGs, including SDG13 on climate change, require sex-disaggregated data collection on areas relevant to disaster and climate resilience. This will provide a body of sex-disaggregated data that can support countries' implementation of their obligations under the CEDAW, SDGs, and Sendai Framework. SDG5 also seeks to achieve gender equality and empowerment for women and girls, with related reporting requirements.[58] For example, indicator 5.1.1 calls for legal frameworks "to promote, enforce and monitor equality and non-discrimination on the basis of sex" (footnote 58).

The UNFCCC processes have increasingly integrated gender since the Cancun COP16 in 2010, which recognized the importance of "gender equality and the effective participation of women."[59] The 2014 Lima Work Programme on Gender[60] and 2017 Gender Action Plan translated this principle into concrete action on promoting gender mainstreaming, advancing gender-responsive climate policy, and increasing women's participation in the UNFCCC process.[61] This also reflects a shift away from a purely needs-based approach to women, focusing on their vulnerability to climate change impacts, towards a more rights-based approach that emphasizes women as equal rights holders and agents of change. While the 2015 Paris Agreement was not fully gender mainstreamed,[62] countries have since made significant progress on the integration of gender into their

---

[53] Third United Nations World Conference on Disaster Risk Reduction. 2015. *Sendai Framework for Disaster Risk Reduction 2015–2030*. Geneva.

[54] United Nations General Assembly. *Transforming Our World: The 2030 Agenda for Sustainable Development*, A/RES/70/1. 25 September 2015.

[55] *United Nations Framework Convention on Climate Change*, United Nations Treaty Series, FCCC/INFORMAL/84. 21 March 1994.

[56] UNFCCC Conference of Parties (COP) 21. 2015. *Paris Agreement in Report of the Conference of the Parties on Its Twenty-First Session, Held in Paris from 30 November to 13 December 2015. Addendum Part Two: Action Taken by the Conference of the Parties at Its Twenty-First Session*, Decision 1/CP.21, FCCC/CP/2015/10/Add.1. 29 January 2016. pp. 21–36.

[57] United Nations General Assembly, *Sendai Framework for Disaster Risk Reduction (2015–2030)*, A/RES/69/283. 23 June 2015.

[58] United Nations. 2015. Sustainable Development Goal 5: Achieve Gender Equality and Empower All Women and Girls, in *Transforming Our World: The 2030 Agenda for Sustainable Development*, A/RES/70/1. 25 September 2015. p. 9.

[59] UNFCCC Conference of Parties (COP) 16. 2010. The Cancun Agreements: Outcome of the Work of the Ad Hoc Working Group on Long-Term Cooperative Action under the Convention, in *Framework Convention on Climate Change: Report of the Conference of the Parties on Its Sixteenth Session, Part Two: Action Taken by The Conference of the Parties at Its Sixteenth Session*, Decision 1/CP.1, FCCC/CP/2010/7/Add.1. 15 March 2010. para. 7, with mention of gender also in paras. 12, 72, and 130.

[60] UNFCCC COP 20. 2014. Lima Work Programme on Gender, in *Report of the Conference of the Parties on Its Twentieth Session, Addendum. Part Two: Action Taken by the Conference of the Parties at Its Twentieth Session*, Decision 18/CP.20, FCCC/CP/2014/10/Add.3. 2 February 2015. pp. 35–36.

[61] UNFCCC COP 22. 2017. The Gender Action Plan FCCC/CP/2017/11/Add.1, in *Report of the Conference of the Parties on Its Twenty-Third Session. Addendum. Part Two: Action Taken by the Conference of the Parties at Its Twenty-Third Session*, Annex to Decision 3/CP.23, FCCC/CP/2017/11/Add.1. 8 February 2018. para. 2.

[62] UNFCCC COP 21. 2015. *Paris Agreement in Report of the Conference of the Parties on Its Twenty-First Session. Addendum Part Two: Action Taken by The Conference of the Parties at Its Twenty-First Session*, Decision 1/CP.21, FCCC/CP/2015/10/Add.1. 29 January 2016. paras. 7, 11, and 102; African Working Group on Gender and Climate Change (AWGGCC). 2016. Gender Analysis of the Paris Agreement and Implications for Africa.

intended/nationally determined contributions (I/NDCs). For example, in 2020, 56% of countries were either mainstreaming gender into their NDCs or planned to do so.[63]

Application of International Norms

There are two main ways in which international norms can become part of local or national law:

(i)   In some legal systems, any international agreements, treaties, or conventions (international instruments) to which the country has acceded or ratified are automatically part of domestic law and can be applied in a court of law.

(ii) Other legal systems require special enabling legislation in the country to bring the international instruments into force, such as a constitutional amendment, a law or decree. Until this is done, the international instrument has no legal force domestically. Sometimes this is done by:

    (a)   inserting the international instrument, in its entirety, in a single piece of legislation (sometimes as an annex to the law); and

    (b)   by gradually inserting various provisions to implement the international instrument over time, often using several different laws.[64]

Other ways that countries recognize international norms are discussed in Part 3.

---

[63] WEDO. 2020. *Spotlight on Gender in NDCs: An Analysis of Parties' Instruments, Plans and Actions Supporting Integration of Gender Equality Principles and Practices.* New York.

[64] See discussion in N. Perrault and C. Lundy. 2008. *Assessing Compliance of National Legislation with International Human Rights Norms and Standards.* UNICEF. New York.

Part 3
Good Gender-Sensitive Laws and Lawmaking

Good Constitutional Provisions for Women Relevant to Climate Change and Disaster Risk Management

Context

The national constitution sets out the system of law and governance, social and cultural values, and guarantees basic human rights consistent with international covenants, conventions, treaties, and norms, including international customary law. A constitution should guarantee equality for all and protection against discrimination, particularly against women. As a minimum, it should be consistent with international norms and other international obligations of the country.

In relation to gender equality, a good constitution would include the essential elements of the CEDAW, the international instrument in which women's human rights to equality and nondiscrimination are detailed, and where the nature and meaning of sex-based discrimination and gender equality are most clearly articulated. As stated in the section on application of international laws, there are two main mechanisms for international law to become part of the domestic law of a country. There are also other ways that countries recognize international norms:

> **Notes for Lawmakers**
>
> - Lawmakers can use or adapt the four steps to gender mainstreaming in lawmaking set out in this section when designing or revising constitutions to provide for fundamental human rights relevant to climate change and disaster risk management, as well as to promote equality and prohibit discrimination against women.
>
> - Lawmakers need an appreciation of how good constitutional provisions can enable other laws that may not be gender-sensitive, such as disaster risk management (DRM) and climate change laws, to be used to provide a gender-sensitive basis for their interpretation and implementation.
>
> - Good constitutional provisions enable courts to more easily use international norms to give decisions and provide remedies to women adversely affected by climate change and disasters. Illustrations can be found in this section. For example, provisions in the Constitution that reflect the CEDAW enable courts to more easily use it to interpret laws and make decisions that provide remedies to women complainants. See also the five different country case illustrations described in the *IPU Handbook for Parliamentarians*.

(i) Recent constitutions (or recently amended constitutions) tend to have more embracing provisions related to women's rights across the spectrum of human rights and international norms. Sometimes these are reflected in a Bill of Rights within the constitution itself, or by broadly expressed provisions, or individual articles in the constitution.

(ii) Provisions in a constitution may state that international treaties or conventions that bind a country automatically become part of the domestic law of that country.

(iii) Constitutional provisions may state that if there is any inconsistency between a domestic law and international law, then international law shall prevail, except if it is contrary to the constitution.

(iv)   Some countries have a comprehensive national law on fundamental rights and freedoms that are not part of the constitution, such as a national Bill of Rights, that effectively copies the International Bill of Human Rights as well as the essential elements of the CEDAW (referred to in Background Section (e) of this report). Or in the case of New Zealand, a *Human Rights Act* 1993, which sets out these provisions.

The disadvantage of having a separate Bill of Rights or similar law, is that these laws can be easily amended in comparison with the process required for a constitution. Additionally, they do not have the same standing and importance as a constitutional provision. Thus, if a Bill of Rights article conflicts with the constitution, the constitution usually prevails. It is also important to note that a country can still be held responsible at *international law* if its constitution is not in conformity with an international treaty or convention that the country has ratified.

Another element highly relevant to the guarantees for women's rights contained within constitutions is to ensure a critical mass of women legislators are in legislative assemblies so as to influence their content. In 1995, the United Nations Division for the Advancement of Women (UNDAW) issued a report in which experts regarded 30% as a minimum critical mass for women to exert a meaningful influence as a group in legislative assemblies.[65] As presented in Part 2, the share of women in national parliaments remains low in relation to men. Of 14 countries in the Pacific region, only three countries exceed this 30% target for women's representation in their lower or single house of parliament,[66] and in Asia, only three countries had surpassed the 30% mark.[67] The countries with the best results regarding representation of women in parliament have used temporary special measures or affirmative action initiatives to set a minimum quota for a gender. In some cases, this is set out in the constitution and examples are set out below.

International Norms

(i)   Universal Declaration of Human Rights (UDHR), Article 2

(ii)   International Covenant on Civil and Political Rights (ICCPR), Articles 2 and 26

(iii)   Optional Protocol to the ICCPR

(iv)   International Covenant on Economic, Social and Cultural Rights (ICESCR), Articles 2(2), 6 and 7

(v)   Optional Protocol to the ICESCR

(vi)   CEDAW, Article 1

(vii)   CEDAW Committee General Recommendation 28 (2010) on the Core Obligations of States Parties under Article 2 of the Convention on the Elimination of All Forms of Discrimination against Women, para [9]

(viii)   International Labour Organization (ILO) Convention 100 (1951) on Equal Remuneration (ILO C100) and ILO Convention 111 (1958) on Discrimination (Employment and Occupation) Convention (ILO C111)

---

[65] United Nations Division for the Advancement of Women (UNDAW). 2005. Equal Participation of Women and Men in Decision-Making Processes, with Particular Emphasis on Political Participation and Leadership. Report of the Expert Group Meeting Addis-Ababa, Ethiopia, EGM/EPDM/2005/REPORT. 24–27 October 2005.

[66] New Zealand (48.3%) and Australia (31.1%). Inter-Parliamentary Union (IPU). 2021. *Women in Parliament 2021.* Geneva.

[67] Timor-Leste (38.5%), Nepal (32.7%), and Uzbekistan (32.7%). IPU. 2021. *Women in Parliament 2021.* Geneva.

Key Elements of Good Laws

Key Elements of Good Constitutional Provisions

The constitution guarantees equality for women and men across the range of human rights set out in the International Human Rights Bill and the CEDAW, in particular, (i) rights to a clean and safe environment; (ii) right to life and health; and (iii) rights to economic, political empowerment, including representation in parliament.

These guarantees are set out either in a Bill of Rights in the constitution or articles in the constitution.

- Specifically prohibits discrimination against women.
- Provides for temporary special measures to promote advancement of women.
- Provides a clear mechanism for incorporation into domestic law of international human rights treaties and conventions to which the country has acceded.
- Provides for a minimum representation of women in parliament.

Examples of Good Laws

There are four different types of examples of good laws described: (i) Bill of Rights in the Constitution: Kenya and South Africa; (ii) Articles in the Constitution: Mongolia and Nepal; (iii) International law becoming part of domestic law: Kenya, Mongolia, and South Africa; and (iv) Constitutional provisions for minimum representation of women in parliament: Kenya and Nepal.

Example of Type 1: Bill of Rights in the Constitution

Kenya Constitution, 2010

Kenya is a good law example because it has a comprehensive Constitution, particularly on the guarantees of basic human rights. The Constitution itself has a "Bill of Rights" contained in Chapter Four with a scope of guarantees of rights and freedoms. The Bill of Rights portion is divided into two. (i) The first deals with general provisions that cover the spectrum of fundamental freedoms and rights. (ii) The second refers to the application of those fundamental freedoms and rights, and to certain groups of persons, for example: children, persons with disabilities, minorities and marginalized groups, and older members of society (women are not specifically mentioned). Each article in the Bill of Rights is set out in detail.	The articles relevant to women in climate change and disaster situations are: **Article 26:** Right to life **Article 27:** Equality and freedom from discrimination **Article 40:** Protection of right to property **Article 41:** Labor relations **Article 42:** Environment **Article 43:** Economic and social rights **Article 48:** Access to justice

Example of Type 1: Bill of Rights in the Constitution

South Africa Constitution, 1986 (revised 2012)

These Articles of the Constitution are good law provisions because they recognize that the scope of protection for human rights extends beyond a limited interpretation of the Bill of Rights, and embrace other freedoms and rights recognized by customary law to the extent that they are consistent with the Bill of Rights. Also, it requires not only legislators, but also courts, to promote those values. This offers opportunities for women to take action if their rights and freedoms are restricted or impeded in responses to climate change and disasters.

Chapter 2, Articles 7–39 provide a wide range of guarantees of the fundamental human rights of men and women in the country. Some of these articles are also referred to in **Chapter 6** on equality and discrimination. Of note in relation to the scope of protection, are the following Articles:

Article 39(1): when interpreting the Bill of Rights, a court, tribunal, or forum;

(i)   must promote the values that underlie an open and democratic society based on human dignity, equality and freedom;
(ii) must consider international law; and
(iii) may consider foreign law.

Article 39(2): when interpreting any legislation, and when developing the common law or customary law, every court, tribunal, or forum must promote the spirit, purport, and objects of the Bill of Rights.

Article 39(3): The Bill of Rights does not deny the existence of any other rights or freedoms that are recognized or conferred by common law, customary law, or legislation, to the extent that they are consistent with the Bill.

Example of Type 2: Articles in the Constitution

Mongolia Constitution, 2019

This is a good law example because it provides comprehensive guarantees on fundamental rights and freedoms, including health and the environment. It also indicates the process for incorporating international treaties into domestic law (discussed below). Although some of the fundamental principles of equality and nondiscrimination are not set out in the Constitution, they are comprehensively set out in the Law on Promotion of Gender Equality 2011 (LPGE), discussed in **Example of Type 3** below.

Chapter 2 is devoted to guaranteeing human rights and freedoms for citizens of Mongolia.

Articles 14 and 16 provide a menu of the fundamental rights and freedoms in international norms that are guaranteed under the Constitution. There are some 20 provisions and five of them are identified below as having particular importance to support women's equality, empowerment, and resilience to climate and disaster risk.

Article 17 sets out the corresponding duties that a citizen has in relation to the state and other citizens.

The most relevant Constitution provisions are:

(i)   **Article 14(1)** requires equality before the law and the courts; Article 14 (2) prohibits discrimination on a range of grounds, including sex.
(ii) **Article 16(2)** confers a right to a healthy and safe environment, and to be protected against environmental pollution and ecological imbalance.
(iii) **Article 16(3)** gives a right to fair acquisition, possession, and inheritance of movable and immovable property.

Example of Type 2: Articles in the Constitution

(iv) **Article 16(11)** establishes that men and women enjoy equal rights in political, economic, social, cultural fields, as well as in marriage.

(v) **Article 17(2)** provides that every citizen has a sacred duty to work, protect their health, bring up and educate their children, and protect nature and the environment.

In the context of climate change, **Articles 16(2) and 17(2)** are good law examples of a mutual right to a healthy and safe environment and an obligation to protect nature and the environment.

Nepal Constitution, 2015

This is a good law example because it is comprehensive and it includes important elements of environment and health, as well as a right to compensation. It also refers to the difficulty of balancing environment and development. It is not gendered, but could potentially be linked to Article 38, specifically on the rights of women, described below.

Part 3 sets out the Fundamental Rights and Duties of citizens. There are some 32 separate articles on those rights, each of which are detailed and include:

(i) **Article 18:** Right to equality
(ii) **Article 25:** Right to property
(iii) **Article 30:** Right regarding a clean environment
(iv) **Article 33:** Right to employment
(v) **Article 35:** Right to healthcare
(vi) **Article 37:** Right to housing
(vii) **Article 38:** Right of women
(viii) **Article 46:** Right to constitutional remedy
(ix) **Article 47:** Implementation of fundamental rights

Of these, the following good law examples are highlighted:

Article 30 on the right regarding a clean environment that provides:

(i) Each person shall have the right to live in a healthy and clean environment.
(ii) The victim of environmental pollution and degradation shall have the right to be compensated by the pollutant as provided for by law.
(iii) Provided that this Article shall not be deemed to obstruct the making of required legal provisions to strike a balance between environment and development for the use of national development works.

Article 38 is a good example of law.

(i) First, because it expressly recognizes rights as being specific to women, whereas it is more common for such provisions to be expressed in gender-neutral terms, or only to women in the context of protecting motherhood and the family.

(ii) Second, the article prohibits oppression and violence against women, and gives them the right to be compensated for such acts. Often within a country, such provisions are not expressed in a Constitution, but are set out in a separate law.

Article 38 on the right of women provides for rights relating to:

(i) lineage without any gender discrimination;
(ii) safe motherhood and reproductive health;
(iii) prohibiting violence against women, which is punishable and gives a right to compensation;
(iv) right to access and participation in all state structures and bodies based on proportional inclusion;

Example of Type 2: Articles in the Constitution

(iii) Third, the importance of these rights is accentuated by their inclusion in the Constitution, although it requires other laws, regulations, or similar for implementation purposes and to expand their operation in practice.

See further discussion on this Article in **Sections 4.1 and 5**.

(v) granting women the right to special opportunities in education, health, employment, and social security based on positive discrimination; and

(vi) granting both spouses equal rights in property and family affairs.

Example of Type 3: International Law Becoming Part of Domestic Law

Mongolia Constitution, 2019

These two Articles are good law provisions as together, they clearly state Mongolia's obligations in relation to an international treaty or convention and how that takes effect. They enable a person to directly pursue fundamental human rights within the Mongolian Courts.

Article 16(14) could potentially be used in the context of climate change or in situations of disaster, if women are subject to discriminatory deprivation of property or treatment in comparison with men.

Article 10 provides that Mongolia (i) adheres to the universally recognized norms and principles of international law, (ii) fulfills in good faith its obligations under international treaties to which it is a Party, (iii) provides that international treaties to which it is a Party become effective as domestic legislation upon the entry into force of the laws on their ratification or accession, and (iv) that it may not abide by any international treaty or other instruments incompatible with its Constitution.

Article 16(14) provides that if a person considers that rights or freedoms have been violated, as spelt out by the Mongolian law or an international treaty, there is a right to appeal to the court for protection.

South Africa Constitution, 1986 (revised 2012)

Each of these three Articles is good law as each specifies the ways in which international agreements may bind the country, other than by specific ratification or accession.

These provisions make South Africa unique within the common law jurisdictions, such as Australia, Canada, Fiji, India, Malaysia, New Zealand, and the United Kingdom, that normally require not only ratification, but also adoption of a treaty or convention by a specific domestic law.

Furthermore, it directs courts as to how to address apparent inconsistencies between international law and domestic law to enable consistency to be achieved by preferring a reasonable interpretation.

Article 231 on international agreements enables international agreements of a technical, administrative, or executive nature, or an agreement that does not require either ratification or accession to bind the Republic on conditions. Furthermore, any self-executing provision of an international agreement approved by Parliament is law in the Republic, unless it is inconsistent with the Constitution or an Act of Parliament.

Article 232 provides that customary international law is law in the Republic unless it is inconsistent with the Constitution or an Act of Parliament.

Article 233 provides that when interpreting any legislation, every court must prefer any reasonable interpretation of the legislation that is consistent with international law over any alternative interpretation that is inconsistent with international law.

Example of Type 3: International Law Becoming Part of Domestic Law	
Kenya Constitution, 2010	
The combination of these Articles in the Constitution is a good law example. (i) First, the protections given appear to be broader than the international treaties and conventions ratified by Kenya, and the "general rules of international law" appear to extend to international norms even if a particular treaty or convention has not been ratified by Kenya. (ii) Second, the Constitution specifically gives jurisdiction to the High Court to hear cases alleging breaches of rights or freedoms set out in the Bill of Rights, which reinforces the importance of these rights and freedoms.	**Article 2(5)** provides that the general rules of international law shall form part of the law of Kenya. (6) Any treaty or convention ratified by Kenya shall form part of the law of Kenya under this Constitution. **Article 21(4)** provides that the State shall enact and implement legislation to fulfill its international obligations in respect of human rights and fundamental freedoms. **Articles 22 and 23** give jurisdiction to the High Court to hear and determine applications for redress of a denial, violation, or infringement of, or threat to, a right or fundamental freedom in the Bill of Rights.

Example of Type 4: Constitutional Provisions for Minimum Representation of Women in Parliament	
Kenya Constitution, 2010	
A good example of a gender quota for representation of women.	**Article 27(8):** A minimum of 33% of each gender.
Nepal Constitution, 2015	
Again, making provision within a Constitution highlights the importance of having women effectively represented at the legislative level, as provided by the CEDAW Article 7. In other countries, laws such as the electoral law provides for a minimum quota.	**Articles 84(8), 176, 222, and 223:** a minimum of one-third women for elected assemblies.

Good National Laws That Promote Equality and Antidiscrimination

Context

This section follows on from the discussion on constitutions and links to the National Good Practice Legislative Framework. National laws may amplify constitutional protections to enable implementation and provide sanctions and remedies for breaches, including justifiable exemptions. They may also provide temporary special measures to address prior disadvantage. This section addresses the promotion of equality and prohibition of discrimination against women and only makes passing reference to discrimination against women in employment or occupation. However, more specific topics such as equal remuneration for work of equal value, sexual harassment in the workplace, and violence against women are addressed later in this report. A number of terms that have specific meanings under international law are used in this section, which are italicized. Readers are recommended to read the Appendix on Terminology for additional definitions.

Many State Parties of the CEDAW confine the interpretation and application of the term *equality* to mean *formal equality* only (equal treatment of women and men). In law, practice, and application, they do not embrace the two additional forms of equality required by the CEDAW, namely, *substantive equality* (equal outcomes or equal results), and *transformative equality* (positively changing and transforming gender roles to promote equality). Incorporating *substantive equality* and *transformative equality* enables laws to address the differing needs of men and women and the disadvantages experienced by women.

Similarly, State Parties often have laws that prohibit discrimination based on sex, but do not specifically prohibit *gender discrimination*, which includes roles socially ascribed to women and men. Furthermore, laws often do not refer to *indirect discrimination*, *temporary special measures*, or *exemption from discrimination*. These concepts are important for designing gender-responsive laws and policies.

> ### Notes for Lawmakers
>
> - When considering revision or development of new national laws on equality and nondiscrimination, lawmakers should note that the research and analysis for this report suggests that having an entire act devoted to a law on gender equality has a powerful influence on all legislation and policies within the country generally.
>
> - A law on equality can be used for gender mainstreaming across the development, design, implementation, and monitoring of all laws and policies. This would include laws on climate change and disaster risk management and environmental management. This is an example of the horizontal application of a law.
>
> - Recognizing that there are difficulties sometimes in expressing all the measures required for equality and discrimination in a law on climate change and disaster risk management, the horizontal use of a law on equality would enable such laws to have a powerful influence more generally to be applied and implemented in the climate change and DRM system.

International Norms

(i)   UDHR, Article 2
(ii)   ICCPR, Articles 2 and 26 and Optional Protocol to the ICCPR
(iii) ICESCR, Articles 2(2), 6 and 7 and the Optional Protocol to the ICESCR
(iv)   CEDAW and the Optional Protocol to CEDAW
(v)   General Assembly resolution res. 34/180, 34 UN GAOR Supp. (No. 46) at 193, UN Doc. A/34/46, entered into force 3 September 1981, Article 1

(vi)   CEDAW Committee General Recommendation 28 (2010) on the Core Obligations of States Parties Under Article 2 of the Convention on the Elimination of All Forms of Discrimination against Women, para. 9

(vii)   ILO C100 and ILO C111

Based on the international law obligations under the CEDAW and ILO C111,[68] as well as other analyses,[69] some key elements of good national laws are identified on gender equality and nondiscrimination to underpin women's resilience to climate change and disasters. Implementation mechanisms such as gender-responsive budgeting should also be part of the legislative framework.[70] A different aspect of implementation should include State Parties ratifying the Optional Protocols to the ICCPR, the ICESCR, and the CEDAW to enable complaints to be made by individuals or groups to those bodies about failure to implement or breaches of the covenant or convention by the state. The CEDAW requires State Parties to address prevailing gender relations and the persistence of gender-based stereotypes and prejudices that violate women's rights. The State Parties are to adopt measures "towards a transformation of opportunities, institutions and systems so that they are no longer grounded in a historically determined male paradigms of power and life patterns."[71] State Parties have three positive obligations to take action, and not simply to refrain from discrimination. The obligations of State Parties[72] are to *refrain*,[73] *respect*,[74] and *fulfill*.[75]

International standards require provisions for *temporary special measures* in appropriate circumstances to accelerate achieving de facto equality of women with men. For example, the disadvantage suffered by women in employment and occupation is so embedded that the most effective means of redressing this imbalance is through legislation that provides for temporary special measures. Both the CEDAW and ILO C111 recognize that women have suffered, and continue to suffer, from various forms of discrimination in employment solely because of their gender, and that temporary special measures are required to address prior disadvantage.

In its Special Survey on Equality in Employment and Occupation, the Committee of Experts on the Application of Conventions and Recommendations (CEACR) (see the description of the CEACR in the **Appendix on Terminology**) drew a distinction between *special measures* provided for in labor standards (for example, maternity protection that requires ongoing differential treatment) and *temporary special measures* designed to meet needs of certain groups for special protection or assistance, by reason of present or past disadvantage, that lasts only until the equality is achieved.[76]

---

[68]   International Labour Conference, *Convention C111—Discrimination (Employment and Occupation) Convention*, 1958 (No. 111). 25 June 1958. Article 1 (2).

[69]   International Commission of Jurists. 2014. International Human Rights Law and Gender Equality and Non-Discrimination Legislation Requirements and Good Practices. Briefing paper. Geneva.

[70]   J. Stotsky. 2016. Gender Budgeting: Fiscal Context and Current Outcomes. IMF *Working Paper* WP/16/149. Washington, DC.

[71]   CEDAW. *General Recommendation No. 25, on Article 4, Paragraph 1, of The Convention on the Elimination of All Forms of Discrimination against Women, on Temporary Special Measures*, A/59/38. 12–30 January 2004. Annex 1 [10].

[72]   CEDAW. 2010. *General Recommendation No. 28 on the Core Obligations of States Parties under Article 2 of the Convention on the Elimination of All Forms of Discrimination against Women*, CEDAW/C/GC/28. 19 October 2010. para. 9.

[73]   To refrain from making laws, policies, regulations, programs, administrative procedures, and institutional structures that directly or indirectly result in the denial of the equal enjoyment by women of their civil, political, economic, social, and cultural rights.

[74]   To respect requires that States Parties protect women against discrimination by private actors and take steps directly aimed at eliminating customary and all other practices that prejudice and perpetuate the notion of inferiority or superiority of either of the sexes, and of stereotyped roles for men and women.

[75]   To fulfill requires that States Parties take a wide variety of steps to ensure that women and men enjoy equal rights *de jure* and *de facto*, including, where appropriate, the adoption of temporary special measures in line with article 4 (1) of the Convention and General Recommendation No. 25.

[76]   CEACR. 1996. Special Survey on Equality in Employment and Occupation in Respect of Convention No. 111. International Labour Conference 83rd Session 1996. Geneva.

The CEDAW Committee has published the most comprehensive standard in its General Recommendation 25 (2004) on Temporary Special Measures.[77] This General Recommendation notes at paragraph 17 that terms such as *affirmative action, positive action, positive measures,* and even *reverse discrimination* (used with regard to proving offenses or discrimination cases in court), are also used in some national legislation to describe temporary special measures taken to reduce the disadvantage or to achieve equality of opportunity.

Both the CEDAW and ILO C111 contain provisions that permit *exemptions* from the application of discrimination in employment. In the case of ILO C111, Article 1(2) provides: "Any distinction, exclusion or preference in respect of a particular job based on the inherent requirements thereof shall not be deemed to be discrimination." The CEACR addressed this topic in its *Special Survey on Equality in Employment and Occupation.*[10] The CEACR indicated that Article 1(2) of ILO C111 should be specific and be interpreted restrictively.

Some of the best examples of laws on equality and nondiscrimination against women can be found in Laws on Equality in various countries. These laws take a more holistic approach because they link equality and its corollary, nondiscrimination. They also set out CEDAW requirements to bring about transformational changes in laws, policies, government, and society for the economic, social, cultural, and political empowerment of women. These represent an essential part of a good legislative framework to strengthen women's resilience to climate change and disaster risk management.

Key Elements of Good Laws

Key Elements of Good National Laws That Promote Equality and Prohibit Discrimination against Women

- The country to ratify the CEDAW and the ILO C111 and the Optional Protocols to the ICCPR, ICESCR, and CEDAW.
- The Constitution and national laws to include principles and definitions of gender equality and prohibition of discrimination on against women grounds of sex or gender consistent with the CEDAW.
- General national laws or constitutional provisions (one or more laws) in place to implement the CEDAW obligations and include:
  - prohibition of discrimination against women, including direct and indirect discrimination, with effective complaint mechanisms and remedies;
  - promotion of both formal and substantive gender equality, including provisions for temporary special measures (including quotas and affirmative action), provisions for special measures (including maternity protection), and effective implementation measures such as gender-sensitive budgeting;
  - provisions requiring gender mainstreaming across all laws and policies;
  - explicitly stating the responsibility of the state to implement CEDAW obligations; and
  - providing for supremacy of international obligations over national laws (excluding the Constitution).

---

[77] Footnote 70.

Examples of Good Laws

Three examples are provided from (i) Viet Nam, (ii) Mongolia, and (iii) Maldives.

There are additional selected examples of good national laws on (i) discrimination: Croatia, (ii) affirmative action: Italy and Namibia, and (iii) exemption from discrimination: Australia.

Example 1: Viet Nam	
Viet Nam Law on Gender Equality, 2006	
This is an early example of a law on gender equality. It is a good comprehensive law example. Specific observations are made about good features of individual articles in the next column. The law has recently been reviewed for its efficacy over a period of 10 years since operation[a] and received a positive evaluation when the Act was compared to the CEDAW requirements. Recommendations were made for future amendments including defining indirect discrimination and providing that sexual harassment be expressed as a form of discrimination. The review is a useful resource on the requirements for good legislation and its Annexure K, contains comparative examples of other laws from other countries.	**Article 1** expresses the scope of the law and it includes all fields of social and family life and the responsibilities of agencies, organizations, families, and individuals to apply gender equality. **Article 3** states that if an international treaty to which Viet Nam is a signatory contains provisions that differ from the law, the provisions of the international treaty shall be applied. This is an important provision that gives *higher status* to international obligations over the national law. **Article 4** states the objectives of gender equality and is a good example of a law as it links the elimination of gender discrimination to the objective of attaining gender equality and refers to "substantial equality" in line with the CEDAW requirement. **Article 5** is a glossary of terms and has a definition of "gender stereotype" and refers to "measures to promote gender equality" aimed at ensuring substantial gender equality. Again, this is a good example in its application of the CEDAW requirement. **Article 7** refers to state policies on gender equality and includes in 7.22 facilitating "man and woman in sharing housework" and in 7.3 "to apply appropriate measures to eliminate backward customs and habits hindering the implementation of gender equality objectives." These are good examples that address the gender roles and stereotypes of women and men. **Article 19** on "measures to promote gender equality" is a gender transformative approach. It includes Article 19.1 (a) to "provide for male and female proportion or to ensure appropriate proportion of female in participation and benefiting"; and Article 19.1 (e) and (f) provide that priority be given to women. These provisions are in effect affirmative measures and could be used to include a quota or similar. **Articles 21 and 22** refer to the mainstreaming of gender equality issues in developing legal documents in some detail and is a good positive measure; **Article 24** refers to the equivalent of setting a gender-sensitive budget.

Example 1: Viet Nam

	Articles 23–32 set out the responsibilities of all government levels and organizations in relation to achieving gender equality.
	Articles 33–34 refer to the responsibility of the families and citizens.
	Chapter V refers to the overall implementation processes of gender equality including complaint processes and the various forms of violation of the law in differing contexts.

ᵃ   United Nations Population Fund (UNFPA) and Viet Nam Ministry of Labour—Invalids and Social Affairs (MOLISA). 2020. *Review of Ten Years of Implementing the Law on Gender Equality*. Ha Noi.

Example 2: Mongolia

Mongolia Law on Promotion of Gender Equality, 2011

The Law on Promotion of Gender Equality (LPGE) is a simply expressed and well-structured Act. This is a good legal provision that gives higher status to international treaties over national law, but not the Constitution.	**Article 2** states that legislation on gender equality is to comprise the Constitution as well as other laws and further states in Article 2.2 that "if an international treaty ratified by Mongolia provides otherwise than this law, the provision of that international treaty shall take precedence."
The LPGE consists of over 27 articles and they specify the objectives, expected outcomes, activities, and roles of lead institutions, as well as the responsibility of each of the organizations involved. It also provides the processes for filing complaints. It is noteworthy that this Act covers not only public, but also private life for all citizens of Mongolia. The law, overall, is a good law example and is gender-transformative. The Articles that best reflect the gender transformative approach are the use of special measures and quotas.	**Article 4** provides good simple definitions of gender, gender equality, gender stereotypes, gender discrimination (both direct and indirect), sexual harassment, gender-based violence, and gender quotas. **Article 5** expresses the "Principles of gender equality." Men and women have opportunities and conditions to enjoy equal rights in political, economic, social, cultural, family and other relations, and to equally participate in social life and equally access the benefits of development and social wealth. **Article 5.1.3** refers to the responsibility of Mongolia to fulfill the commitments provided in the Constitution and international treaties, and be accountable for the results achieved. This places the responsibility on the government, as required by the CEDAW. **Article 5.1.4** refers to the principle of gender mainstreaming regarding laws and policies programs and projects and is a good provision in its breadth. **Article 6.2** recognizes that gender-based violence and sexual harassment shall be seen as constituting gender discrimination. This too is a good law example in recognizing these actions as gender discrimination. **Article 7** details special measures and exemptions from discrimination.

Example 2: Mongolia	
	Article 7.2.2 provides that special measures may be implemented to determine the number of seats or implementing other such quotas aimed at equalizing the representation of men or women are political in decision-making levels. This permits quotas for the number of seats in Parliament for women and men. **Article 10** requires that various quotas be applied in the civil service when the representation of any one sex falls below a named percentage. Depending on the level of the civil service, the quota varies from 15% up to 40%. This is an effective way of attaining gender parity within the civil service at all levels.

Example 3: Maldives	
Maldives Gender Equality Act, 2016	
This is a recent law and the whole of this Act is instructive and overall amounts to good law on gender equality and gender discrimination. However, there are some qualifications. For some years, Maldives had a reservation on Article 16 of the CEDAW,[a] but the government reports that it is working on modifying that reservation. Furthermore, the Act is solely concerned with the equality and nondiscrimination between females and males, and it does not deal with multiple or intersectional forms of discrimination such as age, disability, race, color, or other factors. Overall, this is a good law example with all the key elements addressed. The law has good provisions noted in the next column, particularly its specific reference to the CEDAW and the scope of coverage.	**Article 2** states the objectives of the Act in detail and refers to a requirement to conform with the CEDAW and its Optional Protocol. It seeks to ensure that women enjoy equal terms with men on human rights, fundamental rights, and equal opportunities in their economic, social, cultural, civil, and political life and requires establishing the principles of gender equality in the conduct of state institutions, businesses, civil society organizations, employers, other legal entities and individuals, as well as in policies. **Article 2(g)** expressly refers to ending all forms of violence against women and girls. **Article 3** requires the Act to be interpreted and applied to uphold the principles of the CEDAW and the conventions and treaties to which Maldives is party. **Article 4** defines "gender equality" and in effect it is referring to substantive equality, which complies with the CEDAW requirements. **Articles 7–13** express in detail the meaning and application of "discrimination based on gender." Collectively they amount to good legislation because of their detailed content that includes direct and indirect discrimination and exempt circumstances. **Article 8** provides a good example, not often expressed in a law, which is a definition of Systematic Discrimination. **Article 25(b)** firmly places the responsibility on the Government and State authorities.

Example 3: Maldives	
	Article 44 requires a sufficient budget to achieve its aims including preventing gender-based violence against women and helping victims of such violence.
	Article 45(a) provides that the Act be reviewed every 5 years and to amend the Act if required.

ᵃ The reservations concern constitutional provisions on the equality of men and women in all matters relating to marriage, and family relations "without prejudice to the provisions of the Islamic Shari'ah, which govern all marital and family relations of the 100% Muslim population of Maldives." See CEDAW. 2017. *Concluding Observations on the Combined Fourth and Fifth Periodic Reports of Maldives Addendum Information Provided by the Maldives on the Follow-Up to the Concluding Observations of the Committee*, CEDAW /C/MDV/ CO/4-5/Add.1. 20 October 2017.

Additional Selected Examples:	
Croatia Anti-Discrimination Act, 2008	
<u>Discrimination</u> This is a good law example because of the specific references to all forms of discrimination, as well as providing for compensation for the victim and/or survivor and fines against the perpetrator.	**Sections 2 and 9(1)** define and prohibit direct and indirect discrimination "in all its manifestations," both in the private and public sectors. The legislation also goes beyond international requirements as it creates a category of "more serious forms of discrimination," which includes multiple, repeated, and continued discrimination, and provides that such elements should be considered by the courts when determining the compensation for the victim and the fine for the perpetrator.
Italy Providing Affirmative Action to Achieve Equal Treatment of Men and Women in Employment Act, 1991	
<u>Affirmative Action</u> Although this law was passed 20 years ago, the provisions still have resonance in current work circumstances. It is a good law based on the topic and includes a section that details examples of the obstacles that women face in work and employment, requiring actions to achieve equality.	**Section 1** provides that the Act is intended to promote the employment of women and to attain substantial equality between men and women at work, by the adopting affirmative action in favor of women to eliminate any obstacles that, in practice, are preventing the realization of equal opportunities. Thereafter, detailed reference is made to various forms of work and occupations including the promotion of: diversification in the vocational options available to women; self-employment and access to management; and the integration of women into activities, occupations, and positions in which they are underrepresented, naming high-technology sectors and high positions of responsibility. It also includes promoting a balance between family and occupational responsibilities with better distribution of these responsibilities between men and women, through measures including work reorganization, working conditions, and different work schedules.

Additional Selected Examples:	
Namibia, Affirmative Action (Employment) Act, 1998	
Affirmative Action This is a good law by reason of its topic and also because of its detail and dedication to addressing inequality and discrimination by taking transformative measures. It does not explicitly refer to women, but the examples given of the designated groups would lend themselves to application to women, as well as intersectional groups who may be subject to discrimination.	**Section 17** provides for "affirmative action" designed to ensure that persons in designated groups enjoy equal employment opportunities at all levels of employment and are equitably represented in the workforce of a relevant employer. There are detailed provisions as to the positive measures that can be taken to identify and eliminate employment barriers against persons in designated groups.
Australia Sex Discrimination Act, 1984	
Exemption from Discrimination This is a good law example because the exemptions from discrimination are sufficiently detailed with regard to the particular jobs which may only be performed by men or women. This conforms to the requirements of the CEDAW and the ILO C111.	**Section 30** describes in detail the exemptions from sex discrimination due to genuine occupational qualification. The examples of exemptions are many and include the duties and activities of a person, such as performing in a dramatic performance or other entertainment role, decency or privacy duties, conduct of searches of the clothing or of persons, and working in toilets.

Gender Mainstreaming in Lawmaking

Context

Gender-sensitive laws require a gender-inclusive legislative framework and a gender-sensitive lawmaking process. In recent years, there has been a significant focus on how to make laws work for women and men and what processes are required to achieve that goal. The following are good recent publications on this topic which include guidance for governments and stakeholders and good examples of national practice:

> **Notes for Lawmakers**
>
> - Lawmakers may readily use the key elements and adapt the four-step process to undertake a good gender-sensitive lawmaking process to suit the particular country's legislative system.
>
> - Lawmakers can use any other laws on equality and nondiscrimination in a horizontal way to guide the processes of developing or amending laws.
>
> - This process could be used to develop and/or amend laws on climate change and disaster risk management and environmental management so as to include the essential gender perspective required by the CEDAW.

(i) *Making Laws Work for Women and Men: A Practical Guide to Gender-Sensitive Legislation* published by the Organization for Security and Co-operation in Europe (OSCE) in 2017.[78] This also has a simply expressed Annex II "Self-Assessment Tool on Gender-Sensitive Legislation."[79]

(ii) *Toolkit for Mainstreaming and Implementing Gender Equality: Implementing the 2015 Organisation for Economic Co-operation and Development (OECD) Recommendation on Gender Equality in Public Life.*[80] As the title indicates, this provides guidance on gender mainstreaming of laws.

---

[78] Organization for Security and Co-operation in Europe (OSCE)/Office for Democratic Institutions and Human Rights (ODIHR). 2017. *Making Laws Work for Women and Men: A Practical Guide to Gender-Sensitive Legislation*. Warsaw.

[79] OSCE/ODIHR. 2017. *Making Laws Work for Women and Men: A Practical Guide to Gender-Sensitive Legislation*. Warsaw. pp. 61–65.

[80] OECD. 2018. *OECD Toolkit for Mainstreaming and Implementing Gender Equality. Implementing the 2015 OECD Recommendation on Gender Equality in Public Life*. Paris.

International Norms

(i)   UDHR, Articles 7 and 8

(ii)   ICCPR, Article 2

(iii) ICESCR, Article 2(2) and General Comment N. 16. Article 3: the equal right of men and women to the enjoyment of all economic, social, and cultural rights. paras. [8], [9], [18], and [21]

(iv)   CEDAW, Article 2

Essentially, gender-sensitive lawmaking is applying gender mainstreaming to the process of developing, designing, implementing, monitoring, and evaluating the whole process of lawmaking to achieve the ultimate objective of equality between women and men on the topic addressed by the law.[81] Gender-sensitive lawmaking is not a goal in itself, but a means to achieving equality (footnote 79). A simple description of gender mainstreaming relevant to this context was set out by the United Nations Economic and Social Council (ECOSOC) in 1997:

> Mainstreaming a gender perspective is the process of assessing the implications for women and men of and planned action, including legislation, policies or programmes, in all areas and at all levels. It is a strategy for making women's as well as men's concerns and experiences an integral dimension of the design, implementation, monitoring and evaluation of policies and programmes in all political, economic and societal spheres so that women and men benefit equally, and inequality is not perpetrated. The ultimate goal is to achieve gender equality.[82]

Constitutions and national laws usually contain explicit provisions prohibiting discrimination based on sex. However, the declarative nature of these provisions does not automatically translate into mechanisms to ensure equal opportunities for women to participate on an equal footing with men in all types of social, political, and economic activities. Therefore, mainstreaming gender into all forms of legislation plays a significant role in the process of promoting and attaining the ultimate objective of gender equality.[83]

Many parliaments, especially in European countries, have established committees, subcommittees, or multiportfolio committees to address gender equality concerns. Their mandates are clearly spelled out in rules of procedures, statutes, or other procedural documents. Properly mandated gender committees are empowered to scrutinize all governmental policy and legislation from a gender perspective, to ensure that all laws abide by international gender equality commitments and are aligned with national policies. Importantly, this often includes a mandate to review and amend budget bills.[84] Core functions of gender committees also include monitoring the implementation of gender equality legislation, and ensuring that laws do not directly or indirectly discriminate against women and girls. They also include monitoring adherence to international gender equality obligations, such as the CEDAW and the SDGs.[85] A 2003 guide by the Inter-Parliamentary Union (IPU) addresses the processes required to report on the application of and implementing the CEDAW and its Optional Protocol.[86] Clear mandates and guides exist for addressing gender equality concerns in parliaments.

---

[81] Footnote 79, p. 8.

[82] ECOSOC. 1997. Mainstreaming the Gender Perspective Into All Policies and Programmes in the United Nations System, Chapter IV in *Report of the Economic and Social Council for 1997*, A/52/3. 18 December 1997.

[83] Footnote 79, p. 12.

[84] Footnote 80, p. 52.

[85] Footnote 80, p. 59.

[86] IPU. 2003. *The Convention on the Elimination of All Forms of Discrimination against Women and its Optional Protocol. Handbook for Parliamentarians*. Geneva.

Key Elements of Good Laws

Key Elements of Good National Laws That Promote Equality and Prohibit Discrimination against Women

There can be very many variations on the key elements, but a simple framework for considering the key information required to ensure that the lawmaking process is gender-sensitive, should at least consider these **four basic steps**:

- Obtaining data and information on the needs of women and men on the proposed topic of the law.
  - Data and information on the practical and strategic needs of women and men (including distinctive needs of subgroups, such as ethnicity, disability, and other gender).
  - Both quantitative and qualitative sex-disaggregated data (see the brief description of each in Step 4).
  - Consulting stakeholders about the needs, such stakeholders to include prospective beneficiaries of the law, government representatives, civil society, academia, and media.

- Assessing the gender impacts of a specific law.
  - Using the information obtained in Step 1 to examine whether women and men may be impacted differently by the law.
  - Measuring the short-, medium-, and long-term objectives of the legislation and the various impacts on women and men at each point.

- Designing the law.
  - Designing the law by reference to the information obtained in Steps 1 and 2.
  - Determining how the law can contribute to the elimination of existing inequalities and promote equality between women and men on the topic.
  - Developing a gender-sensitive budget for the entire processes.
  - Additional consultation processes to be held about the draft legislation ensuring women and men are included.
  - Developing a public awareness and education campaign about the law.

- Designing a framework to monitor and evaluate the law.
  - Identifying indicators that can be used to measure the gender impacts of the law.
  - The indicators to include:
    - o Quantitative indicators (numbers of persons affected, typically using sex-disaggregated information obtained from government records or sociological surveys).
    - o Qualitative indicators (assessing people's perceptions on the effectiveness of the legislation from women's and men's perspective, typically, through public hearings, focus groups, attitude surveys, and interviews).

- Identifying a specific body(ies) charged with monitoring the implementation of the indicators and assessing effectiveness.

- Identifying the process required to respond to the outcomes of the evaluation, such as adjustments to the law or improving its implementation to ensure that the overall goal of gender equality is achieved.

Examples of Good Laws

The following examples are provided from (i) Belgium, (ii) Spain, (iii) the Lao People's Democratic Republic (Lao PDR), (iv) Mongolia, and (v) Fiji.

Example 1: Belgium

Belgium Gender Mainstreaming Act, 2007

This is a good law example because gender mainstreaming occurs throughout the whole law and policymaking process, with responsibilities for each ministry.	• Ensures that strategic gender equality objectives are set for each new policy. • Requires that each new bill or proposed policy pass a "gender test," as the federal government is required to define strategic objectives on gender equality at the beginning of the legislative act for every policy area falling under its remit. • Provides for follow-up and evaluation of these actions. • Ministers are required to define gender indicators for use in measuring the achievement of the strategic objectives set, and to submit annual reports on the actions, measures, and projects carried out in pursuit of these strategic objectives. • Overall progress must be measured in terms of the relative societal positions of women and men at the beginning and end of the legislative act.[a]

[a] OSCE/ODIHR. 2017. *Making Laws Work for Women and Men: A Practical Guide to Gender-Sensitive Legislation.* Warsaw. p. 40; OECD. 2018. *OECD Toolkit for Mainstreaming and Implementing Gender Equality. Implementing the 2015 OECD Recommendation on Gender Equality in Public Life.* Paris. p. 58.

Example 2: Spain

Spain Gender Equality Law, 2007

This law is a good law example as it gender mainstreams the whole process of law and policy making, with dedicated units within each ministry to ensure that happens in practice. In particular it: • Institutionalizes gender mainstreaming across all public bodies, requiring its adoption and implementation for all laws and in the formulation and budgeting of all policies, as well as the General Budget Bill; • Includes gender impact assessments to analyze and assess all laws and regulations from the perspective of eliminating inequalities and contributions to achieve equal opportunities and treatment between women and men, based on indicators of the current situation and foreseen impacts; and • Requires the Ministry of Finance and Public Administrations to give guidance on what information the gender impact assessment report should contain.[a]	**Article 20** requires public authorities to systematically include the sex variable in all their statistics, surveys, or data. **Article 77** creates equality units in all ministries to ensure effective gender mainstreaming. The duties of each unit in a ministry includes: providing gender-relevant statistical information; conducting surveys to foster equality between women and men in ministries; providing advice for the gender impact assessment report; improving employees' understanding of the scope and meaning of the principle of gender equality; overseeing compliance of the law and the effective implementation of the principle of equality.[b]

[a] OECD. 2018. *OECD Toolkit for Mainstreaming and Implementing Gender Equality. Implementing the 2015 OECD Recommendation on Gender Equality in Public Life.* Paris. pp. 26, 29, and 32.
[b] Note a, p. 22.

Example 3: Lao PDR

Lao PDR Law on Making Legislation, 2012

The profusion of different laws that have application in the Lao PDR renders the Law on Making Legislation 2012 essential for a cohesive approach in lawmaking. In addition to the Constitution, there are some 10 levels of resolutions, ordinances, decrees, orders and decisions, instructions, and village regulations that are covered by this Law.

This is a good example of a lawmaking process, but it lacks any reference to gender analysis. This could potentially be achieved by either amending the law or horizontally linking it to the new Lao PDR Law on Gender Equality, 2019, to enable the whole process of lawmaking to be gender mainstreamed including involving women at every stage of the process.

Some central provisions include:

Article 7 sets out the Basic Principles for developing legislation. This requires the laws to be consistent with agreements and treaties to which the Lao PDR is a party; ensures transparency, openness, and cooperation with relevant sectors; and requires extensive consultation.

Articles 36, 52, and 53 describe the process of consultations and includes a workshop for members of the National Assembly and others.

Articles 18 and 28 identify the authority in charge of lawmaking and requires the authority to be responsible for a budget plan and appointing a Law Drafting Committee.

Articles 29 and 32 establish the processes for a Law Drafting Committee as well as the requirements for collecting and analyzing information, conducting consultations, and providing an impact assessment of the draft law.

Article 88 requires monitoring of the implementation of legislation by the authority who has overseen the lawmaking. It requires identifying contradictions with other laws including any treaties, or inconsistencies with socioeconomic conditions, and to solve it or propose a solution.

Example 4: Mongolia

Mongolia Law on Legislation, 2015

This is a good technical example of technical lawmaking, but again lacks any gender perspective in the lawmaking processes. However, the existence of the Mongolia Law on Promotion of Gender Equality, discussed above, together with the activities undertaken by the National Commission in Gender Equality, would enable a horizontal process for gender analysis and a gender perspective to be readily undertaken with regard to the Act.

Articles 3 and 4 describe the scope of the law and the general principles that ensure public participation, publicizing, organizing implementation, as well as monitoring and evaluation of the legislation. Transparency and openness are major principles.

Articles 8 and 12 together set out the stages of drafting, require a preliminary study of the needs and requirements of the law, to evaluate the consequences of the implementation of the law legislation. It also includes consultation with citizens and those whose rights and interests are affected.

Article 18 specifically requires expenses to be estimated to include the activities of citizens, legal entities, and government organizations.

Articles 49 to 51 set out a process for monitoring and evaluating the implementation of the law, which may be undertaken by an external organization.

Article 52 requires the results to be shared and to make any necessary amendments or harmonization or other measures as required.

Example 5: Fiji

Government of Fiji and United Nations Development Programme (UNDP). 2017. *Scrutinizing Legislation from a Gender Perspective—A Practical Toolkit*[a]

This is not a law, but a practical guide for Members of Parliament on how to scrutinize legislation from a gender perspective. It was devised by the Fijian Parliament with the assistance of UNDP, to provide guidance to Parliamentary Standing Committees during the legislative process. It is also useful for civil society to make submissions. This is a good simple toolkit for undertaking gender mainstreaming of a law, however, three important topics are missing: (i) requiring a "gender budget" assessment (although that is a term defined within the Toolkit), (ii) processes and responsibilities for monitoring and evaluation, and (iii) a process for public education on the law.	The toolkit follows a four-step process: • Step 1: Identify the issue. • Step 2: Identify the evidence available on the issue (including sex-disaggregated data). • Step 3: Establish whether gender has been mainstreamed in the decision-making process (referring to: gender considerations, consultation processes, whether women will be involved in administering the law, public education, and monitoring and evaluation). • Step 4: Summarizing conclusions and questions that the members should ask.

[a] Government of Fiji and UNDP. 2017. *Scrutinizing Legislation from a Gender Perspective—A Practical Toolkit*. Suva.

Part 4
Gender-Sensitive Disaster Risk Management and Action on Climate Change

Good Laws on Gender-Sensitive Disaster Risk Management

Notes for Lawmakers

The key elements and good law examples on gender mainstreaming in lawmaking, discussed below, demonstrate important mechanisms to make the lawmaking process more inclusive of women and more gender-sensitive, and these should be used whenever disaster risk management (DRM) laws are being revised or written.

In addition, four practical strategies to include the key elements of good laws for gender-sensitive DRM that are set out in this section are:

- When a DRM law is under review or a new DRM law is being drafted, the national disaster management agencies and legislative drafters should:
  - use the key elements as a checklist on what principles and specific mandates need to be included, and how and where special measures may be needed to increase women's participation in DRM;
  - work closely with the ministry responsible for gender equality, and ensure the effective participation of supportive parliamentarians, women's civil society organizations, and women working in DRM governance and civil service at national and community levels; and
  - if the country's style of legislation cannot provide sufficient detail, at a minimum, ensure the key mandates are there to support more detailed secondary legislation such as regulations and decrees, and gender-sensitive and inclusive strategies, policies, and plans.
- If a DRM law does not meet the key elements for good law and is not under review, but there are constitutional rights and/or a good law on gender equality, the responsible ministries for gender equality and DRM should investigate and take measures to ensure they are implemented in the DRM system. This may require, for example, awareness raising of the laws in place, increased commitment and budget allocation for their implementation, secondary legislation to clarify issues, new agreements on horizontal cooperation, establishment and/or use of compliance mechanisms through the courts or human rights commission.
- If a DRM law does not meet the key elements for good law and is not under review, the implementing agencies may still have sufficiently broad powers and discretions to pursue gender equality, nondiscrimination, and protection from gender-based violence. In this situation, the national disaster management agency should:
  - work closely with the ministry responsible for gender equality to strengthen horizontal links and share expertise; and
  - use the many national, regional, and international tools available to develop secondary legislation, national standards, and formal national policies and strategies that include the key elements of good laws for gender-sensitive DRM.
- At times, a sustained awareness-raising campaign will be necessary to address a lack of legislative underpinning for women's resilience in a national DRM system, with the objective to trigger law reform and improve policy and planning. National actors will often find technical and financial support for such campaigns from international agencies with expertise in human rights, gender analysis and gender mainstreaming in DRM.

Context

Legislation has an important part to play in achieving gender equality and empowering women in the face of disaster risk through mandating gender-sensitive DRM. Although they vary in scope and titles, DRM laws generally establish the institutional structures and governance systems, and set the parameters for budgets, decision-making, monitoring, and evaluation in DRM systems. They are the scaffolding for how disaster risks and needs are assessed, for allocating resources for disaster risk reduction, relief, and recovery, and for defining who participates in these decisions and at what level. Recognition of differentiated needs based on gender, and the inclusion and empowerment of women mandated through DRM laws, can be a powerful tool to support gender-sensitive DRM.

An extensive body of research on DRM laws over the last decade indicates that, although many of these laws mention women briefly as a vulnerable group, very few include principles of gender equality or any provisions for representation and/or participation of women in DRM institutions, at either national or local level.[87] For example, a 2014 Multi-Country Report of 31 countries of varying income levels identified this pattern in the 37 national and subnational jurisdictions examined.[88] Within this varied group of countries, the majority of the DRM laws or formal policies did not mention women or gender, a third of them made a general reference to the needs of women, five of them included a commitment to consult with women (Punjab State in India, Namibia, Nepal, the Philippines, Vanuatu), and five had a requirement for representation of one or more women's agencies within the DRM institutions (Hong Kong, China; Kenya; Nigeria; the Philippines; and the United States [US]).[89] Subsequently, Nepal passed the Disaster Risk Reduction and Management Act, 2017 which also provides for representation of women, bringing that number to 6 of the 37 jurisdictions in the multicountry study.

The pattern that DRM laws sometimes identify women as a vulnerable group, but rarely provide for women's representation in DRM governance or staffing, continues to be demonstrated in subsequent research, even with new DRM legislation. A 2017 study of the DRM laws of 10 countries of the Association of Southeast Asian Nations (ASEAN) found that five of them did not address women or gender at all, some recognized that women at times have special needs and vulnerabilities in disasters, and none required monitoring or evaluation of gender equality in DRM.[90] For example, the most recently passed ASEAN country DRM law, the Lao People's Democratic Republic (Lao PDR) Law on Disaster Management 2019, includes the right of disaster victims to receive special services or facilities, especially "pregnant women, children, people with disabilities and the elderly" (Article 43). This is a common type of provision in DRM laws, to recognize pregnant women or women more generally as one of the vulnerable groups. This approach does not recognize differences in disaster impacts based on gender roles, preexisting inequality, or other sexual and reproductive health needs of women.

Within the ASEAN grouping, most of which had revised their DRM laws in the decade prior to the 2017 study, the Lao PDR and the Philippines were also the only two of the 10 countries whose laws required any representation of women in decision-making roles in DRM system institutions (footnote 90). The Philippine law is discussed further below as a good law example. But for the Lao PDR, the new Law on Disaster Management has reduced women's representation through the Lao Women's Union (LWU) to village-level disaster management committees only, whereas when previously it was a member of the central disaster management committee (CDMC). While LWU inclusion in the new village-level committees is a positive

---

[87] Footnote 10.

[88] Algeria, Angola, Australia (Federal, Victoria), Austria, Brazil, the People's Republic of China (PRC; Hong Kong, China), Dominican Republic, Ecuador, Ethiopia, Guatemala, India (Federal, Odisha, Punjab), Italy, Iraq, Japan, Kenya, the Kyrgyz Republic, Madagascar, Mexico, Namibia, New Zealand, Nepal, Nicaragua, Nigeria, the Philippines, St. Lucia, South Africa, Ukraine, Uruguay, the United States (Federal, Illinois, Louisiana), Vanuatu, and Viet Nam.

[89] IFRC, UNDP, and M. Picard. 2014. *Effective Law and Regulation for Disaster Risk Reduction: A Multi-Country Study.* Geneva and New York.

[90] IFRC, M. Picard, and V. Bannon. 2017. *ASEAN Disaster Law Mapping—Implementing AADMER: A Regional Stocktake.* Kuala Lumpur.

legislative provision in its own right, this still leaves the key district, provincial, and central level committees with no mandated representation of women.[91]

The absence of gender inclusion in DRM laws highlights a lack of gender analysis in the lawmaking process about the causes of women's vulnerability to disasters that relate to gender inequality and different gender roles. Simultaneously, there is a failure to recognize the extent of women's actual role in DRM at community level and through civil society.[92] This explains why there is so little focus in the DRM laws on women's role in DRM systems, and indicates there is a need for special measures in the legislation to correct a lack of formal representation and empowerment of women in governance and staffing. Such measures align with the Convention on the Elimination of All Forms of Discrimination against Women (CEDAW) and with country commitments under Sustainable Development Goal (SDG) 5 to achieve gender equality and empower all women and girls, especially SDG5 subgoal 5.5 to "ensure women's full and effective participation and equal opportunities for leadership at all levels of decision-making in political, economic, and public life."[93]

Disasters often reveal the disparities among women's and men's access to land and resources, resulting in differential levels of vulnerability to disaster impacts. Therefore, large-scale disaster reconstruction can be an opportunity to revisit and improve laws on these issues. For example, in Aceh, Indonesia, after the 2004 Indian Ocean Tsunami, the World Bank's Reconstruction of Aceh Land Administration System project used a community land mapping process to determine land titling.[94] Dispute resolution and social protection for women were based on local interpretations of Islamic law and traditional practices, and participants received gender-sensitization beforehand (footnote 94). A high proportion of women participated, using these mechanisms to recover their land and property rights (footnote 94). Additionally, there are distinctly different types of DRM laws.[95] Some DRM laws are comprehensive and address the full spectrum of DRM activities, while others only establish institutions and powers for emergency management. It is not a simple matter to say that one type is better than another, as it depends on the national risk situation and legal system. In particular, it is influenced by other regulations which may be in place to reduce disaster risk in development (e.g., building and planning laws), or to manage the socioeconomic and welfare issues associated with disasters. In fact, the more developed economies examined in the International Federation of Red Cross and Red Crescent Societies–United Nations Development Programme (IFRC–UNDP) Multi-Country Report tended to have narrower specialist emergency management laws rather than comprehensive DRM laws. Other issues were managed by other ministries or local government regulations.

Similarly, when assessing gender equality in DRM laws, some countries have very good laws and enforcement systems on gender equality and nondiscrimination that already apply to DRM laws and institutions. Others do not have applicable human rights and gender equality laws, or there is insufficient horizontal integration between these spheres. Therefore, it is important to look holistically at a country to identify legislative frameworks that support women's resilience to disasters and climate change, which is the approach of this report. Some examples of horizontal integration of gender equality into a DRM law via other legislation are discussed under good laws examples in below, most comprehensively in Mongolia, based on the relationship between the Mongolian Law on Disaster Protection 2003 (2017), the Constitution, and the Law on the Promotion of Gender Equality (2011).

---

[91] There are powers to appoint additional committee members in the DM Law Articles 52–54, or to supplement committees through the National Strategy on Disaster Risk Reduction, which was in drafting at the time of writing. But neither options are as strong as legislatively mandated representation of women at all levels.

[92] Regional Asia-Pacific Conference on Gender and Disaster Risk Reduction. 2016. *Ha Noi Recommendations for Action on Gender and Disaster Risk Reduction*. Ha Noi.

[93] Footnote 58, p. 5.

[94] World Bank East Asia and Pacific Region. n.d. *After the Tsunami: Women and Land Reforms in Aceh*. Washington, DC.

[95] See Chapter 13: A Typology of DRM Laws in: IFRC, UNDP, and M. Picard. 2014. *Effective Law and Regulation for Disaster Risk Reduction: A Multi-Country Study*. Geneva and New York. pp. 41–44.

As explored earlier in the report, gender-based violence (GBV) is also widely recognized as a significant issue for women in disaster situations. However, GBV issues are not addressed by DRM laws. In 2018 in-depth social research done at household level in Indonesia, the Lao PDR, and the Philippines, found that the risks of GBV are exacerbated during disaster situations and that those responding to disasters, and other actors aiming to address the needs of GBV victims and survivors, were not adequately collaborating to reduce these risks. It noted that these trends are applicable to disaster contexts in other countries. While none of these countries included GBV in their main DRM laws, two of the three countries had legal provisions that the study recommended be implemented. These are the section of the Philippines 2008 Magna Carta for Women (Republic Act 9710) on "women affected by disasters, calamities, and other crisis situations" (s.10) and Indonesia's 2014 Head of Badan Nasional Penanggulangan Bencana (BNPB) Regulation (Perka) No. 13 on Gender Mainstreaming in Disaster Management.[96] This indicates that horizontal links with women's equality legislation and secondary legislation in the form of regulations can also be used to integrate gender equality and GBV prevention into DRM systems.

A 2017 global study specifically on laws and policies related to GBV in disasters found that DRM laws did not have specific mandates or resources allocated for this issue, and that there were also not sufficient horizontal links or resource allocations to work with the regular GBV welfare and justice support services for effective prevention and mitigation of GBV during disasters.[97] The same study noted that no DRM law had been identified in any country that identified the prevention or mitigation of gender-based violence as a specific issue of concern in disaster response or recovery. The report made a number of specific recommendations about gender-sensitive DRM laws, as well as how DRM systems could prepare for and make a priority of the issue of gender-based violence along with the relevant health and welfare services, some of which are incorporated into the key criteria below.[98] The 2019 Outcome Statement of the Oslo Conference on Ending Sexual and Gender-Based Violence (SGBV) in Humanitarian Crises,[99] acknowledged that "women and girls are key actors in humanitarian response and must be acknowledged as powerful agents of change in their own lives and communities," and that:

(i)   "Gender inequality and an unequal distribution of power between women and men are root causes of SGBV. A person's risk of SGBV is subject to personal, situational, and social factors, including gender dynamics that place individuals, particularly women and girls, at high risk.

(ii)   We must make concerted efforts to address gender inequality, ensure that human rights are respected, and include local women and women's organizations in decision-making.

(iii)   Governments and international organizations should adopt and implement national and international institutional policies, legal frameworks, and standards to strengthen gender equality and prevent and respond to sexual and gender-based violence" (footnote 99).

A range of international standards on reducing GBV in emergencies are listed under international norms below.

International Norms

DRM treaties and multilateral agreements. There is no binding global treaty that creates specific obligations relevant to DRM legislation at national level, but there are international norms established by agreement, particularly the Sendai Framework on Disaster Risk Reduction 2015–2030. There are also both binding and

---

[96] Footnote 13, p. 15.

[97] Footnote 10.

[98] Footnote 10, pp. 59–63.

[99] Governments of Norway, Iraq, Somalia, United Arab Emirates, United Nations Office for the Coordination of Humanitarian Affairs (UN OCHA), UNFPA, ICRC. 2019. *Oslo Conference on Ending Sexual and Gender-Based Violence in Humanitarian Crises: Co-Host Outcome Statement.* Oslo.

voluntary regional treaties and agreements that play a normative role in DRM in Asia and the Pacific. None of these DRM treaties or agreements are specific to gender or women's empowerment. At best they contain general statements on gender equality and women's participation and, in some cases, they have not yet incorporated gender considerations.

The key norm-setting international and regional DRM agreements in Asia and the Pacific are:

(i) **The Sendai Framework.** Key references to gender are made in para. 19(d) regarding leadership of women and youth, and para. 32 on empowering women and people with disabilities to lead and promote gender equitable and universally accessible DRM. Its most important statement regarding women is in para. 36(a)(i):

Women and their participation are critical to effectively manage disaster risk and designing, resourcing, and implementing gender-sensitive disaster risk reduction policies, plans and programmes; and adequate capacity building measures need to be taken to empower women for preparedness as well as to build their capacity to secure alternate means of livelihood in post-disaster situations.

(ii) **The ASEAN Agreement on Disaster Management and Emergency Response 2005 (AADMER).** It does not address gender issues, but does require State Parties to involve all stakeholders, and this should include women.[100] There is also the ASEAN Committee on Women (ACW), the ASEAN Commission on the Promotion and Protection of the Rights of Women and Children (ACWC), as well as the ASEAN Regional Plan of Action on the Elimination of Violence against Women and the Regional Plan of Action on the Elimination of Violence against Children. However, these gender pillars are not currently integrated with the AADMER workplan or ASEAN-led disaster preparedness, response, and recovery.[101]

(iii) **The South Asian Association for Regional Cooperation (SAARC) Agreement on Rapid Response to Natural Disasters 2011** is concerned entirely with intergovernmental procedures for regional mutual cooperation in disaster response, and does not include any discussion of principles, stakeholders, or gender.[102]

(iv) **The Framework for Resilient Development in the Pacific 2017–2030: An Integrated Approach to Address Climate Change and Disaster Risk Management (FRDP)**[103] provides high-level voluntary strategic guidance to different stakeholder groups—governments, civil society, private sector, and vulnerable groups as key stakeholders. Three of its 10 guiding principles are particularly relevant to gender equality and women's resilience, and these concern the need to: (1) protect human rights, including nondiscrimination and access to basic necessities; (2) prioritize the needs and respect the rights of the most vulnerable, including women, persons with disabilities, children, youth, and older persons, and to facilitate their effective participation in DRM and climate change planning and implementation; and (3) "integrate gender considerations, advocate and support equitable participation of women and men in the planning and implementation of all activities."[104] The FRDP's implementation has been supported by the Pacific Resilience Partnership, a coalition of governmental and nongovernment groups. Information is not yet available to gauge whether it is having an impact on gender considerations in DRM laws in the Pacific.

---

[100] Footnote 90.
[101] Footnote 13, p. 15.
[102] South Asian Association for Regional Cooperation (SAARC). 2011. *SAARC Agreement on Rapid Response to Natural Disasters.* Malé.
[103] Pacific Community, Secretariat of the Pacific Regional Environment Programme, Pacific Islands Forum Secretariat, UNDP, United Nations Office for Disaster Risk Reduction (UNDRR) and University of the South Pacific. 2016. *Framework for Resilient Development in the Pacific: An Integrated Approach to Address Climate Change and Disaster Risk Management (FRDP) 2017–2030.* Suva, Fiji.
[104] Footnote 103, p. 6.

Guidance on gender in DRM laws from the texts of the above international and regional agreements is quite limited, but there is also more elaborated normative guidance, regional resolutions, and initiatives that arise from them, including for example:

(i) The *Ha Noi Recommendations for Action* made by the Regional Asia–Pacific Conference on Gender and Disaster Risk Reduction in 2016, discussed below.

(ii) The "Global Programme in Support of a Gender Responsive Sendai Framework Implementation: Addressing the Gender Inequality of Risk and Promoting Community Resilience to Natural Hazards in a Changing Climate (GIR)," launched by UN Women, the IFRC, and United Nations Office for Disaster Risk Reduction (UNDRR) at the 2017 Global Platform for Disaster Risk Reduction in Cancun, Mexico.

(iii) The *Ulaanbaatar Declaration* of the Asian Ministerial Conference on Disaster Risk Reduction (AMCDRR) 2018, supported by research on country progress from the IASC Asia Partnership (IAP) Gender Stakeholder Group, with its Progress Review on gender equality and social inclusion in implementing the Sendai Framework in Asia,[105] called on all governments and stakeholders to:

> *Promote full and equal participation of women in leading, designing, and implementing gender-sensitive disaster risk reduction policies, plans, and programmes, through joint efforts by public and private sector, supported by appropriate legal frameworks and allocation of necessary resources.*[106]

(iv) The UNDRR series of *Words into Action* guidelines, which are updated regularly and mainstream gender into their guidance on implementing the Sendai Framework. These look at several specific topics, including children and youth, land use and urban planning, developing national and local DRR strategies, and others. As yet, there is not a specific UNDRR guide on mainstreaming gender into DRM.[107]

Gender Equality and Nondiscrimination Treaties and Multilateral Agreements Relevant to Disaster Risk Management

As discussed in Part 1, separate international norms on gender equality also apply to country lawmaking and implementation on DRM. They are important for a full gender analysis of DRM laws. Implementation of these commitments in national legislation can be the basis for horizontal integration to bring legally binding gender equality mandates into DRM systems (especially where DRM laws lack detail on gender or have not yet mainstreamed gender). The two key norm-setting international agreements for gender-sensitive DRM are:

(i) The CEDAW is the binding international treaty on eliminating discrimination against women, and remains the touchstone international norm for countries making and implementing gender-sensitive DRM legislation. The CEDAW Committee General Recommendation 37, also described in the Background Section of this report, provides guidance on how to interpret and apply the CEDAW in DRM and climate change adaptation.[108] It was based on wide consultations with States and submissions from many expert organizations, and emphasizes the impact of preexisting gender inequalities that increase women's risk in disasters and recovery, and heighten the risk of GBV. The solutions, based in the rights of the CEDAW, are highlighted as a need to focus on equality and nondiscrimination,

---

[105] IAP Gender Stakeholder Group. 2018. *Progress Review and the Way Forward: Gender Equality and Social Inclusion in Implementing the Sendai Framework for Disaster Risk Reduction in Asia. Periodic Update to UNDRR Asia Partnership*. Bangkok.

[106] Asian Ministerial Conference on Disaster Risk Reduction. 2018. *Ulaanbaatar Declaration*. Ulaanbaatar. para. 12.

[107] UNDRR. 2019. *Words into Action: Disaster Displacement, How to Reduce Risk, Address Impacts and Strengthen Resilience. A Companion for Implementing the Sendai Framework Target (E)*. Geneva.

[108] CEDAW. General Recommendation No. 37 on Gender-Related Dimensions of Disaster Risk Reduction in the Context of Climate Change, CEDAW/C/GC/37. 13 March 2018.

and women's rights to participation and empowerment, as well as the importance of data collection, monitoring, and assessment of laws.

(ii) *SDG5 to achieve gender equality and empower all women and girls*, and its subgoals and targets, is a newer norm that captures and expands the essence of the CEDAW as part of country commitments under the 2030 Agenda (although it is voluntary rather than a binding treaty).[109] Of particular relevance to DRM laws and their mandates, are the subgoals on the elimination of discrimination (5.1), and of all forms of violence against all women and girls (5.2), ensuring women's participation and opportunities for leadership (5.5), and universal access to sexual and reproductive health (5.6). The three targets are also highly relevant to DRM legislation, especially Target 5.c to "adopt and strengthen sound policies and enforceable legislation for the promotion of gender equality and the empowerment of all women and girls at all levels."

In addition to treaties and agreements, there is also normative guidance from international and regional organizations. Some of this guidance is specific to gender issues in disasters, including GBV, and some guidance mainstreams gender into issues such as displacement, and some provide guidance on DRM lawmaking that mainstreams gender.

Humanitarian Standards that Mainstream Gender

Two key (and related) standards on humanitarian response that mainstream gender include:

(i) *The Sphere Handbook 2018: Humanitarian Charter and Minimum Standards in Humanitarian Response* (Sphere Handbook).[110]

(ii) *The Core Humanitarian Standard on Quality and Accountability* (CHS),[111] which is part of the Sphere Handbook and also widely adopted as a stand-alone standard.

Disaster Displacement

United Nations and other international guidance on disaster displacement that mainstream gender and provide normative guidance to humanitarian responders and countries include:

(i) *Guiding Principles on Internal Displacement 1998* (UN IDP Principles),[112] United Nations principles that remain foundational general guidance to countries and humanitarian responders, based in human rights law.

(ii) *Handbook for the Protection of Internally Displaced Persons 2010*, United Nations.[113]

(iii) *Operational Guidelines on the Protection of Persons in Situations of Natural Disasters 2011*, United Nations.[114]

---

[109] United Nations General Assembly, Sustainable Development Goal 5: Achieve Gender Equality and Empower All Women and Girls, in Transforming Our World: The 2030 Agenda for Sustainable Development, A/RES/70/1. 25 September 2015. p. 5.

[110] Sphere Association. 2018. The Sphere Handbook 2018: Humanitarian Charter and Minimum Standards in Humanitarian Response. 4th ed. Geneva.

[111] CHS Alliance. 2018. Core Humanitarian Standard on Quality and Accountability. Geneva. Developed by the Humanitarian Accountability Partnership, People in Aid, which subsequently merged to form the "Core Humanitarian Standard Alliance," Groupe URD, and the Sphere Project, now the "Sphere Association."

[112] UN OCHA. 2004. Guiding Principles on Internal Displacement 1998. Geneva.

[113] UN IASC. 2010. Handbook for the Protection of Internally Displaced Persons. Geneva. Especially identification of GBV and human trafficking as threats. pp. 167–180 and 215–223, respectively, although gender equality is integrated throughout the guidance. Also see UN OCHA. 2001. Guiding Principles on Internal Displacement 1998. Geneva.

[114] IASC. 2011. IASC Operational Guidelines on the Protection of Persons in Situations of Natural Disasters. Geneva and Washington, DC.

(iv) *Guidance on Protecting People from Disasters and Environmental Change through Planned Relocation, 2015*, UN High Commissioner for Refugees (UNHCR), and Brookings.[115]

(v) *Disaster Displacement—Towards a Protection Agenda for People Displaced across Borders in the Context of Disasters and the Effects of Climate Change, 2016*.[116] This currently active Platform on Disaster Displacement (follow-up to the Nansen Initiative) on climate and disaster displacement, focuses on cross-border displacement, and mainstreams gender into its guidance.

(vi) *Words into Action: Disaster Displacement, How to Reduce Risk, Address Impacts and Strengthen Resilience. A Companion for Implementing the Sendai Framework Target (E), 2019*, UNDRR.[117]

Minimum Standards for Prevention and Response to Gender-Based Violence in Disasters

There is now substantial and detailed international guidance on GBV in disasters to support humanitarian responders, including governments, in interpreting the different needs and their obligations. These norms can be used by countries in formulating gender provisions of DRM laws, and in creating horizontal links between DRM laws and the regular systems of GBV prevention and victim/survivor support. They include:

(i) "Outcome Statement of the Oslo Conference on Ending Sexual and Gender-Based Violence in Humanitarian Crises." May 2019.[118]

(ii) The Global Protection Cluster, 2019, Inter-Agency Minimum Standards for Gender-Based Violence in Emergencies Programming.[119]

(iii) The IFRC 2018 Minimum Standards on Protection, Gender and Inclusion in Emergencies.[120]

(iv) The Global Shelter Cluster 2017 *GBV Risk Reduction in Shelter Programmes—Three Case Studies*,[121] and its guidance on site planning, and handling disclosure of GBV.[122]

(v) The United Nations Population Fund (UNFPA) 2015 *Minimum Standards for Prevention and Response to Gender-Based Violence in Emergencies*.[123]

Guidance on Developing Disaster Risk Management Laws

In terms of specific guidance for good national DRM legislation that mainstreams aspects of gender issues, three generalist sources can be drawn on to identify relevant norms. All three of these resources support gender mainstreaming in DRM laws, but are not detailed guidance on this issue. These are:

(i) The Caribbean Community (CARICOM) 2013 "Model Comprehensive Disaster Management Legislation and Regulations."[124] This is a model law and guidance, used actively by CARICOM and the Caribbean Disaster Emergency Management Agency (CDEMA) members countries, which provides a good law example of systematic gender mainstreaming into a DRM Law. For example, in the model law: the national disaster management committee is to advise the Cabinet on DRM issues including

[115] UNHCR and Brookings Institution. 2015. *Guidance on Protecting People from Disasters and Environmental Change through Planned Relocation*. Geneva and Washington, DC.

[116] Platform on Disaster Displacement (PDD). 2016. *Disaster Displacement—Towards a Protection Agenda for People Displaced across Borders in the Context of Disasters and the Effects of Climate Change*. Geneva.

[117] Footnote 107.

[118] Footnote 99.

[119] UNFPA. 2019. *The Inter-Agency Minimum Standards for Gender-Based Violence in Emergencies Programming*. New York.

[120] IFRC. 2018. *Minimum Standards for Protection, Gender and Inclusion in Emergencies*. Geneva.

[121] Global Shelter Cluster, GBV in Shelter Programming Working Group. 2017. *GBV Risk Reduction in Shelter Programmes—Three Case Studies*. New York.

[122] Global Shelter Cluster. 2021. *Shelter Programming Working Group—Documents*.

[123] UNFPA. 2015. *Minimum Standards for Prevention and Response to Gender-Based Violence in Emergencies*. New York.

[124] Caribbean Disaster Emergency Management Agency (CDEMA). 2013. *Model Comprehensive Disaster Management Legislation and Regulations 2013 and Adaptation Guide*. Bridgetown, Barbados.

gender (Section 6(3)); district disaster management committees need to meet the dietary and health needs of pregnant and nursing mothers and their children (Sections 10 and 20); the National Disaster Management Agency is to collaborate with a wide range of stakeholders to ensure, among other things, that "disaster risk reduction and climate change measures are gender responsive" and this includes an obligation to "institutionalize gender analysis as part of any assessment following the impact of a hazard" (Section 20(1)(j)) and 20(2)). In this model example, the National Disaster Management Agency (NDMA) Director is also required to collaborate with climate change and gender agencies as well as to use "standardized, holistic and gender-sensitive community methodologies for natural and anthropogenic hazard identification and mapping" (Section 22). The model continues in a similar vein with systematic entry points on gender mainstreamed throughout.

(ii)   The 2015 IFRC and UNDP *Checklist on Law and Disaster Risk Reduction: An Annotated Outline*,[125] and its accompanying *Handbook on Law and Disaster Risk Reduction*.[126] This 10-point checklist for lawmakers includes a general on inclusion of nongovernment stakeholders, after which the commentary notes that "specific provisions may also be needed to ensure meaningful engagement of women, minorities, people with disabilities, and older persons."[127] More specifically, question 9 asks "Do your country's laws adequately address gender considerations and the special needs of particularly vulnerable categories of persons?" The checklist guidance notes that:

> Disasters can have disproportionate impacts on certain categories of persons, either due to their particular vulnerabilities and/or the influence of socioeconomic and cultural systems and practices. These categories may vary between countries and localities, but they commonly include women, the very poor, older persons, migrants, children and people with disabilities, among others. Laws can ensure an adequately disaggregated analysis to detect groups facing increased risk and require that certain measures be undertaken to increase their safety and resilience. For example, legislation may require that evacuation centers are made accessible to people with disabilities, or that gender differences are taken into account when developing DRR strategies or contingency plans.[128]

(iii)   The 2019 IFRC Checklist on Law and Disaster Preparedness and Response, also mainstreams gender issues relating to women throughout a 10-point checklist.[129] It emphasizes the importance of involving a wide range of stakeholders in the law development through processes that are inclusive of women and others. Key points where women are specifically mentioned relate to: awareness through training and drills to ensure "trainings include an equal representation of women, men, and other identified vulnerable groups in a particular community;" early warning systems; disaster displacement; shelter assistance; and most comprehensively regarding participation and inclusion of vulnerable groups.[130]

In considering the gaps in DRM legislation on gender and disasters, a useful source of guidance remains the 2016 Ha Noi Recommendations for Action.[131] The identified actions aim to ensure that implementation of the Sendai Framework in Asia and the Pacific are gender-sensitive and inclusive and a number of them are directed to national law and policy. Noting that women play a greater role in risk management and resilience-building than is often acknowledged, the preamble to the outcome document observed that "women in Asia and the Pacific have the lowest decision making and political power in the world, thereby limiting their say and influence in DRR decision making processes."[132]

---

[125]   IFRC and UNDP. 2015. The Checklist on Law and Disaster Risk Reduction: An Annotated Outline. Geneva and New York.
[126]   IFRC and UNDP. 2015. The Handbook on Law and Disaster Risk Reduction. Geneva and New York.
[127]   Footnote 125, p. 16 (Checklist question 8).
[128]   Footnote 125, p. 17.
[129]   IFRC. 2019. The Checklist on Law and Disaster Preparedness and Response. Geneva.
[130]   Footnote 129, pp. 12, 18, 20, 27, 30–34.
[131]   Footnote 92.
[132]   Footnote 92, p. 1.

The Ha Noi Recommendations for Action of particular relevance to law and policy are that governments should seek to:

(i)   Understand risk, by mandating the collection and updating of national and local sex, age, and disability disaggregated data and socioeconomic baselines to inform gender-responsive disaster risk reduction, then conduct gender analysis of disaster risks and use the gender analysis to inform national and local DRR policy development.[133]

(ii)   Implement strong laws that mandate women's participation and leadership in decision-making and also create accountability for implementation.[134]

(iii)   "Invest in social protection and social services that reduce gender inequality and other inequalities and enable at-risk groups of women and men to mitigate disaster risks and adapt to climate change."[135]

(iv)   "Implement women-led security and protection interventions that reduce current risks and prevent creation of new risks to gender-based discrimination and violence." This would include accessible service and referral mechanisms on GBV, women's refuges and safe spaces, and accountability indicators for security and protection in the national monitoring and reporting.[136]

(v)   "Institutionalize the leadership of women and diverse groups in disaster preparedness (including inclusive and accessible early warning systems) response, recovery, and reconstruction at all levels." It proposes that women and diverse groups must be represented at least 40% in national and local mechanisms responsible for developing disaster preparedness, response and recovery decisions (footnote 136).

To date, these remain the most comprehensive guidance on how to integrate gender equality and gender sensitivity into national DRM laws, especially under the Sendai Framework, and they form an important core of the elements of good DRM law to support women's resilience set out below.

Key Elements of Good Laws

Key Elements of Good Laws for Gender-Sensitive Disaster Risk Management

Legislation supports women's resilience most effectively if DRM laws—or gender equality laws applicable to the DRM system—include the following key elements:

- Clear principles of sex or gender equality and nondiscrimination that align with the CEDAW and must be applied in disaster risk reduction, preparedness, response, recovery, and reconstruction from national to local level.

- Language and concepts that are gender-inclusive.

- Legal mandates, mechanisms, and budget to implement gender equality principles, including requirements and resource allocation for:
    - gender-sensitive policy development;
    - gender mainstreaming in planning and implementation;
    - capacity building for policy makers and implementers on gender-sensitive DRM;
    - gathering, analysis, and reporting of all disaster-related statistics on the basis of sex-disaggregated data; and,
    - targets, indicators, monitoring, evaluation, and reporting on gender issues in DRM policy, planning, and implementation.

continued on next page

---

[133] Footnote 92, pp. 3–4.
[134] Footnote 92, p. 4.
[135] Footnote 92, p. 6.
[136] Footnote 92, pp. 7–8.

continued

Key Elements of Good Laws for Gender-Sensitive Disaster Risk Management

- Promotes participation and empowerment of women as key stakeholders in national and local DRM institutions, including:
  - representation of women's organizations, and a minimum of one-third women overall, in DRM governance, including key policy and disaster management committees, councils, and technical advisory bodies;
  - inclusion of a wide cross-section of nongovernment stakeholders in participatory approaches to DRM policy development and implementation; and
  - targets for gender parity in all employment in the DRM institutions, with a temporary minimum quota of one-third women overall, while taking positive measures to increase women's presence in leadership roles.
- Recognizes potential gender differences in disaster impacts and requires implementing authorities to take account of these in DRM policy and planning, response, recovery, and reconstruction mechanisms, including:
  - risk assessments and needs assessments that take account of the range of possible different impacts based on gender roles and preexisting inequality or discrimination (e.g., carer responsibilities, degree of personal autonomy, access to warnings and means of evacuation, restrictive factors due to types of clothing and physical skills, access to risk knowledge and education, and gendered roles in response and recovery);
  - provision of goods and services relating to women's sexual and reproductive health and sanitation during disasters (e.g., culturally appropriate sanitary products and contraception, basic hygiene kits, ante-natal and post-natal healthcare, nutritional needs of pregnant and nursing mothers, access to safe sanitation facilities);
  - prevention, mitigation, and response to increased sexual and gender-based violence in disaster situations as a central issue for women's rights, health, and safety, (e.g., training of responders to recognize and refer, mobilization of specialist support services, mechanisms for access to justice);
  - avoidance of direct and indirect sex discrimination in delivery of humanitarian relief, recovery, and reconstruction assistance, (e.g., assumption that heads of households are men, registration criteria that fewer women can meet such as property titles);
  - awareness of national or local practices relating to birth or identity documentation, evidence of marriage and/or title to marital property, to ensure fair and rapid means for women to establish their identities and title to land and property for disaster relief and reconstruction; and
  - recognition that preexisting socioeconomic disadvantage from gender inequality affects many women's capacity to adapt and recover, and may require special measures to support women's economic recovery (e.g., the gender pay gap leading to women having fewer economic resources on average, counting disaster losses of income and nutrition from women's informal and family labor, and ensuring access to disaster risk financing and business recovery loans for women-led MSMEs).

Examples of Good Laws

As noted above, gender equality in DRM, and the representation or empowerment of women, are rarely mentioned in DRM legislation. More frequent mentions of women's different needs are couched in terms of women as a vulnerable group, which is only part of the picture, and situation-specific. Therefore, it is difficult to identify DRM laws that meet all of the key criteria, so most of the following examples are provisions within laws rather than entire laws. There are also suggestions on how to achieve horizontal integration between DRM legislation and national human rights laws on gender, using country examples.

In cases where the DRM laws do not meet the key elements for good law, and if there is also little appetite for a major review of the law (e.g., when it is a newly passed law), there is the possibility to strengthen horizontal links with other good laws or provisions on gender. For example, this might be done through minor amendment to the DRM law, the use of secondary legislation in the form of regulations or decrees, or institutional enforcement of constitutional rights or existing powers in a gender law.

Five country examples are provided from (i) the Philippines, (ii) Bhutan, (iii) Nepal, (iv) Indonesia, and (v) Mongolia.

Example 1: The Philippines

Two good Philippine laws reinforce each other to provide a basis for gender-sensitive DRM: the **Philippine Disaster Risk Reduction and Management Act, 2010 and the Magna Carta for Women 2008**.

Philippine Disaster Risk Reduction and Management Act, 2010

This Act is an example of a good gender-sensitive law because it includes gender equality principles, provides for specific representation of women's agencies in its institutions, adopts a participatory model that gives other opportunities for women's inclusion, and indicates the need to investigate how and when women's needs may differ from men.

It:

(i) Includes gender equality principles and mainstreaming through **Sections 2, 9, and 12**.

(ii) Provides for representation of women's offices at national and local level in **Sections 5 and 11**.

(iii) Multistakeholder participation also increases opportunities for women to have a voice, as provided in **Sections 5, 6, and 11**.

The Act, therefore, has a number of the key elements which, taken together, make it the best overall example identified. It could certainly be improved by requiring a minimum proportion of women and/or men on the committees, assuming there is a need for such a special measure based on current proportions of representation.

Gender equality principles and mainstreaming:

Section 2 policy objective to "Ensure that disaster risk reduction and climate change measures are gender responsive, sensitive to indigenous knowledge systems, and respectful of human rights."

Section 9(1)(m) requires the Office of Civil Defense to "conduct early recovery and post-disaster needs assessment implementing gender analysis as part of it."

Section 12(16) ensures immediate delivery of basic necessities to women (and children) during emergencies, and this can also be used to ensure that women have access to products required for their sexual and reproductive health during disasters.

Representation of women:

Sections 5 and 11 provide for representation of the Chairperson of the Philippine Commission on Women on the National Disaster Risk Reduction and Management Council (DRRMC), and the Head of the local Gender and Development Office in each Local DRRMC.

Multistakeholder participation:

Section 6(d): National DRRMC must "Ensure a multistakeholder participation in the development, updating, and sharing of a Disaster Risk Reduction and Management Information System and Geographic Information System-based national risk map as policy, planning, and decision-making tools."

Sections 5 and 11 provide for representation in both the National DRRMC and the Local DRRMCs of Philippine Red Cross, four accredited civil society organizations and one private sector representative—an additional six positions that can also potentially add to the number of women.

Example 1: The Philippines

Philippine Magna Carta for Women 2008 (Republic Act 9710)

The Philippine Magna Carta for Women 2008 includes a **Section 10** on women affected by disasters, calamities, and other crisis situations, although it had not yet been operationalized in the DRM system in 2018.[a]

It also includes a general provision, **Section 11**, on women's participation, representation, and empowerment in the DRM system as civil service staff and in governance policy and decision-making bodies It then continues with subsections on international bodies, political parties, and the private sector.

This is a good law because:

(i)   It recognizes women's particular needs in disasters from a gender perspective, including the increased risk of gender-based violence, and sets out the types of prevention and support services needed;

(ii) It supports gender parity for women in the civil service, a minimum of 40% women in development councils and planning bodies and representation of women's organizations in other policy and decision-making bodies, all of which are highly relevant to DRM governance; and

(iii) Although it is not part of the Disaster Risk Reduction and Management (DRRM) Act, its provisions apply generally to the DRM system and its institutions.

Section 10: "Women have the right to protection and security in times of disasters, calamities, and other crisis situations especially in all phases of relief, recovery, rehabilitation, and construction efforts. The State shall provide for immediate humanitarian assistance, allocation of resources, and early resettlement, if necessary. It shall also address the particular needs of women from a gender perspective to ensure their full protection from sexual exploitation and other sexual and gender-based violence committed against them. Responses to disaster situations shall include the provision of services, such as psychosocial support, livelihood support, education, psychological health, and comprehensive health services, including protection during pregnancy."

Section 11: Participation and representation—"The State shall undertake temporary special measures to accelerate the participation and equitable representation of women in all spheres of society particularly in the decision-making and policy-making processes in government and private entities to fully realize their role as agents and beneficiaries of development.

The State shall institute the following affirmative action mechanisms so that women can participate meaningfully in the formulation, implementation, and evaluation of policies, plans, and programs for national, regional, and local development:

(i)   Empowerment within the Civil Service—Within the next 5 years, the number of women in third level positions in government shall be incrementally increased to achieve a 50–50 gender balance;

(ii) Development Councils and Planning Bodies— To ensure the participation of women in all levels of development planning and program implementation, at least 40% of membership of all development councils from the regional, provincial, city, municipal, and barangay levels shall be composed of women;

(iii) Other Policy and Decision-Making Bodies— Women's groups shall also be represented in international, national, and local special and decision-making bodies..."

[a]   IFRC. 2018. *The Responsibility to Prevent and Respond to Sexual and Gender-Based Violence in Disasters and Crises*. Kuala Lumpur. pp. 15, 38.

Example 2: Bhutan

Bhutan Disaster Management Act, 2013 (DM Act)

The Disaster Management Act of Bhutan 2013 has provisions which address representation of women on Disaster Management Committees as well as the concept of women having special needs during disasters, which is titled "Affirmative Action."

The use of the term "affirmative action" aligns with the CEDAW Article 4 concept of special measures to address prior inequality. This needs to be applied to disaster management committees in most countries, because they are frequently all male or have a very small proportion of women. The provision in **Article 133** would be improved by specifying a minimum percentage for adequate representation, but it clearly establishes the principle, and its implementation can be argued in practice.

This is a good law because it both recognizes that women have certain vulnerabilities and different needs in disasters and establishes the important principle of women's "adequate representation" in all the statutory disaster management committees, which are at national, provincial, and district levels.

Article 133: Due care shall be taken to ensure that women are adequately represented on Disaster Management Committees established under this Act.

Article 134: Special care shall be taken of children, women, elderly persons. and persons with disability during rescue, response, and relief operations.

Example 3: Nepal

In Nepal, the good law **Nepal Disaster Risk Reduction and Management Act 2017** is further reinforced by rights for women in the **Constitution**.

Nepal Disaster Risk Reduction and Management Act 2017 (DRRM Act 2017)

The DRRM Act 2017 is a good law to promote gender-sensitive DRM because it takes women's right to participation seriously, by including the women's ministry in both the executive committee and the larger National Council.

In addition, it requires a minimum of one in three of the DRM experts to be women. The inclusion of nongovernment stakeholders is also a positive provision because it indicates a broadly inclusive approach and is also another opportunity for appointment of women and inclusion of gender issues.

The DRRM Act does not establish a minimum percentage representation of women and it is not yet clear how women's constitutional right to "proportional inclusion" is to be implemented in DRM system governance, as discussed in the next example.

Article 3: provides that the National Council for Disaster Risk Reduction and Management is to include the Minister of Government looking after the portfolio for women, as well as "three persons including one woman" appointed for their expertise in disaster management.

The Executive Committee of the National Council must also include the Secretary of the women's ministry, as well as social welfare; and from outside the government, the Nepal Red Cross, and private sector organizations, which also have the capacity to nominate women.

Example 3: Nepal	
Nepal Constitution 2015	
Constitution **Article 38** on the Rights of Women is a good law to support gender-sensitive DRM, because it states specific rights for women in the highest law of the country, and all other legislation must comply with it. Constitution **Article 38(4)** is effectively a target of 50% women in state structures and bodies. This is higher than the Constitution's minimum of one-third women to be nominated for the national assembly.[a] The other most relevant rights of women in DRM are in **Articles 38(2)–4)**. They support women's sexual and reproductive health in disasters, and the responsibility to prevent, mitigate, and respond to all forms of GBV in disasters. These rights could be used as the basis for institutional mechanisms and policies within the DRM system. If that avenue is not open, an individual or group of women could potentially make a legal claim that their constitutional rights were not being upheld in the DRM system. Nepal is gradually establishing court processes for individuals to claim violations of constitutional human rights, although it is not clear from English language sources whether the mechanism is yet in place.	**Article 38(4)**: The rights of women include "access and participate in all state structures and bodies on the basis of the principle of proportional inclusion." **Articles 38(2)–(4)**: rights to "safe motherhood and reproductive health" and to be free from "any physical, mental, sexual, or psychological or any other kind of violence against women, or any kind of oppression based on religious, social, and cultural tradition, and other practices" (with such acts punishable by law).

[a] Nepal Constitution 2015 [Unofficial Translation]. Section. 84 (8). pp. 176, 222, 223.

Example 4: Indonesia	
In Indonesia, secondary legislation in the form of a **Badan Nasional Penanggulangan Bencana (BNPB) Regulation** has been used to add gender mainstreaming into the **Disaster Management Act 2007**.	
Disaster Management Act 2007	
The Disaster Management Act includes reference to women as a vulnerable group.	**Article 55**: includes pregnant women or nursing mothers as a vulnerable group, but does not provide for representation of women or otherwise address gender issues.
Indonesia Head of BNPB Regulation (Perka) No.13 on Gender Mainstreaming in Disaster Management 2014	
The national disaster management authority has passed a regulation that governs gender mainstreaming in DRM. As yet, it has not been operationalized, but it does provide a foundation for gender-sensitive DRM, including in relation to GBV.[a]	[Not translated]
This is a good law example because legislation in the form of a regulation has been used to retrofit and expand the gender sensitivity of a relatively old DRM law, and it is gender positive by promoting gender mainstreaming.	

[a] IFRC. 2018. *The Responsibility to Prevent and Respond to Sexual and Gender-Based Violence in Disasters and Crises*. Kuala Lumpur. p. 15.

Example 5: Mongolia

Mongolia's legal framework is an example where greater horizontal integration of a good law on gender equality with the DRM law and its implementing institutions, could enhance the legal foundation for women's disaster resilience. This requires making stronger links between the **Law on the Promotion of Gender Equality, 2011** and the **Law on Disaster Protection 2017**.

Mongolian Law on the Promotion of Gender Equality, 2011

The Law on the Promotion of Gender Equality is a good law to support gender equality in DRM because it offers three mechanisms to bring gender equality and nondiscrimination principles and action into the DRM system:

- First, the law provides that other laws or legal provisions "shall not weaken or worsen the gender equality norms adopted in this law," (**Article 2.3**). At the broader level, all revised Mongolian laws are required to include an Article 2 which states which other laws form the relevant legal framework on the subject matter. These always include the constitution and any relevant treaties, as well as any higher laws on the same subject. While other laws cannot weaken the gender equality law, they can be strengthened by direct reference to the Law on the Promotion of Gender Equality as part of their Article 2 references.
- Second, the law puts direct obligations on each central and local government agency, local self-governing body, and the Civil Service Commission, to ensure gender equality (**Articles 19, 20, and 21**). Among other things, this is also the source of government agencies' obligations to produce sector gender strategies and to ensure quotas for women in employment.[a] The Law on the Promotion of Gender Equality also has gender quotas for civil servants, although the National Emergency Management Agency is substantially exempt from these because it is part of the national security system.
- Third, the law gives the National Human Rights Commission mandates to hear complaints of violations of gender inequality, which can be made by individuals, trade unions, and nongovernment organizations (NGOs), (**Article 23**) in which it can also hold government and private sector employers liable (**Articles 23 and 25**); and also to "provide independent oversight of the enforcement of the gender equality related provisions of the Constitution, other laws, and international treaties" and receive and resolve complaints on violation of them (**Article 24**). Both of these options give the National Human Rights Commission oversight capacity over gender equality implementation in DRM under the Law on Disaster Protection, by way of hearing complaints or by proactive oversight. This is different from the advocacy and development role of the National Committee on Gender Equality, but would need additional budget resources.

Mongolian Law on Disaster Protection 2017

This law uses gender neutral language on the whole, and provides for citizen involvement at many stages, but it does not expressly address gender issues. It has indirect provisions on gender equality because it incorporates the constitution and the CEDAW by reference in its **Article 2**, but it does not mention the Law on the Promotion of Gender Equality, even though technically it applies.

A minor amendment to **Article 2** of the Law on Disaster Protection could make sure the gender law is mentioned, as a way to expressly bring it to the attention of implementers. This would be a starting point for guidance on gender in DRM by pointing to the applicable principles of gender equality, nondiscrimination, and special measures (affirmative action) in the gender law, which, in turn, are based on the CEDAW.

---

[a] It seems from LPGE Article 10.1.3 that the gender quota of 40% minimum women in the civil service does not apply to emergency agencies. However, they are not exempt from the law's gender equality and nondiscrimination obligations.

Good Laws for Gender-Sensitive Action on Climate Change

Notes for Lawmakers

As a whole, climate change and environmental laws do not provide any specific framework for gender-sensitive action on climate change. The two main areas with most scope for immediate improvement are:

- where there are requirements for multistakeholder community consultations already in environmental laws, that could be slightly amended or made subject to secondary legislation to ensure they are inclusive and gender-sensitive; and
- where new comprehensive climate change laws are being drafted that focus on and regulate the broad socioeconomic implications of climate change and the national response to it, such as the Fiji Climate Change Bill.

The elements of good law to support women's resilience are clear, but need to be implemented by policy makers, drafters, and legislators at the country level. The good laws on gender mainstreaming in lawmaking are an important mechanism to make the normal lawmaking process more inclusive of women and more gender-sensitive, and these should be used whenever climate change and related laws are being revised or new laws made.

Practical strategies to include the key elements of good laws for gender-sensitive action on climate change are very similar to those for DRM laws.

- When a law is under review or a new law is being drafted, the relevant ministries national climate change or disaster management agencies and legislative drafters should:
  - use the previous key elements as a checklist on what principles and specific mandates need to be included, and how and where special measures may be needed to increase women's participation in government climate action;
  - work closely with the ministry responsible for gender equality, and ensure the effective participation of supportive parliamentarians, women's civil society organizations, and women working in climate change and environmental governance and civil service at national and community levels; and
  - if the country's style of legislation cannot provide sufficient detail, at a minimum, it should ensure their key mandates support more detailed secondary legislation such as regulations and decrees, as well as gender-sensitive and inclusive strategies, policies, and plans.

- If a law does not meet the key elements for good law and is not under review:
  - there may be constitutional rights and/or a good law on gender equality, which the responsible ministries for gender equality and climate change or environment should investigate and take measures to ensure they are implemented in the sector;
  - the implementing agencies may still have sufficiently broad powers and discretions to pursue gender equality, nondiscrimination and protection from gender-based violence, working closely with the ministry responsible for gender equality to strengthen horizontal links and share expertise; and
  - policy makers can use the many national, regional, and international tools available to develop secondary legislation, national standards, and formal national policies and strategies that include the key elements of good laws for gender-sensitive action on climate change.

- At times, a sustained awareness-raising campaign will be necessary to address a lack of legislative underpinning for gender-sensitive action on climate change, with the objective to trigger law reform and improve policy and planning. National actors will often find technical and financial support for such campaigns from international agencies with expertise in human rights, gender analysis, and gender mainstreaming in action on climate change..

Context

The legislative base for achieving gender equality and empowering women in the face of climate change is more complex than stand-alone climate change laws. Many countries have not passed specific laws on climate change and have chosen to manage the national response through existing environmental, energy, and planning laws and institutions. For example, a recent ADB report indicates that 24 of 32 Asia and the Pacific countries surveyed have chosen to regulate climate action through existing laws.[137] This situation is unsurprising, as until a decade ago, most stand-alone climate laws were made in developed economies, primarily to implement their treaty obligations under the United Nations Framework Convention on Climate Change (UNFCCC) and fulfill their climate change mitigation obligations under the Kyoto Protocol,[138] and these did not include gender equality.[139] Even where climate change laws are in place, laws on environmental management, development planning, natural resource management, and energy remain a critical aspect of managing both climate change mitigation and adaptation. All these laws are required to establish the institutional and regulatory framework for responding to risks from climate change, reducing carbon emissions, undertaking specific climate change adaptation—including planned relocation—and ensuring planning approvals support climate-resilient development. Countries are addressing climate change through a range of environmental, energy and planning laws and institutions, all of which need to mainstream gender.

Since 2009, there has been an increasing focus on climate change adaptation, with 91 countries now having at least one law that addresses adaptation.[140] Adaptation-focused laws are less driven by treaty commitments and more focused on national governance and planning across sectors. This is especially so in low-emission developing economies that primarily wish to focus on climate change adaptation and sustainable development. More recently, there is a sign that a newer type of national climate change law may be emerging that is aimed at all aspects of action on climate change, as exemplified in Fiji's approach discussed below.[141]

There is a significant gap in climate change and environmental law provisions to ensure gender equality principles and practice, and to ensure women's participation at national and local levels in staff and governance roles. There is also often a need for special measures to correct a lack of formal representation and empowerment of women in governance and staffing. No legislative examples were identified that authorize special measures to address past gender inequality in relation to climate change and environmental law implementation and practice, particularly to ensure women's equal and effective participation in public life.[142] There are now two main global databases on climate law, one including laws, policies, and litigation;[143] and the other focusing on litigation;[144] plus a small number of published global analyses of climate laws and policies that include environmental and energy laws.[145] These do not use gender criteria as a key element for searching or reporting. Also, they do not always distinguish between law and policy in the statistical and content analysis. In some cases, it is not clear whether gender is absent from reports because it was not considered, or because there is nothing to report due to a lack of gender inclusion in the laws themselves.

---

[137] ADB. 2020. *Climate Change, Coming Soon to a Court Near You: National Climate Change Legal Frameworks in Asia and the Pacific, Report 3*. Manila. p. 12.

[138] M. Nachmany, R. Byrnes, and S. Surminski. 2019. *National Laws and Policies on Climate Change Adaptation: A Global Review: Policy Brief*. Grantham Research Institute on Climate Change and the Environment and Centre for Climate Change Economics and Policy, London School of Economics and Political Science (LSE). London.

[139] B.P. Resurrección et al. 2019. *Gender-Transformative Climate Change Adaptation: Advancing Social Equity*. Rotterdam and Washington, DC. p. 37.

[140] Footnote 138, p. 2.

[141] Government of Fiji, Ministry of Economy. 2019. *Background Note: Draft Climate Change Bill 2019*. Suva, Fiji.

[142] Footnote 109, p. 5.

[143] LSE Grantham Research Institute on Climate Change and the Environment. 2021. *Climate Change Laws of the World (Database)* (accessed 18 January 2021). On date accessed, the database listed a total of 2,092 national and subnational laws and policies and 420 litigation cases.

[144] Sabin Center for Climate Change Law. n.d. Climate Change Litigation Databases (accessed 18 January 2021).

[145] Footnote 138 (Based on the LSE Grantham database).

ADB's 2020 report on *National Climate Change Legal Frameworks in Asia and the Pacific* analyzes national climate change law and policy in 32 Asia and the Pacific countries.[146] Although it identifies a number of national climate change strategies and policies that include significant provisions on gender, it does not report any examples of climate change-related legislation that do so, including in the eight countries that have passed specific climate change laws rather than relying on existing legislation.

The absence of gender inclusion in climate change and environment laws suggests a failure to undertake gender analysis during the lawmaking process when developing or amending climate change laws or environmental laws. The problem with this situation is that the resulting laws do not integrate gender considerations and do not:

(i)   address the causes of women's vulnerability to climate change that relate to gender inequality and different gender roles;

(ii)   enable women to have equal rights to a healthy environment;

(iii)   enable equal and effective participation in public life;

(iv)   recognize the specific importance and benefits of ensuring women's equal participation in climate change and environmental management, including in all aspects of decision-making, governance, and employment in climate change and environmental law and policy implementation;

(v)   draw on the diverse capacities and knowledge base of women to assist in reducing risk; and

(vi)   empower women to gain access to the benefits of adaptation and emerging economic opportunities in areas such as renewable energy.

The reasons for slow progress on gender mainstreaming in climate change were well summarized in a recent Irish Aid analysis which noted a continuing power imbalance of poor representation of women at national and global levels where key decisions are made. As a result, gender dimensions are rarely prioritized in national policies and implementation priorities. There is also a lack of capacity to implement effective gender-inclusive programs, as government officials "lack the technical capacity to meaningfully analyze gender issues and break it down into tangible messages for decision-makers," as well as a lack of access to good data, and a need to "strengthen accountability for climate and gender goals where data does exist."[147]

Gender Issues Related to Environmental Laws and Sustainable Development

The main national laws on environmental management are particularly important for climate change adaptation and sustainable development in the face of climate change. However, as with the international climate change frameworks discussed in Part 2, national environmental laws evolved from a technical approach to management "the environment"—meaning the natural environment. This characterizes the environment as an entity separate from human communities and their built and social environments. Some more recent environmental laws include aspects of the social environment or human interactions with the natural environment. However, the more traditional approach creates a tendency to overlook gender considerations in laws and policies because the underlying assumptions are that (i) regulation is about how people act on the environment (to protect it, or to reduce emissions into it); and (ii) to the extent that regulation needs to be concerned with impacts on human communities, it assumes that everyone is affected in the same way regardless of unequal starting points.

Many practical climate change adaptation decisions are made in the form of local decisions on development planning approvals, especially environmental impact assessments (EIAs). EIAs have an impact on sustainable development planning and natural resource management that are essential underpinnings of effective action

---

[146]   Footnote 137.

[147]   Irish Aid. 2018. *Women as Agents of Change: Towards a Climate and Gender Justice Approach*. Dublin: Irish Aid, Department of Foreign Affairs and Trade, Ireland. pp. 15–16.

on climate change. Although good EIA laws take account of socioeconomic impacts and include provisions for community consultations, there is no guarantee that women within a given community have equality of participation and influence in decision-making roles. Additionally, EIAs typically focus on project-level impacts and may, therefore, miss systemic issues affecting power relations between men and women in a community.

The Framework Principles on Human Rights and the Environment proposed by the United Nations special rapporteur in 2018 set out states' environmental responsibilities to people resident in their territory according to international human rights obligations. They do not mention sex or gender specifically, but they do focus on prohibiting discrimination; equality in access to a safe, clean, healthy, and sustainable environment; public access to information, public participation, and "additional measures to protect the rights of those who are most vulnerable to, or at particular risk from, environmental harm, taking into account their needs, risks, and capacities."[148]

Gender and Particular Climate Change Impacts

Other gender factors that are integral to climate change, the environment, and sustainable development, include management of land and natural resources, including fisheries, forests, water, and agriculture. Each of these have important gendered impacts for women and are referred to in the CEDAW Committee General Recommendation 37 [69–71]. Some important gender issues in relation to land are addressed later in this report, but others are well beyond the scope of this report.

Climate displacement and relocation are most urgent issues for small island states and other countries with low and extensive coastlines. These countries are already dealing with the impacts of sea level rise such as salination, king tides, erosion, and the disappearance of small islands and coastal areas. Climate displacement may also arise from greater and more frequent weather extremes, such as cyclones or droughts, that eventually make some areas too high risk and no longer viable for housing and/or agriculture. Gender-sensitive resettlement legislation is essential and should include gender equality principles and requirements for women's inclusion in community consultations, GBV prevention and response, consideration of different impacts due to gender roles, access to medical, welfare, and education services, and women's access to livelihoods in the new location.

Climate Change Laws, Human Rights Laws, and Court Litigation

Climate change-related laws are also often underpinned by constitutional and/or human rights legislation that define rights to a clean and safe environment, or participation in public institutions, as well as gender equality and nondiscrimination. As discussed in the section concerning DRM laws, the vertical and horizontal linkages to such human rights legislation is often unclear and can be strengthened. Similarly, greater linkages can be made to enable climate change laws to be applied and implemented in a gender-sensitive and gender mainstreamed way though constitutional provisions and laws on gender equality. As will be discussed later in the report, employment law can ensure that gender-sensitive measures for a just transition away from fossil fuels are applied and implemented.

Also, individual or group claims through the court systems to assert these legal rights is an important aspect of the law in many national jurisdictions. Therefore, judges' interpretations of legislative rights and government obligations is an additional area to consider, although to date, there is very little specific case law on issues of gender and climate change. The London School of Economics and Political Science (LSE) Grantham Institute

---

[148] United Nations Human Rights Council. 2018. *Framework Principles on Human Rights and the Environment—The Main Human Rights Obligations Relating to the Enjoyment of a Safe, Clean, Healthy and Sustainable Environment, A/HRC/37/59.*

2020 global snapshot on climate litigation reported only one case related to gender,[149] and the ADB 2020 report on climate litigation reported a small number in Asia and none in the Pacific.[150] This issue is examined specifically below.

International Norms

Climate Change, Gender Equality, and Nondiscrimination Treaties and Multilateral Agreements

(i) Paris Agreement 2015

(ii) Conference of Parties (COP)24 Paris Implementation Guidelines 2018

(iii) UNFCCC Gender Action Plan 2017

(iv) UNFCCC Lima Work Program 2014

(v) CEDAW, as the binding international treaty on eliminating discrimination against women, and the key norm for gender-sensitive climate change legislation

(vi) CEDAW Committee General Recommendation 37

(vii) Sustainable Development Goal (SDG) 5 to achieve gender equality and empower all women and girls, especially subgoals 5.1, 5.2, 5.5, and 5.6 with Target 5.c to "adopt and strengthen sound policies and enforceable legislation for the promotion of gender equality and the empowerment of all women and girls at all levels."

(viii) SDG13 on climate change with Target 13.b on capacity building in developing economies "focusing on women, youth, and local and marginalized communities."

(ix) Framework Principles on Human Rights and the Environment (proposed)—The main human rights obligations relating to the enjoyment of a safe, clean, healthy, and sustainable environment. Report of the UN Special Rapporteur 2018, (A/HRC/37/59).[151]

(x) Gender Analysis and NDCs: Short Guidance for Government Stakeholders, UNDP, 2019.[152]

International Guidance and Tools on Climate Displacement

To date, the African Union's 2009 Kampala Convention on internally displaced persons (IDPs) is the only binding treaty on this issue. There is also United Nations and other international guidance on climate displacement that mainstream gender and provide normative guidance. These focus mainly on displacement in emergency contexts, and in that regard are the same as those cited for DRM. But they also include guidance on planned relocations to humanitarian responders and countries and include:

(i) UN Internally Displaced Persons (IDP) Principles[153] that remain foundational general guidance to countries and humanitarian responders, based in human rights law.

(ii) *Kampala Convention—African Union Convention for the Protection and Assistance of Internally Displaced Persons in Africa 2009*, is the only binding treaty on this issue, and largely codifies the UN IDP Principles.[154]

[149] J. Setzer and R. Byrnes. 2020. *Global Trends in Climate change Litigation: 2020 Snapshot*. London. p. 24. (Union of Swiss Senior Women for Climate Protection v. Swiss Federal Council and Others—see Chapter 10 of this report.).

[150] There were no gender and climate change cases identified in the Pacific, in: Women and Climate Change in Asia, in ADB. 2020. *Climate Change, Coming Soon to a Court Near You: National Climate Change Legal Frameworks in Asia and the Pacific, Report 2*. Manila. pp. 207–210.

[151] UN Human Rights Council. 2018. Report of the Special Rapporteur on the Issue of Human Rights Obligations Relating to the Enjoyment of a Safe, Clean, Healthy and Sustainable Environment: Framework Principles, A/HRC/37/59.

[152] UNDP. 2019. *Gender Analysis and NDCs: Short Guidance for Government Stakeholders*. New York.

[153] Footnote 112.

[154] African Union, African Union Convention for the Protection and Assistance of Internally Displaced Persons in Africa (Kampala Convention), 23 October 2009.

(iii) *Handbook for the Protection of Internally Displaced Persons* 2010, United Nations.[155]

(iv) *Disaster Displacement—Towards a Protection Agenda for People Displaced across Borders in the Context of Disasters and the Effects of Climate Change, 2016.*[156] This currently active Platform on Disaster Displacement (follow-up to the Nansen Initiative) focuses on cross-border climate and disaster displacement, and also mainstreams gender into its guidance.

(v) Peninsula Principles on Climate Displacement within States.[157]

(vi) *Guidance on Protecting People from Disasters and Environmental Change through Planned Relocation,* United Nations High Commissioner for Refugees (UNHCR), and Brookings, 2015.

(vii) *Words into Action: Disaster Displacement, How to Reduce Risk, Address Impacts and Strengthen Resilience. A Companion for Implementing the Sendai Framework Target (E),* United Nations Office for Disaster Risk Reduction (UNDRR), 2019.

Key Elements of Good Laws

Key Elements of Good Laws for Gender-Sensitive Action on Climate Change

- Constitutional protection of:
  - the general right to a clean, safe, and healthy environment;
  - the precautionary principle and the principle of intergenerational equity concerning action on climate change and potentially irreversible environmental damage;
  - women's rights to equality and nondiscrimination and to participation in governance; and
  - women's rights to equal access to land and natural resources, including the benefits of communal property and entitlements under customary law.

- National legislation on climate change mitigation and adaptation, whether stand-alone climate change laws or other relevant environmental laws to:
  - authorize and regulate national climate change mitigation and adaptation policies, measures, and institutions that are inclusive of a wide cross-section of stakeholders and support equitable and sustainable development in the face of climate change;
  - include the precautionary principle and intergenerational equity in relation to action on climate change and assessment of environmental risks from development;
  - include principles of gender equality and nondiscrimination with mechanisms and budget for monitoring and evaluation and special measures to achieve substantive equality for women in climate change adaptation, mitigation, and emerging opportunities in renewable energy and sustainable environmental and natural resource management;
  - use gender-inclusive language and concepts;
  - avoid any direct or indirect discrimination in the text on the basis of sex or gender, while allowing for special measures and initiatives to promote gender equality and adjust for past disadvantage;
  - ensure representation of women's organizations and a minimum of one-third women overall in climate change governance, including policy committees, councils, technical advisory bodies from national to local level, and national delegations to international climate change fora; and
  - ensure placement of women in decision-making roles in relevant civil service and community positions, with a clear target of gender parity in sector employment and a mandatory minimum of one-third women overall.

- Environmental impact assessments to:
  - assess impacts of proposed new developments and investment projects on natural ecosystems, shared natural resources, and the social and built environments of stakeholder communities;
  - take account of projected climate change and disaster impacts on the viability of proposed new developments and investment projects;

continued on next page

---

[155] UN OCHA. 2001. *Guiding Principles on Internal Displacement 1998.* Geneva.

[156] PDD. 2016. *Disaster Displacement—Towards a Protection Agenda for People Displaced across Borders in the Context of Disasters and the Effects of Climate Change.* Geneva.

[157] Displacement Solutions. 2013. *The Peninsula Principles on Climate Displacement within States.* Geneva.

continued

Key Elements of Good Laws for Gender-Sensitive Action on Climate Change

  - – apply principles of gender equality and nondiscrimination, the precautionary principle and intergenerational equity;
  - – require impact assessments to examine differential socioeconomic impacts based on gender and other relevant factors; and
  - – require stakeholder and community consultations with specific mechanisms to ensure women have a voice.

- Legislation supports community-based natural resource management, such as forest and water resources, that empowers local community organizations and ensures women have an equal role in communal management institutions and decision-making.
- Legislation mandates social protection and safeguards to protect procedural and substantive rights of people who are internally displaced by disasters or climate change to:
  - – implement safeguards and procedures to govern planned relocations, including community consultations on resettlement, just compensation, and secure access to alternative land and housing, livelihoods, education, and social welfare services;
  - – create mechanisms to ensure that people who are temporarily displaced or have relocated autonomously have access to safe land and housing, livelihoods, education, and social welfare services;
  - – apply principles of gender equality and nondiscrimination, including special measures and initiatives to ensure gender equality in the outcomes and prevent and respond to gender-based violence; and
  - – require stakeholder and community consultations with specific mechanisms to ensure women have a voice.

Examples of Good Laws

Examples of good laws or legal provisions, regulations, or mechanisms that support gender-sensitive action on climate change are given below under the following general categories: (i) comprehensive climate change laws and regulations: Fiji; (ii) framework climate change laws and regulations: Kenya, the Philippines; (iii) environmental laws and environmental impact assessments: India, Lao People's Democratic Republic (Lao PDR); (iv) constitutional rights and gender equality combined with environmental laws: Mongolia; and (v) codified rights to a clean, safe, or healthy environment: Nepal.

Example of Type 1: Comprehensive Climate Change Laws and Regulations

In Fiji, the proposed **Climate Change Act (Draft Bill 2019)** promises to break new ground as the most comprehensive national law on all aspects of a country's response to climate change. It also gives a solid legal base for participation and empowerment of women and gender-sensitive climate action. This would combine with secondary legislation in the form of the existing **Planned Relocation Guidelines: A Framework to Undertake Climate Change Related Relocation 2018** which will be made as regulations under the new Act, to address a crucial issue for Fiji in way that is gender sensitive.

Fiji Draft Climate Change Bill 2019 (not yet tabled in Parliament as of January 2021)

This Draft Bill was intended for tabling in the Fiji Parliament in May 2020, but was delayed by coronavirus disease (COVID-19) lockdowns. It currently remains a draft bill that may be revised as a result of consultations. The version used is the official consultation version Draft 1 and the included background note posted online by the Ministry of Economy.[a]

The Draft Bill is lengthy and comprehensive, comprising 17 parts that include establishment of the national governance structure, mainstreaming climate change into a whole-of-government approach, an agenda for development of a series of key climate change policies, action on mitigation, adaptation, planned relocations, and enforcement mechanisms.

It addresses both international and domestic obligations and plans, aiming to signal Fiji's commitment to the international community and "provide a comprehensive framework that will guide Fiji's response to climate change" (Background Note).

The Fiji Draft Bill has seven notable good law elements which are set out below.

Example of Type 1: Comprehensive Climate Change Laws and Regulations	
1. Recognition of gender as a climate change issue This is a good law statement of principle on how climate change impacts women's equality and rights.	**Section 5**: on Principles includes 11 principles that are both broad in scope and important underpinnings for the Act as a whole and its implementation. Key is: **Section 5(h)**: "there are inextricable links between gender equality and the Sustainable Development Goals, and when taking action to address climate change, Fiji will respect, promote, and consider gender equality and responsiveness, women's human rights and the empowerment of women, including in the areas of formal sector employment and livelihoods, participation in decision-making and access to services, health, education, water, sanitation, housing, and transport."
2. The inclusion of constitutional equality and nondiscrimination principles This is a good-law constitutional provision for the breadth of its definitions on gender, discrimination, and equality. Inclusion of it as an overarching principle in a Climate Change Act would be a good law because it clearly imports these rights into all of the Government of Fiji's policies and actions on climate change.	**Section 5 (a)**: Refers to the Constitution Chapter 2, an extensive Bill of Rights, that includes Article 26— the "right to equality and freedom from discrimination" which prohibits both direct and indirect discrimination on grounds that include "actual or supposed personal characteristics or circumstances, including…sex, gender, sexual orientation, gender identity and expression…marital status or pregnancy."
3. Codification of planned relocations that requires gender responsive consultations This is a very significant requirement because community consultations in relation to relocation are a key part of the existing policy framework in Fiji, and the specific inclusion of gender-responsive consultation and participation processes are essential for effective gender mainstreaming and empowerment of women in the difficult process of uprooting people's lives and reestablishing their community and livelihoods elsewhere.	**Part 13, Section 81**: on displacement, requires that for relocation of at-risk communities, the Minister must ensure "inclusive and gender responsive consultation and participatory processes."
4. Mainstreamed principles into decision-making criteria Gender is better integrated into the Draft Bill than at first appears, because **Sections 5(a) and 5(h)** (described above) are mainstreamed throughout the law, as are all 11 principles. The main challenge with this style of drafting is that decision-makers need to keep all 11 principles in mind at each of these points. This also assumes that policy makers and implementers know what it means to apply the gender principles in practice. There is no mechanism in the Draft Bill to require gender assessments or gender analysis, and it is likely that most implementers will not be gender experts and will require further guidance. Making this a central element of the decision-making process will require political will, capacity	Many of the provisions in the Draft Bill require decision-makers to act in accordance with these principles including: **Section 9(5)**: Development of standards and codes of practice in governance. **Part 5, Sections 16, 18, and 21**: All State entities and decision-makers are required to take climate change into consideration with reference to the objectives and principles of the Act, for "any decision made, and any policy, program, or process developed or implemented by the State entity," including Government procurement decisions." **Sections 42 and 43**: The Minister must "be informed by" the principles in areas such as: preparation of the Low Emission Development Strategy, regulations, measures, and actions on mitigation.

Example of Type 1: Comprehensive Climate Change Laws and Regulations	
building and resource allocation, but the broad legislative powers for gender-sensitive action on climate change exists.	**Sections 71, 72, and 76**: preparation of National Adaptation Plans by the NAP Steering Committee, and Ministerial regulations on adaptation measures and the National building Code. **Sections 87 and 97**: the forthcoming Oceans Policy and Mechanisms for Climate Finance.
5. Other inclusive environmental law provisions The Draft Bill also includes other good law elements that support inclusive environmental management that is informed by climate change and climate action. These are good law provisions because they are state-of-the-art environmental law principles that support broader population resilience to climate change, including women.	**Section 5**: recognizes indigenous ownership and culture and captures important international environmental law principles, including intergenerational equity, the precautionary principle, and sustainable development.
6. Indirect inclusion of Climate Change Act gender principles into EIAs This would be a good law provision because proposed amendments to the EIA criteria would take account of climate risk, and the Climate Change Act principles would apply in the environment sector.	The Draft Bill proposes consequential amendments to the Environment Management Act 2005 by seeking to amend the EIA criteria to include whether a development "may result in material greenhouse gas emissions or could be adversely affected by the impacts of climate change." This would make clear the nexus between development decisions and climate change. Then, given the general obligation on all government entities set out in the Draft Bill Part—to take climate change into consideration with reference to the objectives and principles of the proposed Climate Change Act—this would also bring the **Sections 5(a) and (h)** gender principles into EIAs.

Fiji Planned Relocation Guidelines: A Framework to Undertake Climate Change-Related Relocation 2018

Fiji's *Planned Relocation Guidelines: A Framework to Undertake Climate Change-Related Relocation* 2018 currently has the status of policy, but the Draft Climate Change Bill (Section 80) proposes this will be mandated under the new Climate Change Act.

The Guidelines draw on international best practices[b] and on lessons learned from Fiji's own experience of a small number of Government-led relocations where "community movements have been associated with numerous social, cultural, gender, economic, and environmental issues relating to tensions over land, dislocation of communities, inadequate resources, and unsuitable sites."[c]

Fiji's experience has highlighted the importance of gender-inclusive consultation and decision-making processes to ensure that all women's as well as men's socioeconomic and cultural needs are met in the relocation process and access to livelihoods afterwards.[d]

Gender and inclusive processes are an integral part of the Scope and Purpose of the Planned Relocation Guidelines, as follows (*italics added*):

"This document provides guidance for the Government of the Republic of Fiji and all Other Stakeholders present in Fiji, to consider planned relocation solutions for the affected communities as part of their adaptation strategies in relation to disasters and climate change related slow-onset events occurring on the territory of Fiji.

Example of Type 1: Comprehensive Climate Change Laws and Regulations

The purpose of this document is:

- To ensure an *inclusive and gender responsive consultative and participatory process* to strengthen communities' riposte to climate change impacts and ensure community engagement and ownership in the relocation process.
- To serve as a coordination mechanism to *enhance the involvement and collaboration of all range of stakeholders, namely: affected communities,* government ministries and agencies, trade unions and employers' organizations, intergovernmental organizations, regional and international organizations, the private sector, *civil-society organizations, women's organizations,* faith-based groups, and academia.
- To facilitate the use of clear, inclusive, and comprehensive procedures, while assessing and responding to potential relocation risks, in order to respect, protect, and fulfill the needs of the relocated communities.
- To recognize the richness of the indigenous knowledge, the multicultural and interfaith composition of the Fijian population, when addressing communities experiencing uncertainty about their future due to climate change."[e]

The Guidelines must also be supported by standard operating procedures (SOPs), in which the government must ensure that the values and principles and the relocation stages set out in the Guidelines are included.

The Guidelines are based on **three policy pillars for relocations**, based around the processes of (1) decision, (2) planning for a sustainable relocation, and (3) implementation in line with human rights and protection standards, including the process of physical relocation and long-term follow-up and monitoring.[f] These are to be embedded in implementation along with the five principles.

The **five principles** are also important because they are based on an inclusive and human rights-based approach, and can be summarized as:

- A human-centered approach to ensure that the community bottom–up perception is prioritized.
- A livelihood-based approach to adaptation (rather than a sector approach) to ensure that people who have relocated are not negatively affected and can contribute to the process of "migration as adaptation."
- A human rights-based approach, "ensuring that men, women, elderly, and persons with disabilities are meaningfully engaged and participate in the decision-making, planning, and implementation related to the planned relocation." This also implements the Paris Agreement Articles 8, 13, and 14 on participation and consultation processes and its transparency concept.
- A preemptive approach to ensure that any potential humanitarian crises are avoided, to "create an efficient response to environmental scenarios and protect the vulnerable groups on a medium- and long-term basis, contributing inter alia, to successful adaptive measures, decreasing potential risks and building resilience at the new destination"; and
- A regional approach, due to the high probability of cross-border movement or integration of people in hosting foreign societies.[g]

While the **Scope and Purpose** make a clear commitment to "ensure an inclusive and gender responsive consultative and participatory process" in **Part I** of the Guidelines, this is shortened in the body of the document to simply "inclusive."

The detailed guidance on processes set out in **Part II** "Stages of Planned Relocation and Stakeholders involved" uses this abbreviation and therefore does not specifically draw attention to gender-inclusiveness.

The Fiji Planned Relocation Guidelines provide a good law example of (proposed) secondary legislation because:

- The scope and purposes are:
  - specifically gender-inclusive and responsive, also mentioning collaboration with women's organizations as a key stakeholder; and
  - committed to meaningful community participation and collaboration with a wide range of stakeholders, including trade unions and civil society organizations, that may also represent women effectively in relocation processes.

Example of Type 1: Comprehensive Climate Change Laws and Regulations

- The definition of "community" used is inclusive, referring to "villages, formal settlements, informal (squatter) settlements, and subcommunities within larger urban areas," which recognizes a wide range of forms of occupation of land and housing and does not limit planned relocation rights to holders of formal property title.[h]
- The principles that must be applied by the Government in SOPs and implementation are rights-based and specifically mention the rights to participate of "men, women, elderly, and persons with disabilities."

The Guidelines as a whole assume that implementers understand the practical elements of a gender-responsive consultative and participatory process, which will require capacity building and resource allocation to ensure implementers understand and have the skills to implement inclusive and gender-responsive processes.

[a] Government of Fiji, Ministry of Economy. 2019. *Fiji Climate Change Bill 2019 (Draft)*. Suva, Fiji.
[b] See for example: UNHCR and Brookings Institution. 2015. *Guidance on Protecting People from Disasters and Environmental Change through Planned Relocation*. Geneva and Washington, DC. See the most recent developments at: Internal Displacement Monitoring Centre. 2019. *Global Report on Internal Displacement*. Geneva.
[c] Government of Fiji, Ministry of Economy. 2018. *Planned Relocation Guidelines: A Framework to Undertake Climate Change Related Relocation*. Suva, Fiji. p. 8.
[d] ADB. *Gender Analysis of Fiji's Laws and Policies that Support Women's Resilience to Climate Change and Disasters*. Unpublished.
[e] Note c, p. 3.
[f] Note c, p. 8.
[g] Note c, pp. 8–9.
[h] Note c, p. 3. n. 1.

Example of Type 2: Framework Climate Change Laws and Regulations

Kenya Climate Change Act, 2016

An example of good law provisions on including gender mainstreaming in the aims of the law and the role of the National Climate Change Council.	**Article 3-2**: One of the aims of the Kenya Climate Change Act No. 11 of 2016 is to "mainstream intergenerational and gender equity in all aspects of climate change responses." **Article 6**: Establishes a high-level National Climate Change Council as an overarching national climate change coordination mechanism. It must "approve a national gender and intergenerational responsive public education awareness strategy and implementation programme."

Philippine Climate Change Act of 2009 (RA 9729)

The Philippine Climate Change Act 2009 RA 9729 and its implementing regulations creates the Climate Change Commission. This is a good law because it: (i) includes a key national women's organization in the Climate Change Commission; (ii) recognizes that there are differential impacts of climate change on women, men, and children; and (iii) identifies rural women as a priority	**Sections 2 and 3**: This policy clause includes the precautionary principle and one of the aims is gender mainstreaming, a defined term. **Section 5**: The Chairperson of the National Commission on the Role of Filipino Women is a member of the Climate Change Commission. **Section 9**: The Climate Change Commission has responsibility to mainstream climate change into all sectors, including disaster risk reduction and management. **Section 13(c)**: Requires the development of a National Climate Change Action Plan that includes the "identification of differential impacts of climate change on men, women, and children." **Sections 15 and 18**: Rural women are named as a priority for allocation of climate change funding, including microcredit schemes.

Example of Type 2: Framework Climate Change Laws and Regulations	
Philippine Magna Carta for Women 2008 (Republic Act 9710)	
The Philippine Magna Carta for Women 2008 also underpins the Climate Change Act.	Its two most relevant provisions: **Section 10**: "Women Affected by Disasters, Calamities, and Other Crisis Situations" **Section 11**: "Participation and Representation" (both are reproduced in Chapter 8).
These are good law provisions because they: • Recognize women's particular needs in climate-related disasters and resettlement from a gender perspective, including the increased risk of gender-based violence, and sets out the types of prevention and support services needed. • Support gender parity for women in the civil service, a minimum of 40% women in development councils and planning bodies and representation of women's organizations in other policy and decision-making bodies, all of which are highly relevant to gender-sensitive action on climate change. • Apply generally to the administration of the Climate Change Act, even though it is not directly linked through a legislative provision.	

Example 3: Environmental Laws and Environmental Impact Assessments	
India Environment (Protection) Act 1986	
India's Environment (Protection) Act 1986 does not include references to women or gender, but its definition of the environment is otherwise a good law provision because it includes human beings and their property, as well as the natural environment. This means these factors can be considered in policy and EIAs, an important underpinning for gender-sensitive action on climate change under the law.	**Section 2(a)**: "environment" includes water, air, and land and the interrelationship which exists among and between water, air, and land, and human beings, other living creatures, plants, microorganism and property…"
Lao PDR Law on Environmental Protection, 2012 and Decree on Environmental Impact Assessment, 2010	
The law and decree are state-of-the-art in their inclusion of climate and natural hazard risks as part of the criteria for assessing new development proposals. The law very specifically refers to both natural hazards and climate change risks as the basis for EIAs, which is good practice from the climate resilience perspective. The law and decree do not refer directly to women or gender, but there are provisions in the law that recognize socioeconomic considerations and provide for consultations as one of its underlying "Principles of Environmental Protection." This is a good law example for participatory environmental management and EIAs that take account of climate and disaster risks. These are important pre-conditions for gender-sensitive environmental management. Although	The law has a specific provision on impacts on both the social and natural environment: **Article 10**: An impact on social environment is an adverse impact on human life and health, properties. and livelihoods, including shelters of people, and on cultural and historical heritages. **Article 11**: An impact on the natural environment is an adverse impact on natural ecological fundamentals, natural resources, biodiversity, arable land, water sources, climate change. and natural heritages. In addition to the mention of climate change in Article 10, it also includes preventive measures against natural hazards (disasters). The law further includes preemptive forms of EIA including:

Example 3: Environmental Laws and Environmental Impact Assessments

the law and decree do not consider gender or women, there also EIA Guidelines which do provide some guidance on this, including consultation with the Lao Women's Union and consideration of factors such as the livelihoods of both women and men.[a]

(i) **Article 19**: A Strategic Environmental Assessment (SEA) is a process of anticipating an impact that may affect social and natural environment. By conducting the SEA, there shall be participation by organizations, local concerned authorities, and people, who are directly or indirectly affected by the sector policies, strategic plans, and programs.

(ii) **Articles 21 and 22** on Initial Environment Examination and EIAs follow the same participatory model.

[a]   Lao PDR. 2012. *Environmental Impact Assessment Guidelines*. Vientiane.

Example of Type 4: Constitutional Rights and Gender Equality Combined with Environmental Laws That Have Not Yet Mainstreamed Gender

Mongolia Law on the Promotion of Gender Equality, 2011 and Environment Protection Law, 2012

As discussed in Section 4.1 of this report, it is a requirement of Mongolian law to import the Constitution and international treaties to which Mongolia is a party, including the CEDAW, in a standard Article 2.

While there is no separate climate change law, the following environmental laws also include this Article 2:

(i)   Environment Protection Law, 2012
(ii)   Environmental Impact Assessments Law, 1998

This means that gender equality and nondiscrimination are part of the legal framework. However, this indirect inclusion does not give specific guidance on how to implement gender-inclusive environmental protection or impact assessments, or decisions on climate change adaptation or mitigation that fall under these powers. These do not address gender issues at all in the body of their texts.

Mongolia also has the global good practice Law on the Promotion of Gender Equality 2011 which clearly applies to the environmental sector, including minimum quotas for either gender in the civil service. While the mechanism for the general application of the gender law requires clarification, one aspect of its implementation is very clear, and that is the requirement for sectors to develop and implement gender strategies.

The Environmental Sector Gender Strategy 2014–2030 was the first sector strategy adopted in Mongolia under the Law on the Promotion of Gender Equality and it has faced some implementation challenges in a sector that is reportedly gender-segmented in work and access roles. A midterm evaluation of the forestry sector, for example, found that the forestry business was regarded— especially by men—as male-dominated and women's participation in environmental decision-making was lower than that of men. However, this is a good practice example of how a law on gender equality can be translated horizontally into the environment sector to support gender-sensitive action on climate change.

Example of Type 5: Constitutional or Other Codified Rights to A Clean, Safe, or Healthy Environment Combined with Gender Equality

Nepal Constitution, 2015

Within the Constitution, **Part 3** on Fundamental Rights and Duties sets out a very comprehensive bill of rights, mentioned in this report in the section on good constitutional provisions and in this report concerning women's rights to participate in DRM governance institutions. Many of these rights are relevant to women's socioeconomic resilience to climate change.

In this table, three key sets of rights in three Articles of the Constitution are discussed together, as they can be seen as a positive obligation for a government to: first, take action on climate change; and, second, ensure that such action is gender-sensitive.	**Article 30**: the right to a healthy and clean environment **Article 18**: the right to equality **Article 38**: the rights of women Each is discussed in more detail below.
Article 30 does not refer directly to climate change, but it does refer to the right to a "healthy" environment and to a right of a "victim of environmental pollution and degradation" to be compensated. The Supreme Court of Nepal interpreted this provision to include environmental justice by relating it to the constitutional right to social justice, also related to the right to live a dignified life, giving rise to a state responsibility to restrict adverse effects on the environment.[a] A recent Asian Development Bank (ADB) report on climate change litigation details similar interpretations of the right to a healthy environment have been made by the highest national courts in other Asian countries, including India, Malaysia, Pakistan, the Philippines, and Sri Lanka.[b] That report notes that these build on the concepts of environmental constitutionalism and the right to life.	**Article 30(1)**: Each person shall have the right to live in a healthy and clean environment. **Article 30(2)**: The victim of environmental pollution and degradation shall have the right to be compensated by the pollutant as provided for by law. **Article 30(3)**: Provided that this Article shall not be deemed to obstruct the making of required legal provisions to strike a balance between environment and development for the use of national development works.
The key elements to draw from **Article 18** are that: first, there is a general right to equality and to be free from discrimination on the grounds of sex, gender, marriage, and pregnancy in the application of general laws—such as climate change and environmental laws; and, second, that while the State is not permitted to discriminate on these grounds, it is permitted to make special provisions for the protection, empowerment, and advancement of women who are disadvantaged and pregnant women.	**Article 18(1)**: All citizens shall be equal before law. No person shall be denied the equal protection of law. **Article 18(2)**: There shall be *no discrimination in the application of general laws* on the grounds of origin, religion, race, caste, tribe, *sex*, physical conditions, disability, health condition, *matrimonial status, pregnancy,* economic condition, language or geographical region, or ideology or any other such grounds. **Article 18(3)**: The *state shall not discriminate among citizens on grounds of* origin, religion, race, caste, tribe, *sex*, economic condition, language or geographical region, ideology and such other matters. *Provided that nothing shall be deemed to bar the making of special provisions by law for the protection, empowerment, or advancement of the women lagging behind socially and culturally...pregnant* [persons]..."

Example of Type 5: Constitutional or Other Codified Rights to A Clean, Safe, or Healthy Environment Combined with Gender Equality

Article 38 is also discussed in Section 4.1 of this report as being an example of good law and in each case, the points made are equally relevant to gender and climate change.	**Article 38**: on the right of women then builds on these general rights to equality and nondiscrimination and the recognition that positive measures to correct prior disadvantage are valid policy responses and are not unlawful discrimination.
An additional sub-article of importance is **Article 38(4)** which supports gender parity in women's participation in governance and all state action on climate change. The term "proportional inclusion" would also appear to mean 50%, since that is women's proportion of the population. The provision for "positive discrimination" to create special opportunities for women in education, health, employment, and social security also recognizes prior disadvantage, in line with the CEDAW.	**Article 38 (4)** Women shall have the right to access [and] participate in all state structures and bodies on the basis of the principle of proportional inclusion.

In summary, the preceding Articles read together provide a good law example to support gender-sensitive climate action because:

- There is a positive obligation on the state to uphold these constitutional rights in the way it applies and makes legislation and policy; and
- State institutions administering environmental and climate change laws are bound by the constitution, as the superior law of the nation. This is the case even if the specific laws they are administering have not yet mainstreamed gender, or do not include some aspects of the rights, such as gender parity ("proportional inclusion") for women in all state structures and bodies.

[a] Citing the cases of Advocate Raju Prasad Chapagain vs. Government of Nepal, Ministry of Agriculture and Cooperatives and Others 2009, and Advocate Prakash Mani Sharma vs. Godavari Marble Industries Pvt. Ltd. and Others 2015 in: ADB. 2020. *Climate Change, Coming Soon to a Court Near You: National Climate Change Legal Frameworks in Asia and the Pacific, Report 2.* Manila. p. 34.

[b] ADB. 2020. *Climate Change, Coming Soon to a Court Near You: National Climate Change Legal Frameworks in Asia and the Pacific, Report 2.* Manila. pp. 33–35.

Emerging Case Law on Women, Disasters, and Climate Change

Context

Climate change case law is growing internationally, reflecting the mounting injuries and damage it causes.[158] As people increasingly feel the effects of climate change or witness their governments' inadequate responses to climate change, citizens look to protect their rights and litigation is one mechanism for doing that.

Within Asia, claims based on constitutional legal rights are prevalent because climate change is impacting people's fundamental and constitutional rights, such as their rights to life, environment, food, water, equality, and security.[159] Claims based on constitutional rights are also popular in jurisdictions with fewer climate change laws or commitments. Having a constitutional legal right provides a party with a legal right to sue even if there are no other legal rights. Constitutional claims also frequently allow people to commence their action directly with their national supreme court, leapfrogging over the courts of lower jurisdiction, avoiding lengthy appeals and saving time and money.

Rights-based legal claims are a growing trend internationally. Around 35% of all climate change cases globally relate to rights.[160] The connection between rights and climate cases is unsurprising.

> **Notes for Lawmakers**
>
> Although there are still very few examples of climate change litigation based on gender arguments, the foregoing overview of recent and emerging case law demonstrates the great potential for climate justice drawn from constitutional provisions and international human rights. It illustrates some of the arguments made in court proceedings on why governments should undertake gender-sensitive climate action and environmental management to support women's resilience. These have included:
>
> - specific impacts of climate change on women and the resulting positive obligation on governments to mitigate global warming;
> - an obligation to implement DRM laws to adequately prepare for and respond to natural hazards such as floods, and to include special measures for widows and orphans;
> - stressing the need to safeguard the population, including women and children suffering abuse, during economic stress from water scarcity; and
> - the important role in climate justice of women's involvement in sustainable development decisions through EIA consultations.
> - Although not yet reflected in case law, there are clear benefits to women and the general population in supporting a significant role for women in food production through ensuring their rights to land and inheritance, as well as resources and technology for adaptation.

Advancements in scientific knowledge, synthesized by the Intergovernmental Panel on Climate Change, provide persuasive evidence of the future anticipated effects of climate change. They also shine a light on governments' collective responsibility to limit global warming to 1.5°C above preindustrial temperatures. Such information provides useful evidence to support claims that climate change undermines life and other fundamental rights and that governments should, therefore, ramp up their climate change mitigation and adaptation.

This discussion applies the definition of "climate litigation" used by the Asian Development Bank in its recent report series *Climate Change, Coming Soon to a Court Near You*.[161] Report Two in that series explained that climate litigation could be a case before judicial courts or other specialized tribunals that "(i) raises climate change as

---

[158]   The Climate Change Litigation Databases, maintained by the Sabin Center for Climate Change Law, is one of the leading websites tracking climate litigation. The databases contained 1,715 climate change cases, as of 6 January 2021.

[159]   For further analysis of developments in climate litigation in Asia and the Pacific, see: ADB. 2020. *Climate Change, Coming Soon to a Court Near You: Climate Litigation in Asia and the Pacific and Beyond*. Manila. p. 7.

[160]   C. Rodríguez-Garavito. The Rights Turn in Climate Litigation. In World Commission on Environmental Law. 2020. *Webinar 4: Climate Change in the Courts*. (43:47).

[161]   ADB. 2020. *Climate Change, Coming Soon to a Court Near You: Climate Litigation in Asia and the Pacific and Beyond*. Manila.

a central issue; (ii) raises climate change as a peripheral issue; or (iii) does not explicitly raise climate change, but has ramifications for climate change mitigation or adaptation efforts, e.g., recognition of intergenerational responsibility."[162]

National legal and policy frameworks domesticate international legal commitments, laying the groundwork for homegrown climate action. As courts interpret, enable, and assist with implementing laws and other legal obligations, they have a critical role in supporting national and global climate action (footnote 162). Many courts internationally and in Asia have accepted that human-caused greenhouse gas emissions are causing the Earth's climate to change and that climate action is urgent.[163] As a result, judges in various jurisdictions have ordered governments to enhance their climate action, with these decisions frequently relying on rights.[164] Such findings underscore the capacity of courts to shape the law and domestic legal and policy frameworks, making litigation pertinent to any discussion of climate legal and policy frameworks. This section discusses some globally significant rights-based climate change cases below.

Gender-specific climate litigation is rare globally, including in Asia. The authors know of two cases globally where petitioners specifically built a case around climate change impacts on women and girls.[165] In addition to these cases, there are a number of cases which, although they are not particular to climate change, have outcomes that build the capacity of women and girls to adapt. Within the small selection of gender-relevant climate cases, the following themes are emerging:

(i)   gender-specific cases against governments for the protection of a right;
(ii)   cases where courts observe the need for special protections for women;
(iii) cases where courts observe the need for female participation; and
(iv)   rights-based litigation with outcomes that are beneficial for women and girls.

In addition to these cases, this discussion also covers some groundbreaking rights-based climate cases to demonstrate how litigation can clarify and enforce these rights, including the positive obligations of governments to legislate, make policy, and act on it.

Foundational Climate Change Cases

Protecting the Rights of Family in the Netherlands

Urgenda Foundation v. The State of the Netherlands (Ministry of Infrastructure and the Environment)[166] created a ripple effect globally in the world of climate litigation, making it a relevant and essential decision to consider in this section. While the case is not a gender-specific climate case, the courts took into account the impacts of climate change on family life. Women are predominantly society's caregivers, so decisions protecting family life have benefits for them. The Urgenda Foundation argued that the government's proposed emission levels would

---

[162] Intergenerational responsibility refers to the responsibility of each generation to protect the environment for future generations. ADB. 2020. *Climate Change, Coming Soon to a Court Near You: Climate Litigation in Asia and the Pacific and Beyond.* Manila. p. 7

[163] M.L. Banda. 2020. *Climate Science in the Courts: A Review of U.S. and International Judicial Pronouncements.* Washington, DC. See footnote 160.

[164] *The State of the Netherlands (Ministry of Economic Affairs and Climate Policy) v Urgenda Foundation,* Case No. 19/00135, ECLI:NL:HR: 2019:2007, Supreme Court of the Netherlands, 20 December 2019 (unofficial translation), *Advocate Padam Bahadur Shrestha vs Prime Minister and Office of Council of Ministers and Others,* Case No. 074-WO-0283, Supreme Court of Nepal, 25 December 2018 (2075/09/10 BS); *Leghari v. Federation of Pakistan,* PLD 2018 Lahore 364, discussed below.

[165] *Maria Khan et al. v. Pakistan et al.,* Writ Petition No. 8960 of 2019, High Court of Lahore; *Union of Swiss Senior Women for Climate Protection v. Swiss Federal Council and Others,* petition to the European Court of Human Rights, 26 November 2020.

[166] *Urgenda Foundation v The State of the Netherlands (Ministry of Infrastructure and the Environment),* HA ZA 13-1396, C/09/456689, ECLI:NL:RBDHA:2015:7145 (translation).

contribute to dangerous climate change, undermining citizens' right to life and family life. Dutch citizens have the right to life under article 2 and right to family life under article 8 of the European Convention on Human Rights (ECHR). The case focused on the dangerous nature of climate change and its impact on the rights of present and future generations.

The Hague District Court found that articles 2 and 8 of the ECHR (the rights to life and family life) imposed on the government a positive duty to safeguard residents' lives and family lives from dangerous activities or natural disasters. The court reasoned that the government owed a duty of care for a safe living climate across the Netherlands. It concluded that the state must do more to avert the imminent danger posed by climate change.

The Hague Court of Appeal described climate change as such a "serious risk that the current generation of citizens will be confronted with loss of life and/or a disruption of family life."[167] Therefore, "it follows from Articles 2 and 8 ECHR that the State has a duty to protect against this real threat" (footnote 167). The court ordered the Government of the Netherlands to reduce its national emissions targets by at least 25% compared to 1990 by the end of 2020.

The Supreme Court of the Netherlands agreed with the appeal court, but focused less on the duty of care to avoid hazardous climate change.[168] It affirmed that the government must contribute to global climate action in line with its commitments under the UNFCCC and the ECHR. Such obligations required the government to do its part and to act consistently with widely accepted scientific opinion and internationally recognized standards on climate change. Scientific opinion has stressed the necessity of reducing carbon emissions by 25%–40% by 2020.[169] The court considered that failing to meet these emissions, reduction targets and timeframes would expose communities to the risk of abrupt climate change.

Urgenda is the first example globally of courts ordering a government to set specific emissions reduction targets for reasons other than statutory mandates.

Creating a Climate Change Commission in Pakistan

Leghari v. Federation of Pakistan[170] was instrumental in driving Pakistan's policy response to climate change. Leghari sued the federal government for not implementing the National Climate Change Policy 2012 and its Framework for Implementation of Climate Change Policy 2013. He argued that such failures affected Pakistan's water, food, and energy security, undermining his fundamental right to life.

Viewing climate change as a defining challenge of our time, the court found for Leghari. It interpreted the constitutional rights to life and human dignity (Articles 9 and 14 of Pakistan's Constitution) broadly, reasoning that they incorporated a right to a healthy and clean environment.[171] As citizens held these rights, the government was obligated to progress its climate policy and implementation framework, something it had not done.

---

167   *The State of the Netherlands (Ministry of Infrastructure and the Environment) v Urgenda Foundation*, HA ZA 13-1396, C/09/456689, ECLI:NL:GHDHA:2018:2591, Hague Court of Appeal, 9 October 2018 (unofficial translation), p. 13, para. 45.

168   *The State of the Netherlands (Ministry of Economic Affairs and Climate Policy) v Urgenda Foundation*, Case No. 19/00135, ECLI:NL:HR:2019:2007, Supreme Court of the Netherlands, 20 December 2019 (unofficial translation).

169   The court referenced IPCC. 2007. *Climate Change 2007: The Physical Science Basis. Contribution of Working Group I to the Fourth Assessment Report of the Intergovernmental Panel on Climate Change.* Cambridge and New York. See footnote 183, para. 71 of the unofficial translation.

170   *Leghari v. Federation of Pakistan*, PLD 2018 Lahore 364.

171   This reasoning followed established precedent such as *Shehla Zia and Others v. WAPDA*, PLD 1994 SC 693. The court also considered that a broad interpretation should take into account (i) the constitutional values of democracy, equality, and social, economic, and political justice; and (ii) international environmental principles of sustainable development, precautionary principle, intergenerational and intragenerational equity, and the doctrine of public trust. See footnote 170, para. 12.

The Supreme court constituted the Climate Change Commission to oversee the execution of the government's policy, a watershed in climate litigation globally. The court ordered the commission to provide regular progress updates, only dissolving the commission when the government had achieved 66% of the priority items under the climate policy. After disbanding the commission, the court constituted a standing committee, creating an enduring link between the court and the executive. This case is significant for (i) showing courts' ability to hold government accountable for meeting climate policy commitments[172] and (ii) recognizing the need to involve many stakeholders in climate planning and implementation.

Requiring a Climate Law in Nepal

Nepal's Supreme Court recently ordered the national government to pass a climate change law immediately in *Advocate Padam Bahadur Shrestha vs Prime Minister and Office of Council of Ministers and Others*.[173] Shrestha's case centered on climate change's existential threat and his associated rights. He argued that the government's failure to pass a climate change law exacerbated the danger of climate change, violating his constitutional rights to (i) live with dignity, (ii) live in a healthy and clean environment, (iii) access essential healthcare services, and (iv) food and protection from starvation.[174]

Climate Change and Human Rights Law in the Philippines

In the Philippines, the Commission for Human Rights is considering whether major fossil fuel emitters (carbon majors) have violated Filipinos' human rights to life, health, and self-determination.[175] The commission released preliminary findings in December 2019 during the 25th Conference of the Parties of the UNFCCC.[176] While international law may not have the mechanisms to hold major emitters accountable under existing human rights law, the commission believes domestic courts may make such findings subject to existing laws. The range of potential liability is broad. Fraudulent company officers may be subjected to criminal penalties, for example. The value of the commission's findings, when published, will likely be its exhaustive assessment of the linkages between climate change and human rights. Asian courts might rely on these findings when dealing with rights-based cases.

Gender-Specific Rights-Based Litigation against Governments

Globally, there are only two gender-specific lawsuits, in Pakistan and Switzerland. Both allege that the petitioners' governments should adopt more aggressive climate action because climate change disproportionately affects women. Neither case is decided. Another case from South America asks the Inter-American Commission on Human Rights to investigate how climate change impacts the human rights of Indigenous peoples, women, children, and rural communities.

---

[172] Since the *Leghari* case, the United Kingdom (UK) Court of Appeal recently set aside the Government of the United Kingdom's approval of a third runway at Heathrow Airport because it failed to consider its climate change policy. See R (Friends of the Earth) v Secretary of State for Transport & Others [2020] EWCA Civ 214.

[173] Advocate Padam Bahadur Shrestha vs Prime Minister and Office of Council of Ministers and Others, Case No. 074-WO-0283, Supreme Court of Nepal, 25 December 2018 (2075/09/10 BS).

[174] Nepal Constitution 2015. Articles 16, 30, 35, and 36.

[175] Case No. CHR-NI-2016-0001, Commission on Human Rights Philippines.

[176] J. Paris. 2019. CHR: Big Oil, Cement Firms Legally, Morally Liable for Climate Change Effects. *Rappler*. 11 December.

Women Seeking Energy Emissions Reductions in Pakistan

Five women in Pakistan have sued the national government for failing to pursue emission reductions consistent with its first nationally determined contribution (NDC) (see **Maria Khan et al. v. Federation of Pakistan et al.**)[177] Khan et al. argue that decreased energy sector emissions are critical to achieving a 20% reduction of projected greenhouse gas (GHG) emissions by 2030, committed in Pakistan's first NDC. The government, asserts the petitioners, has a positive duty to "encourage and support the development of renewable energy projects to reduce GHG emissions and mitigate climate change impacts."[178] Notwithstanding this obligation, the government had not approved any renewable energy power projects in the 14 months before the petition.

The petition stresses that the government's inaction disadvantages women (mothers of future generations of women). Gender, they say, is a crucial determinant of vulnerability to climate change. Social norms limit women's participation in political and household decision-making processes and access to education, finance, and social resources. Furthermore, "women's productive and reproductive activities make them disproportionately vulnerable to changes in biodiversity, cropping patterns, and insect and disease vectors."[179]

Constitutional rights sit at the heart of this claim. Khan et al. argue that the government's climate failings violate their constitutional rights to equality before the law, life, liberty, and dignity (articles 4, 9, 14, and 25 of the Pakistan Constitution). Khan et al. also argue that the national government has violated the public trust doctrine, the principle of intergenerational equity, and the concept of climate justice developed in *Leghari v. Federation of Pakistan* (footnote 170). The petitioners seek orders declaring that the government must support renewable energy projects and enforce the Paris Agreement in letter and spirit. This case has not yet been decided.

Women Seeking More Ambitious Climate Targets in Switzerland

A group of senior women lodged a petition to the European Court of Human Rights after unsuccessful litigation in their national courts.[180] The women pursued rights-based litigation against the Government of Switzerland in 2016.[181] They argued that the government's emission reduction targets of 20% by 2020, and 30% by 2030, were not on track to limit global warming to the Paris Agreement goal of well-below 2°C, which violated their constitutional and human rights. The women cited the Swiss Constitution on the right to life, the sustainability principle, and the precautionary principle (Articles 10, 73, and 74). They also relied on articles 2 and 8 of the European Convention on Human Rights, the articles considered in the *Urgenda* case. The case stressed the vulnerability of older women to heatwaves. The women sought orders to compel the legislature and federal agencies responsible for transportation, environmental protection, and energy to adopt regulatory approaches to achieve GHG emission reductions of at least 25% below 1990 levels by 2020 and 50% below 1990 levels by 2050.

Gender-based arguments did not persuade the Swiss national courts. The Federal Administrative Court of Switzerland dismissed the lawsuit in 2018, reasoning that women over 75 years of age were not the only population affected by climate change. Hence, the injury and remedy were not specialized to the petitioners. The Supreme Court of Switzerland later denied an appeal in May 2020. It concluded that the plaintiffs' asserted rights had not been sufficiently affected and that the women should seek their remedy via political means.

---

[177] *Maria Khan et al. v. Pakistan et al.*, Writ Petition No. 8960 of 2019, High Court of Lahore. para. 2.
[178] Footnote 177, para. 18.
[179] Footnote 177, para. 25.
[180] *Union of Swiss Senior Women for Climate Protection v. Switzerland*, application to the European Court of Human Rights. 26 November 2020.
[181] *Union of Swiss Senior Women for Climate Protection v. Federal Department of the Environment, Transport, Energy and Communications*, Federal Supreme Court of Switzerland, Public Law Division I, Judgment 1C_37/2019 of 5 May 2020.

On 26 November 2020, the Union of Swiss Senior Women filed an application to the European Court of Human Rights. They cite three main complaints: (i) Switzerland's inadequate climate policies violate their right to life and health under articles 2 and 8 of the ECHR; (ii) the Supreme Court of Switzerland rejected their case on arbitrary grounds, in violation of their right to a fair trial under article 6 of the ECHR; and (iii) the Swiss authorities and courts did not deal with the content of their complaints, in violation of the right to an effective remedy in article 13 of the ECHR.

Investigating the Impacts of Climate Change on People Who Are Vulnerable to Its Impacts

In September 2019, civil society organizations petitioned the Inter-American Commission on Human Rights to analyze the impacts of climate change on human rights and propose humane measures for responding to climate change.[182] These measures should consider the needs of indigenous peoples, women, children, and rural communities, a fundamental requirement of the Paris Agreement.[183]

As the petition is not solely focused on women, it seeks a range of recommendations, including that the commission:

(i)   call on states to ramp up ambition in their second or updated NDCs in 2020;
(ii) emphasize the responsibility of businesses to respect human rights in the context of climate change;
(iii) urge states to promote energy transition models that guarantee economic, social, cultural, and environmental rights, especially of indigenous peoples, children and youth, women, and rural communities; and
(iv) advocate that states promote gender equality.

The investigation is ongoing.

Protecting Women in Disasters and during Resource Scarcity

Within Asia, courts have recorded the need for special protections for women in post-disaster responses and situations resulting in resource scarcity.

Disaster risk reduction plans and their implementation were at issue in **Gaurav Kumar Bansal v. Union of India & Ors**.[184] Following the unprecedented flood and landslide disaster in Uttarakhand in 2013, the petitioner asked the Supreme Court of India to direct the national and state governments to properly prepare for disasters and implement the Disaster Management Act, 2005. Accepting the petition, the Supreme Court managed the case over several hearings, prodding the government to ensure compliance with the law. During the matter, the national government confirmed that it had instructed all state governments to prepare minimum standards and guidelines for disasters covering food, water, sanitation, medical cover for disaster-affected persons affected. Furthermore, state governments were required to create special provisions for the needs of widows and orphans in post-disaster situations.

BELA Vs. Bangladesh[185] was not a disaster case, but considered the impact of water scarcity on neighboring communities in the Bay of Bengal, an expected climate change impact across Asia. BELA sued to protect mangrove forests from shrimp farms, which were causing mass deforestation, polluting water bodies, and

182 Sabin Center for Climate Change Law. Hearing on Climate Change Before the Inter-American Commission on Human Rights (accessed 22 December 2020).
183 Paris Agreement, Paris, 12 December 2015, *United Nations Treaty Series*, No. 54113, p. 2, para. 11 of the Preamble.
184 *Gaurav Kumar Bansal v. Union of India and Others*, Civil Appeal No. 444 of 2013 (Supreme Court, 8 May 2017).
185 *BELA Vs. Bangladesh*, WP No. 57 of 2010, D-/01-02-2012.

causing salinity intrusion to more than 60% of cultivable land in the three districts of the Bay of Bengal. Conflicts over water and land access had eroded law and order and led to the abuse of women and children.

The court expressed concern over the impacts on women of resource scarcity caused by salinity intrusion. It said: "In view of declining supply of eggs and milk from household poultry and fish and water from the ponds, women not only have to walk miles to collect drinking water for their families, but are also compelled to engage in shrimp fry/seed collection for extra earning to meet the family demands."[186] The court did not make any gender-specific orders, but expressed concern for the gender-related impacts of water scarcity. It ordered the government to regulate shrimp farming and limit the use of saline water in cultivation practices.

Gender and Participatory Rights in the Climate Context

No lawsuits specifically detail the need for special protections for women; lesbian, gay, bisexual, transgender, queer, and intersex (LGBTQI) people; and gender minorities in consultations for climate-related projects such as energy, transport, or resettlement projects. Limited numbers of lawsuits likely reflect the lack of special protections for women and other genders in most EIA laws.

A recent study assessed the EIA laws in 12 countries in Africa and India. It found that only one-third of the countries had schemes that mainstreamed gender.[187] International development agencies such as ADB require meaningful consultation in connection with environmental and Indigenous peoples' safeguards.[188] However, unless such rights are embedded within domestic legal frameworks, it is challenging for injured parties to sue for exclusion from a consultation. Given the lack of gender-specific litigation relating to participatory rights, it is useful to consider existing jurisprudence on participatory rights in climate litigation.

Imrana Tiwana v. Province of Punjab[189] reinforced the importance of community participation in EIAs concerning a 7 kilometer (km) expressway in Lahore. The petition challenged defective consultation processes and the credibility of the project's emissions forecasts, which estimated that the project would result in decreased emissions. The court stressed that EIAs are a fundamental element of sustainable development because they integrate "environmental considerations into socioeconomic development and decision-making processes."[190] Public participation was, therefore, such an integral part of the EIA process that it was "akin to environmental democracy."[191] Hence, the failure to seek public comment and the decision to commence construction before obtaining regulatory approval violated the citizenry's right to life and dignity and were fatal flaws. The court also held that the permission offended environmental justice and due process, which were protected under articles 4 and 10A of the Constitution of Pakistan. The principles established in this case apply in the gender context. A lawyer might successfully argue that a right to environmental democracy, when combined with a right to equality before the law, affords women and other minority gender groups a right to participate.

The Supreme Court of Sri Lanka in **Bulankulama and Others v. Secretary, Ministry of Industrial Development**[192] has also expressed its displeasure at the lack of gender-inclusiveness in laws, including EIA laws. The case centered around the government's plan to enter into a mining agreement covering phosphate deposits in Eppawela. Nearby farmers objected to the proposed agreement due to the lack of a feasibility or environmental impact assessment. The community members argued that the contract would offend their

186   Footnote 185, p. 205.
187   S.K. Singh and V. Wankhede. 2018. *Inclusion of Gender in Environmental Impact Assessment. Centre for Science and Environment.* New Delhi.
188   ADB. 2009. Safeguard Policy Statement. Manila.
189   Imrana Tiwana v. Province of Punjab, PLD 2015 Lahore 522.
190   Footnote 189, p. 4. para. 35.
191   Footnote 189, p. 53. para. 41.
192   Bulankulama and Others v. Secretary, Ministry of Industrial Development, (2000) 3 Sri LR 243.

rights to equality before the law, freedom of profession, and freedom of movement.[193] The court agreed. It directed the government to refrain from entering into a mining contract until an environmental survey was published and discussed.

It was the court's observations regarding the language of EIA laws that are relevant to this report. The law required the Sri Lankan Central Environmental Authority to make available copies to any person interested to enable "him or her to make copies" or to make "his or its comments."[194] The court stated:

> I might observe, in passing, that it is time, indeed it is high time, that the laws of this country be stated in gender neutral terms and that laws formulated in discriminatory terms should not be allowed to exist, although protected for the time being as "existing law" within the meaning of Article 16 of the Constitution. The argument advanced that the provision in the law relating to the interpretation of statutes that "his" includes "her" is clearly insufficient: it displays, in my considered opinion, a gross ignorance or callous disregard of such a matter of fundamental importance as the fact that there are two species of humans.[195]

Protecting Women's Inheritance Rights Has Climate Co-Benefits

In its recent report on regional climate litigation, ADB highlighted women's capacity to boost climate solutions.[196]

As explored in **Part 2**, ensuring women's capacity to own or hold legal tenure to land brings benefits for climate change mitigation and adaptation. Asia has a few examples of cases where courts have protected women's constitutional right to inherit land despite social and cultural practices barring such rights.

In **Jance Faransina Mooy-Ndun v. Junus Ndoy et al.,**[197] the Supreme Court of Indonesia invalidated a customary rule that women's inheritance rights were not equal to those of men. The court held that the customary law violated the principles of equality before the law and nondiscrimination under the Constitution of Indonesia.

The Supreme Court of Myanmar in **Daw San Lwin v. Daw Than (aka) Daw Than Than,**[198] recognized a widow's right to inherit her late husband's inherited property from her former father-in-law. The court held that the widow's later remarriage did not extinguish her right to inherit the land because she held primogeniture rights (an exclusive right to inherit belonging to a firstborn son).

---

[193] Democratic Socialist Republic of Sri Lanka Constitution, 1978. Articles 12(1), 14(1)(g) and 14(1)(h).
[194] Footnote 192, p. 311.
[195] Footnote 192, p. 312.
[196] Footnote 162.
[197] Supreme Court of Indonesia, Decision No. 1048/K/Pdt/2012, *Jance Faransina Mooy-Ndun v. Junus Ndoy et al.* (2012).
[198] *Daw San Lwin v. Daw Than (aka) Daw Than Than,* Case No. 19/2007, Special Civil Appeal Case, Supreme Court, Myanmar Law Report 2007.

Part 5
Good Lawmaking to Improve the Overall Resilience of Women

Good Laws to Combat Violence against Women

Context

Violence against women is a form of gender discrimination that reduces women's health and wellbeing, impacts their livelihoods through lost time in work or education, and increases their vulnerability to shocks such as the impacts of climate change and disasters. Global data on the prevalence of gender-based violence (GBV) against women reveals that 35% of women have experienced physical and/or sexual violence, mostly by intimate partners[199] and less than 40% of women who experience violence seek help of any sort.[200] As Sandie Okoro, Senior Vice President and General Counsel of the World Bank Group, stated in 2019: "[i]t is undisputed that domestic violence against women and girls remains one of the most extreme forms of gender inequality, a violation of human rights, and a development issue."[201] International evidence demonstrates that domestic violence and sexual violence increase following disasters, as Part 1 explores in depth.

Comprehensive legislation is fundamental for an effective and coordinated response to GBV. States have clear obligations under international law to enact, implement, and monitor legislation addressing all forms of violence against women (VAW). At least 155 countries have passed laws on domestic violence and 140 countries have laws on sexual harassment in the workplace, according to the World Bank.[202] Unfortunately, many laws on the prevention of GBV are already limited or flawed and prevent women's access to justice through limited prosecution of GBV cases and obtaining protection orders. These inadequacies can be magnified under the additional stresses of climate change and disaster risk management. Therefore, GBV is a high-priority issue for these contexts.

Notes for Lawmakers

As women facing climate change and disaster risk are especially vulnerable to GBV, the following practical key elements of good laws are recommended:

- Include broad, clear definitions of violence against women.
- Ensure protection, support, and assistance to victims and survivors through comprehensive and integrated support services, such as a "one-stop shop" approach.
- Clearly specify the duties for specially trained police and prosecutors judicial officers, including a range of protection orders and enforcement options.
- Ensure all disaster risk management (DRM) plans include special arrangements for women such as:
  - highly visible dedicated service points to enable women to make complaints and receive urgent services and protection;
  - advance planning between relevant disaster, health, and social services, including arrangements for post-disaster shelter, to ensure that assistance for women meets international guidance; and
  - ensure the above measures are linked to mainstream services as the situation normalizes.

---

[199] World Health Organization. 2017. *Violence Against Women*. Geneva.
[200] United Nations Department of Economic and Social Affairs (UN DESA). *The World's Women 2015: Trends and Statistics*. New York. p. 159.
[201] World Bank. 2019. Compendium of International and National Legal Frameworks on Domestic Violence. Washington, DC. (Vol. I of V) p. iii.
[202] World Bank. 2020. *Women, Business and the Law 2020*. Washington, DC.

It should be noted that laws are not the only strategy required to address VAW. A national action plan and strategy also need to complement the laws as part of an overall approach to prevent, protect, support, and assist victims and survivors of GBV. Other measures may include awareness raising, education, and community sensitization, however, these are not the focus of this report.

International Norms

(i)   Universal Declaration of Human Rights (UDHR), Articles 7 and 8
(ii)   Declaration on the Elimination of Violence against Women (1993) Resolution No. 48/104 adopted by the General Assembly on 19 December 1993, Article 4
(iii)   Convention on the Elimination of All Forms of Discrimination against Women (CEDAW), Articles 1, 2, 3, 4, 15
(iv)   CEDAW Committee General Recommendation 12 (1989) on Violence against Women
(v)   CEDAW Committee General Recommendation 19 (1992) Gender-Based Violence paras. [6], [7], [11], [17], [14], [23], [24]
(vi)   CEDAW Committee General Recommendation 33 (2015) Women's Access to Justice paras. [3], [5], [9], [13], [22], [27], [62], [63]
(vii)   CEDAW Committee Recommendation No. 35 (2017) on Gender-Based Violence Against Women, updating General Recommendation No. 19
(viii) Committee against Torture General Comment No. 2 (2008) para. 22
(ix)   Regional Instrument: Declaration on the Elimination of Violence Against Women and Elimination of Violence Against Children in ASEAN 9, October 2013

In addition to these international norms, there are numerous sources that provide guidance on good laws to combat VAW. Two major publications are: *United Nations (UN) (2010) Handbook for Legislation on Violence against Women (UN Handbook)*;[203] and the more recent World Bank (2019) *Compendium of International and National Legal Frameworks*,[204] comprising five volumes of laws from some 160 countries. The *UN Handbook* advocates a Model Framework for Legislation and many key elements set out below have been drawn from that publication.

Good laws should include broad definitions of GBV, notably the definition of domestic violence. It should also address cyber GBV, which is rapidly increasing over social media and the internet. It can be perpetrated remotely by sending a picture, video, or text to a targeted individual's device or account or shared on a public online platform, causing acute and long-lasting psychological effects on victims and survivors.

Good laws should be accompanied by the implementation of specific measures to address situations of VAW. These can be set out either in other laws, policies, regulations, or other publications, as appropriate. The *UN Handbook* makes a number of recommendations in this regard including:

(i)   Legislation or subsidiary legislation to ensure the designation or strengthening of specialized police and prosecutor units, including through training and adequate funding.[205]
(ii)   Provisions ensuring that victims and survivors have the option of communicating with female police officers or prosecutors.
(iii)   The creation of specialized courts or court proceedings, supported by training, which guarantee the timely and efficient handling of cases of violence against women.

---

[203] United Nations Department of Economic and Social Affairs (UN DESA). 2010. *Handbook for Legislation on Violence against Women.* New York.
[204] Footnote 201.
[205] Footnote 203, Section 3.2.4.

Gender-sensitive specialized courts avoid re-victimizing victims and survivors during court processes. A growing number of countries have now adopted this approach, including Brazil, Spain, Uruguay, Venezuela, the United Kingdom, and many states of the United States. The Asian Development Bank (ADB) has supported the establishment of GBV Courts in Pakistan and conducted GBV training in Afghanistan with judges and prosecutors from Elimination of Violence against Women Courts (EVAW Courts) as well as the Supreme Court, criminal court, appeal court, and other courts, commencing in December 2018 and finishing in September 2019 with Train the Trainers.[206]

Another good measure is to ensure that the availability of alternative dispute settlement procedures do not restrict women's rightful access to judicial and other remedies, notably in situations of domestic violence.[207] The UN Handbook also includes provisions to this effect.[208] An increasing number of countries, such as Spain, are prohibiting all mediation in cases of violence against women.[209] CEDAW Committee General Recommendation 33 on women's access to justice, makes important observations about alternative dispute resolution processes in the context of family law, domestic violence, and other matters:

> 57. Many jurisdictions have adopted mandatory or optional systems for the mediation, conciliation, arbitration, collaborative resolutions of disputes, facilitation, and interest-based negotiation. Such alternative dispute resolution processes are sometimes referred to as informal justice which are linked to, but function outside formal court litigation processes. Informal alternative dispute resolution processes also include non-formal indigenous courts, as well as chieftaincy based alternative dispute resolution where chiefs and other community leaders resolve interpersonal disputes. The Committee observes that while such processes may provide greater flexibility and reduce costs and delays for women seeking justice, they may also lead to further violations of their rights and impunity for perpetrators due to the fact that these often operate with patriarchal values, thereby having a negative impact on women's access to judicial review and remedies.

> 58. The Committee recommends that States Parties:

> (a) Inform women of their rights to use mediation, conciliation, arbitration, and collaborative dispute resolution;
> (b) Guarantee that alternative dispute settlement procedures do not restrict access by women to judicial or other remedies in any area of the law and do not lead to further violations of their rights;
> (c) Ensure that cases of violence against women, including domestic violence, are under no circumstances referred to any alternative dispute resolution procedure."[210]

However, alternative processes are a sensitive topic in some contexts. As noted above, they can also be influenced by customary and/or religious law. This is also referred to in the UN Handbook with the recommendation at that: "[l]egislation should state that: where there are conflicts between customary and/or religious law and the formal justice system, the matter should be resolved with respect for the human rights of the survivor and in accordance with gender equality standards; and the processing of the case under customary and with/or religious law does not preclude it from being brought before the formal justice system."[211]

---

[206] ADB placed on hold its assistance in Afghanistan effective 15 August 2021.
[207] CEDAW. *General Recommendation No. 33 On Women's Access to Justice*, CEDAW/C/GC/33. 3 August 2015. Articles 57, 58.
[208] Footnote 203, Section 3.9.
[209] Organic Act 1/2004 of 28 December, on Integrated Protection Measures against Gender Violence. 29 December 2004.
[210] CEDAW. General Recommendation No. 33 On Women's Access To Justice, CEDAW/C/GC/33. 3 August 2015.
[211] UN DESA. 2010. Handbook for Legislation on Violence against Women. New York. Section. 3.1.5.

Key Elements of Good Laws

Key Elements of Good Laws on Gender-Based Violence

Laws should include:

- Explicit recognition that violence against women is a violation of human rights and is a form of gender-based discrimination.
- Broad definitions of all forms of violence against women with specific definitions for gender-based violence to include domestic violence and sexual violence, trafficking, and cyber gender-based violence (GBV).
- Protection, support, and assistance to victims and survivors through comprehensive and integrated support services, such as a "one-stop shop" approach.
- Creating specialized GBV Courts (or providing special GBV-sensitive laws and procedures for courts) to enable victim and survivors of GBV to get access to justice. The laws to require specially trained police and prosecutors or early investigative judicial officers and judges involved in GBV cases.
- Simple complaint mechanisms with expressed time limitations for each stage of a complaint, from filing of complaints, investigation, and reference to courts, as well as the trial process.
- Temporary and permanent protection orders including their scope and enforcement, as well as the right of a woman to remain in the family dwelling.
- Availability of civil lawsuits as a supplement or alternative to criminal prosecution, including civil protection orders and other legal remedies such as compensation for victims and survivors.
- Ensure that alternative dispute procedures are not mandatory, do not restrict women's access to judicial or other remedies, and are not applied to GBV criminal offenses.
- Effective sentencing options including reference to particular types of sentences for certain types of crimes.
- Comprehensive and regular monitoring and data collection to ascertain the implementation and effectiveness of the laws.
- Link to a comprehensive national action plan with a budget to include training, as well as awareness-raising campaigns and educational material.
- Recognition that violence against women is a heightened risk during disasters and recovery periods, climate change relocation or displacement, and requiring institutional arrangements to ensure complaint mechanisms and victim and survivor support services remain available, and that emergency or temporary accommodations do not increase this risk.

Examples of Good Laws

The following three country examples are provided: (i) Spain, (ii) Timor-Leste, and (iii) Mongolia. Each is very different, but provide valuable learning for lawmakers when drafting or amending laws related to violence against women.

Example 1: Spain

Spain Organic Act on Integrated Measures against Gender Violence, 2004

This Act is the most comprehensive of the three examples. It takes an integrated approach to prevention, protection, detection, intervention, and sensitization measures to address violence against women. This is achieved across a broad range of areas including education, advertising, and health measures. The Act is organized into five titles with 20 additional provisions. A few are highlighted and summarized here.	**Preamble** of the Act is broadly expressed, acknowledging that violence against women is "the most brutal symbol" of inequality and that gender violence is one of the most flagrant attacks on the basic rights of freedom, equality, life, integrity, and nondiscrimination. **Article 2** sets out the guiding principles including guaranteeing mainstreaming of the measures.

Example 1: Spain

There are also linkages to other Acts including the **Penal Code, 1995 (revised 2015)** Articles 173 and 177, regarding particular offenses and their penalties including community work as well as the **Law on Criminal Procedure, 1882 (revised 2015)**.

In summary, this is a good law because of its comprehensive integrated approach to domestic violence against women, which lends itself to a broader range of responses to be modified and utilized during disaster situations.

Title I: refers to (i) the duty to instill values and respect for the dignity of women and equality as an essential goal of education for children in early and later education, (ii) health measures including early detection and assistance to victims and setting of institutional bodies, and (iii) requiring that all advertising materials must respect the dignity of women and not be stereotyped or discriminatory.

Title II: refers to the rights of women as victims of gender violence and includes: (i) the right to information, (ii) the right to integrated social assistance, (iii) legal aid, (iv) employment and social security rights, and (v) labor and economic rights.

Title III: refers to institutional protection.

Title IV: deals with protection under criminal law and creates a specific category of serious assault. There are increased penalties when the injury is done to the wife or former wife of the accused, or a woman with whom he shares or has shared a relationship with or without cohabitation.

Title V: refers to judicial protection and the measures of specialization in specific violence against women courts and refers to mediation that guarantees due legal process.

Example 2: Timor-Leste

Timor-Leste Law against Domestic Violence, 2010

This entire Act is instructive and takes an integrated approach that is expressed in simple terms and addresses many key elements of good law.

Overall, it is a good example, although it would be improved if the detailed preamble emphasized that women are predominantly the victims of domestic violence, as they are only specifically referred to in the body of the Act in the context of rape.

Preamble: refers to domestic violence as being "a long-standing problem and perhaps one of the most complex social problems of our time." It refers to three major international covenants and conventions as well as the principles of human rights set out in its own Constitution. It expresses that there is a special duty of protection and defense of "vulnerable groups such as women, children, the elderly, and disabled from all forms of violence, exploitation, discrimination, neglect, oppression, sexual abuse, and other ill treatment." It further prescribes that the protection should not be limited to "within families," but that "[a]ll citizens are bound by the obligation to prevent acts of domestic violence and to facilitate assistance to the victims..."

Article 2: refers to the concept of domestic violence. "Psychological violence" has an expanded definition to include "conduct that causes emotional harm and reduces self-esteem, aimed at degrading or controlling the actions, behavior, beliefs, and decisions of another person through threats, coercion, humiliation, manipulation, isolation, constant surveillance..." and more. Similarly, "economic violence" has an expanded description.

Example 2: Timor-Leste	
	Articles 9–12: continue the integrated approach, addressing awareness raising, information, prevention, identification of domestic violence factors, education, particularly schools, as well as study and research.
	Chapter III: refers to institutional cooperation and the role of the state, including having a National Action Plan.
	Chapter IV: refers to support for victims that includes shelters, social assistance, police roles, legal assistance, social reintegration of victims, and support for offenders (Article 27).
	Article 37: enables a judge to order the removal of the perpetrator from the family residence when there are indications that acts of aggression may occur again.
	Article 39: refers to witness protection. There is also a connection with the Penal Code, 2009 and, in particular, article 52 which refers to general aggravating circumstances, of which domestic violence is one aspect.

Example 3: Mongolia

Mongolia Law to Combat Domestic Violence, 2005 (revised 2016)

This revised law is one of the more recent national laws on this topic. The objectives of the law are to establish the legal framework to detect and bring domestic violence to an end.[a] It is to be read in conjunction with other laws that address the serious issue of gender-based violence against women and girls in Mongolia, including:

(i) **Criminal Code 2002 (revised 2015)**, which contains several articles to prevent crimes violating women's rights, criminalizes domestic violence and prohibits discrimination on various grounds;[b]
(ii) **Law on Victim and Witness Protection 2013**, which provides protection to victims of violence; and
(iii) **Law on Combating Human Trafficking 2012**.

This law takes an integrative approach to domestic violence. It regulates the participation of all levels of government, as well as nongovernment organizations (NGOs) and citizens, to prevent and respond to domestic violence. It requires national and local governments to allocate budgets and undertake public education, awareness, and other programs to combat domestic violence.[c] It also includes comprehensive definitions of domestic violence including on: physical violence, emotional abuse, economic abuse, and sexual abuse.

The good law examples set out within the law include:

Article 4.1.1: the principle of respect for dignity of the victim, nondiscrimination, and no victim blaming in any form.

Article 4.1.6: the principle of zero tolerance of violence.

Articles 6.6, 25, 31 onward: the conduct of "risk assessments" of the circumstances of victims.

Article 8.1.9: the requirement for an employer to keep a victim's employment position open throughout the period that they are under protection under the law.

Articles 12, 15, and 36: the setup, management, and coordination of one-stop centers.

Article 20: the role of multidisciplinary teams.

Article 23: requiring a citizen or legal entity to report domestic violence to the police and other named persons.

Example 3: Mongolia	
The focus of the law is on protecting and giving security to victims and survivors by using risk assessments, providing temporary shelters, one-stop service centers, and services from multidisciplinary teams. In addition, behavior-change training programs are provided for the perpetrators of domestic violence, either on a voluntary or a mandatory basis through court orders. Overall, this law is a good example that contains many of the key elements set out above. The shortcomings relate to: the limited sanctions that appear to minimize the seriousness of domestic violence, and the gender-neutral language which makes no reference to the fact that women are disproportionately the victims and survivors of domestic violence. Finally, there are also concerns with its implementation in practice,[d] but this is not unique to Mongolia, as all countries have the same issue for differing reasons.	
Criminal Code 2002 (revised 2015)	
The Law to Combat Domestic Violence (page 79) does not provide sanctions or criminalize domestic violence, but there are several articles in the Criminal Code that apply, in particular, **Article 120**. It is noted, however, that the penalties for domestic violence do not appear to be commensurate with the severity of the violent act. The Criminal Code also has a good practice example that recognizes the legitimacy of self-defense for the victims and survivors of abusive spouses who are exposed to constant abuse and harassment. The legitimacy of self-defense is retroactive, with the effect that women currently charged under the revenge provision will have their sentences recalculated, with some having their sentences reduced or their being released.	**Articles 120.1 and 120.2**: provide administrative measures (fines or warnings) that apply to the first instance of domestic violence, and only if violence continues will it be considered a criminal offense. If it is a criminal offense, the Criminal Code penalizes offenses by enabling orders of restriction of movement or imprisonment, as follows: (i) for less grave offenses, 1 week to 3 months; (ii) for more grave offenses, 1 month to 6 months; and (iii) if the victim is "systematically beaten, treated with heightened brutality, cruelty causing sufferings, or the right to possess, use, and dispose of separate and communal property is violated," it is 6 months to 1 year.

[a]   Mongolia Law to Combat Domestic Violence 2005 (Revised 2016).
[b]   The Criminal Code of Mongolia 2002, as revised in 2015, is not available in English.
[c]   W. Zeldin. 2017. Global Legal Monitor. Mongolia: Domestic Violence Made a Criminal Offense. *Library of Congress—Law*. 12 April.
[d]   Government of Mongolia, National Committee on Gender Equality. 2019. *Mongolia Gender Situational Analysis: Advances, Challenges and Lessons Learnt Since 2005*. Ulaanbaatar. pp. 59–69.

Good Laws to Improve Women's Rights to Decent Work

Part of the National Good Practice Legislative Framework refers to building women's economic resilience to disasters and climate change though national laws to promote equality and eliminate discrimination against them in work and employment. Women face multiple forms of discrimination and inequality in work and employment, and this can impact on their ability and flexibility to respond to climate changes and the effects of disasters. Women are subject to various forms of employment discrimination such as sexual harassment in the workplace and lower remuneration for work than men. They also require decent work conditions and fair minimum wages to protect them in low-paid jobs where they are disproportionately represented.

"Decent work" is an expression that has been promoted by the International Labour Organization (ILO). The term decent work has been taken up more broadly and is identified as one of the key objectives in the Sustainable Development Goals (SDGs). SDG8 calls for "sustained, inclusive, and sustainable economic growth; full and productive employment and decent work for all" and highlights the importance of achieving equal pay for work of equal value and protecting labor rights. SDG10 seeks to "reduce inequality within and among countries," including through income growth for the bottom 40% of the population, the elimination of discrimination, as well as the adoption of policies to progressively achieve greater equality.

Major decent work standards relevant to women's situation in climate change and DRM include the following ILO conventions:

(i)   Elimination of Discrimination (employment and occupation) Convention 1958 (No. 111)[212]
(ii) Equal Remuneration Convention 1951 (No. 100)[213]
(iii) Labour Inspection Convention (No. 81) and the Labour Inspection (Agriculture) Convention (No. 129)[214]
(iv) Minimum Wage Fixing Convention 1970 (No. 131)
(v)   Violence and Harassment Convention 2019 (No. 190)[215]

Governments that ratify and adopt the ILO Conventions are obliged to comply with their content in law and in practice. The conventions and the laws that implement them, in turn, become a source of international law and support good laws on the topic. Even if countries have not ratified conventions, ILO member states still have obligations to report any barriers to ratification to the ILO Conventions.

The ILO has produced reports on climate change and decent work. The ILO report *Working on A Warmer Planet* highlights impact of heat stress on labor productivity and decent work, expressing concern that:

> heat stress could entrench existing inequalities in the world of work, notably by worsening the working conditions of the many women working in agriculture, and of male workers on construction sites. It may also act as a push factor for migration by prompting people to leave rural areas in search of better prospects in the cities of their country or in other countries. Different countries have different levels of public, financial, institutional, and technological capabilities to deal with heat stress.[216]

The *ILO Guidelines for a Just Transition*[217] also provide practical guidance for addressing the national labor market implications of climate change. It refers to the inclusion of women in green jobs and skills development and notes some of the differential effects of climate change on women, particularly related to pregnancy.[218] These guides provide a helpful starting point for understanding the relationship between gender equality, decent work, and climate change.

---

[212] This is one of eight fundamental conventions of the ILO out of 190 Conventions. This is an indication of its relative standing and importance in the ILO.
[213] This is one of eight fundamental conventions of the ILO.
[214] This is one of the four priority conventions of the ILO. After the fundamental conventions, the priority conventions are next in the ranking of importance.
[215] This is the most recent ILO convention.
[216] ILO. 2019. *Working on A Warmer Planet. The Impact of Heat Stress on Labour Productivity and Decent Work.* Manila.
[217] ILO. 2015. *Guidelines for a Just Transition towards Environmentally Sustainable Economies and Societies for All.* Manila.
[218] Footnote 216, p. 14.

This section discusses four topics related to decent work for women: sexual harassment in the workplace, equal remuneration for work of equal value, minimum wage setting, and monitoring and enforcement of labor conditions through labor inspectors. Each include key elements and examples of good laws.

Sexual Harassment in the Workplace

Context

Women may be in employment before a disaster occurs, and their employment may change during and after disasters. Women may also work in places or in certain sectors that may be adversely affected by climate change. One significant barrier for women is the high and pervasive level of sexual harassment in the workplace, even without stressful events such as disasters and climate change impacts. Sexual harassment in the workplace also affects men, but it is overwhelmingly women who are the victims and survivors. It is a form of human rights violation[219] and a form of gender-specific violence and discrimination.[220]

> **Notes for Lawmakers**
>
> The key elements for good laws are provided in detail in this section, but it is recommended in addition that lawmakers:
>
> - develop a stand-alone law and not have the legal provisions as an insert as part of another law;
> - develop handbooks and similar materials, preferably involving all stakeholders, notably workers, and employers;
> - accompany the law with effective awareness-raising, not only within employment or workplace environs, but more generally within the community.

Data reveals that sexual harassment in the workplace affects women across every socioeconomic level in every country.[221] National data for the prevalence of sexual harassment against women in Asia is scarce and often does not differentiate between sexual harassment in public spaces and sexual harassment in the workplace. The following are some statistics drawn from recent publications:

United States	60% of women reported being sexually harassed at work, with three in four failing to report.[a]
European Union	55% of women reported being sexually harassed at work, and in top management jobs, 75% over their lifetime.[b]
Australia	39% of women reported being sexually harassed at work during the previous 5 years to 2018.[c]
Bangladesh	One-third of women reported sexual violence in the workplace as a likely occurrence.[d]
India (Delhi)	66% of all women and girls experienced sexual harassment in public places.[e]
Pakistan (Peshawar City)	One in three women faced sexual harassment in public spaces.[f] Most sexual harassment is at bus stops and in buses.[g] Therefore, even before women get to work, they may have already been subjected to sexual harassment.

[a] US Equal Employment Opportunity Commission. 2016. *Select Task Force on the Study of Harassment in the Workplace*. Washington, DC.
[b] European Union Agency for Fundamental Rights. 2014. *Violence against Women: An EU-Wide Survey. Results at A Glance*. Luxembourg.
[c] Australian Human Rights Commission (AHRC). 2018. *Everyone's Business: Fourth National Survey on Sexual Harassment in Australian Workplaces*. Sydney.
[d] Government of Bangladesh, Bangladesh Bureau of Statistics. 2016. *Report on Violence against Women (VAW) Survey 2015*. Dhaka.
[e] Jagori and UN Women. 2011. *Safe Cities Free of Violence against Women and Girls Initiative. Report of the Baseline Survey Delhi 2010*. New Delhi.
[f] M.B. Orlando, R.P. Pande, and U. Quresh 2020. Sexual Harassment In Asia: What Recent Data Tells Us. *World Bank Blogs*. 25 November.
[g] In a Pakistan study in Lahore, 82% of women experienced sexual harassment at bus stops and 90% on buses. Women Development Department Punjab, UN Women Pakistan, and Aurat Foundation. 2018. *Women's Safety Audit in Public Transport in Lahore*. Islamabad and Lahore.

---

[219] CEDAW. 1989. General Recommendation No. 12 on Violence against Women (1989).
[220] CEDAW. 1992. General Recommendation No. 19 on Violence against Women (1992).
[221] Footnote 202.

Having an effective law on sexual harassment in the workplace is essential for ensuring the economic resilience of women subjected to climate change and disaster risk. The World Bank Group publication on *Women, Business and the Law 2020*[222] collects and analyzes data from 190 economies across a range of indices including on sexual harassment in the workplace. Legal provisions on sexual harassment in the workplace may be found in criminal and civil laws, labor codes, equality laws, antidiscrimination laws, or laws against gender-based violence. In addition, they can be accompanied by codes or guidelines. The World Bank Group has published five volumes of a *Compendium of International and National Legal Frameworks on Sexual Harassment in the Workplace* setting out the laws from almost 150 countries.[223] This is an invaluable resource on the topic. The *Handbook Addressing Violence and Harassment against Women in the World of Work* published by ILO and UN Women is another excellent resource.[224]

Despite the prevalence of laws on this topic, one common limitation is their use of gender-neutral language, which fails to recognize that women are the predominant victims and survivors. Some provisions on sexual harassment in the workplace are simply included as another example of unfair labor practices, which does not reflect the very special nature of sexual harassment in a workplace environment. Furthermore, some laws are contained in a penal code only, which is a very blunt instrument for addressing the subtleties and nuances of the treatment of victims and survivors, thus, it is unsurprising that many women do not report violations. Best practice indicates that a stand-alone law enables true focus to be given to this important form of violent discrimination against women.

Sexual harassment in the workplace has serious implications for women, employers, and society at large. The impact on victims and survivors include personal consequences such as physical and mental health problems and professional effects including abandonment of careers, forced job changes, lost or reduced professional advancement and opportunities, lower earnings and work performance, limited employment options, and career interruptions. On a larger scale, this contributes to lost productivity, unemployment, and persistent gender wage differences.[225]

For employers, the impact of sexual harassment in the workplace includes security issues, absenteeism, high turnover, negative effects on staff morale and productivity, and substantial legal costs.[226] For communities, the global cost of violence and harassment against women at work has been estimated at approximately $1.5 trillion and, in some countries, it is estimated to cost 3.7% of gross domestic product.[227] Furthermore, there is a direct correlation between gender inequality and discrimination in the labor market and the absence of legislation protecting women from sexual harassment.[228]

International Norms

(i)   UN Declaration on the Elimination of Violence against Women 1993, Article 2
(ii) Convention on Preventing and Combating Violence against Women and Domestic Violence (Istanbul Convention)
(iii) CEDAW
(iv) International Covenant on Civil and Political Rights (ICCPR), Article 26
(v)   ILO C111

---

[222] Footnote 202.
[223] World Bank. 2019. *Compendium of International and National Legal Frameworks on Sexual Harassment in the Workplace*. Washington, DC.
[224] UN Women and ILO. 2019. *Handbook Addressing Violence and Harassment against Women in the World of Work*. New York.
[225] Footnote 223; Footnote 223, p. 9.
[226] Footnote 223, pp. ix.
[227] Footnote 224, p. 10.
[228] Footnote 202, p. 15.

(vi) CEDAW Committee General Recommendation 12 (1989); CEDAW Committee General Recommendation 19 (1992), Articles 11 (17), and 24 (j) and (t); and CEDAW General Recommendation 24 (1999), Article 12

(vii) ILO Convention 130 (2019) on Violence and Harassment and Its Related Recommendation 206 (2019)

Key Elements of Good Laws

Key Elements of Good Laws on Sexual Harassment in the Workplace

- The core elements should cover prevention, prohibition, protection, remedies, and responsive assistance, as well as a requirement for regular monitoring and assessment of the effectiveness of the implementation of the law.
- The law and associated documents should take account of the cultural and deeply rooted social norms and practices in the country.
- Definition of sexual harassment should be broad and the basic definition should include any unwelcome sexual advance, act, or behavior, either directly or by implication, whether it is a physical, verbal, nonverbal, or written communication of a sexual nature and cyber or digital pictures or messaging of a sexual nature. It should also include creating an "intimidating or hostile or offensive working environment."
- Definitions of workers and other named categories of persons connected with the workplace should be broad and include all sectors of employment, whether private or public, formal and informal economy, in urban or rural areas.
- Definition of workplace should be broad and include both organized and unorganized sectors, public and private spaces, and when commuting to and from work.
- The law should stipulate simple and appropriate mechanisms to enable complaints to be made by victims and survivors which are both within and external to the workplace including access to courts or tribunals. There should be multiple reporting options and any time limits should be reasonable and enable extension on reasonable grounds.
- Data, both quantitative and qualitative, should be collected and monitored by relevant authorities of the state including labor inspectorates.
- Complaint bodies addressing the complaints should include women.
- The law should also place an obligation on all employers to inform every employee that there is zero tolerance of sexual harassment in the workplace, and how and where complaints can be made.
- Employers of a named size of employees should have a sexual harassment policy and be required to set up a simple internal complaints system with effective remedies and dispute resolutions.
- Victims and survivors should have options as to whether to pursue formal or informal processes and enable confidentiality.
  - Formal processes should include making a complaint through an employer or through a government body or taking a complaint under a criminal code (for example, criminal offenses of sexual assault, stalking, insult to the modesty of a woman, exploitation of sexual imagery, or cyber stalking crimes).
  - Informal processes should include alternative dispute resolution, however, there should be no mediation of sexual harassment which amounts to a criminal offense.
- Redress for sexual harassment should not be limited to action taken against the individual perpetrator, but also against the employer if the employer has not taken adequate measures to prevent it.
- The law should provide for inspection of workplaces and regular monitoring of sexual harassment claims.
- Sanctions include penalties against the perpetrator, but also against the employer if they have not taken adequate steps in advance to prevent the violence and harassment in the first place. The sanctions to be appropriate to the seriousness and may include criminal proceedings for an offense.
- Remedies should be available to the victims and survivors and include damages and compensation and other employment remedies.
- Responsive assistance to the victims and survivors of violence and harassment should include information, counselling, emergency services, medical care and treatment, psychological support, legal and social support.

The previous key elements could be included in a combination of legislation, as well as guidelines, codes of conduct, handbooks or other associated documents, including emerging policies in support of a just transition.

Examples of Good Laws

One major example of a good law from (i) India is provided here, as it addresses most of the key elements including an associated handbook. Other short examples are from: (ii) Australia, (iii) the Philippines, and (iv) Pakistan.

Example 1: India
India Sexual Harassment of Women at Workplace (Prevention, Prohibition, and Redressal) Act, 2013[a]

This law is to be considered in conjunction with the detailed *Handbook on Sexual Harassment in the Women at Workplace (Prevention, Prohibition, Redressal) Act, 2013* (2015)[b] published by the Ministry of Women and Child Development:

Introduction to the Handbook: addresses the cultural and social norms and practices that devalue women. The introduction perceptively encapsulates that "[s]exual harassment constitutes a gross violation of women's right to equality and dignity, it has its roots in patriarchy and its attendant perception that men are superior to women and that some forms of violence against women are acceptable. One of these is workplace sexual harassment, which views various forms of such harassment, as harmless and trivial. Often, it is excused as "natural" male behavior or "harmless flirtation which women enjoy."

This is a good law as it allows for decentralization for the receiving and hearing of complaints. Also, the Local Complaints Committee is able to receive complaints of sexual harassment when an employer has not set up an Internal Complaints Committee (e.g., the company has less than 10 workers), or if the complaint is against the employer personally.

The inclusion of women and vulnerable and minority persons on both Committees is an important and empowering mechanism to increase their trust in the decision process and outcome, and encourage them to come forward.

Title of the Act: the name of the Act, the preamble, and the content refer to protection, prevention, and redressal of complaints.

Articles 2(n) and 3: define "sexual harassment" simply, but broadly in an inclusive way and these definitions are explained by the Handbook which also includes examples and drawings.

Article 2(f): defines "employee" broadly and includes a person working, whether for remuneration or not, or working on a voluntary basis. A domestic worker is also protected by the law in Article 2(e) and defines a "domestic worker" widely, but does not include any member of the family of the employer. The inclusion of a domestic worker is a highly important aspect of the law as domestic workers are frequently not covered by protective legislation.

Article 2(o): defines "workplace" inclusively and names government departments in all their forms. It also particularizes a spread of private sectors, which is important as some laws do not cover educational institutions, for example, Pakistan (referred to page 87).

Article 2(v): includes any place visited by the employee "arising out of or during the course of employment" including transportation by the employer for undertaking such journey and **Article 2 (vi)** includes a dwelling place or a house.

Chapters II and III provide for two complaint mechanisms:

Chapter II, section 4: provides that an employer is obliged to set up an "Internal Complaints Committee" to consist of no less than two members from amongst employees "preferably committed to the cause of women or who have had experience in social work or have legal knowledge." The presiding officer is to be a woman employed at a senior level at the workplace and at least one-half of the total members shall be women.

Example 1: India

Chapter III, section 5: provides that a "Local Complaints Committee" be set up in every district. It is to consist of: a female chairperson; one member to be nominated from among women working in a ward or municipality; two members, of whom one shall be a woman, nominated from among nongovernment organizations or associations committed to the cause of women, or a person familiar with the issues relating to sexual harassment. At least one of the nominees should preferably have a background in law or legal knowledge. Also, one of the nominees shall be a woman from the scheduled Castes, Tribes, or other "Backward Classes" or minority.

Chapter IV Section 9: addresses how complaints can be made in writing within a period of 3 months, or as extended. It also permits assistance to be given to a woman when making a complaint in writing. Good practice suggests a longer time should be expressed in law as women often delay in taking action. Furthermore, good laws should enable multiple reporting options other than in writing such as verbal complaints, as well as utilizing digital forms.

Section 10: enables conciliation, but only if a woman wishes it and provides that no monetary settlement shall be a basis for conciliation. This is a good provision in that a woman is not required to be involved in a conciliation, as is the case under many laws. Furthermore, forbidding payment of money addresses pressure or inducements that are often placed on a woman to settle.

Section 15: enables an internal Committee or a Local Committee to grant compensation and expresses that it is to have regard to the mental trauma, pain, suffering, and emotional stress caused to the aggrieved woman, the loss of career opportunity, medical expenses incurred for physical or psychiatric treatment, income and financial status of the employer, and the feasibility of payment in lump sums or in installments. This is a good provision in that it takes a broad account of the impacts that sexual harassment has on the woman.

Section 19: details the duties of an employer and includes providing assistance to the woman if she wishes to make a complaint for an offense under the Penal Code.

Section 22: requires employers to provide an annual report to the District Officer on the number of cases filed. This process would enable data to be collected for monitoring purposes.

[a] India Sexual Harassment of Women at Workplace (Prevention, Prohibition and Redressal) Act 2013.
[b] Government of India. 2015. *Handbook on Sexual Harassment in the Women at Workplace (Prevention, Prohibition, Redressal) Act, 2013.* New Delhi.

Other Examples
2. Australia Sex Discrimination Act, 2010
Article 106: This is not an entire law on the topic, but has a critical provision that requires employers to take all reasonable steps to prevent an employee or an agent from committing an act of sexual harassment and makes them vicariously liable if they fail to do so. This is a good example of a legal provision that places responsibility on employers, as well as employees or agents who commit the act.
3. Philippines Anti-Sexual Harassment Act, 1995
Article 5: includes a provision on vicarious liability of the employer expressed in terms similar to Australia.
4. Pakistan Prohibition against Harassment of Women at the Workplace Act, 2010
Overall, this is a good recent example of an entire law that contains many, but not all, of the key elements set out above. In particular, it lacks broad sector coverage, e.g., education institutions with the unique feature of students presence on workplace campuses are not covered, and a more limited definition of worker.

Equal Remuneration for Work of Equal Value

Context

Providing for equality in remuneration between women and men is a major step toward overall equality. Pay differentials between women and men is one of the most tangible and measurable manifestations of discrimination against women. The ILO C100 is a Fundamental Convention of the ILO,[229] and is the primary source for the relevant principles on equal remuneration for work of equal value. ILO C100 has been ratified by 173 countries, however, a majority have not fully reflected the principle of "equal remuneration for men and women for work of equal value" in their national legislation.[230] Countries continue to refer only to expressions such as "equal pay for equal work"; or they may have correctly introduced the principle, but subsequently narrowed the scope of the expression "work of equal value" to mean only "equal work." This has a particularly important effect, as it accounts for a significant portion of the "gender pay gap" (referring to the differential in remuneration paid to men in comparison with women). Globally, women get 77 cents for every $1.00 that a man earns. In Southeast Asia, women earn 66 cents and in East Asia and the Pacific, women earn 68.5 cents for every $1.00 earned by a male.[231] This is a major cause of lifetime income inequality.

Notes for Lawmakers

- It is important for lawmakers to ensure that the national law explicitly requires that there be "equal remuneration for work of equal value" or equivalent wording. This is not a matter of pedantry and the important requirement is reference to "work of equal value." This requires more than applying equal remuneration to "equal work," but additionally, it applies to work that may be very different, but have an equal value.

- A good law or secondary regulations should require using an objective job analysis to assess the relative value of work.

- Lawmakers should refer to the ILO published guidelines to assist with the drafting of the law and its implementation.

- This international norm is extremely important for women as they are usually the losers if it is not implemented. This is what contributes to the gender wage gap between women and men.

- Although the international responsibility rests with the State, the domestic legal responsibility rests with employers. Therefore, lawmakers should set up a national process requiring employers to report data to the government on gender participation in the workplace and remuneration disaggregated by sex. This would be a good law requirement.

[229] ILO. 2012. *General Survey on the Fundamental Conventions Concerning Rights at Work in the Light of the ILO Declaration on Social Justice for a Fair Globalisation.* International Labour Conference 101st Session 2012. Geneva. pp. 271–272.
[230] ILO. 2007. *General Observation CEACR Report 111 (Part 1A).* ILC Conference 96th Session 2007. Geneva.
[231] World Economic Forum. 2019. *Global Gender Gap Report 2020.* Cologny and Geneva, Switzerland.

The particular relevance of equal remuneration in climate change and disaster situations is that the undervalued and underpaid labor of women already places them in the most vulnerable segments of society. Women's economic recovery capacity is impaired compared to that of men, as it can be more difficult to continue or obtain new avenues of work during or following disasters. Even when employment is secured, the gender pay gap means that women will take longer to economically recover than men from the adverse impacts of climate change and disaster situations.

International Norms

(i)   ILO C100, Articles (1)(b) and (2) and Recommendation (R90)
(ii)   International Covenant on Economic, Social and Cultural Rights (ICESR), Article 6
(iii)   CEDAW, Article 11(1)(d)

Key Elements of Good Laws

Key Elements of Good Law on Remuneration for Work of Equal Value

- National law should provide for "equal remuneration for men and women for work of equal value."

- The term "remuneration" should be defined in legislation to include not only "the ordinary, basic or minimum wage or salary," but also any "additional payments whether in cash or in-kind, for example fringe benefits, bonuses, or transport payments." It is not limited to money payment for the actual work performed.

- National law or regulations should require a determination process to assess "work of equal value" by using objective job analyses and evaluation of the particular tasks required to be performed in a job, without discrimination on the basis of sex.

- National law should deem that failure to provide equal remuneration for men and women for work of equal value is unlawful and should include penalties for employers who breach the law.

The ILO Committee of Experts on the Application of Conventions and Recommendations (CEACR) published a General Observation giving guidance on how "work of equal value" could be assessed.[232] The ILO has published two guidelines to assist that process namely:

(i)   ILO *Promoting Equity, Gender-Neutral Job Evaluation for Equal Pay: A Step-by-Step Guide*, 2008;[233] and
(ii)   ILO *Equal Pay: An Introductory Guide*, 2013.[234]

This General Observation and the publications were used to identify the previous key elements for good laws on equal remuneration.

---

[232] Footnote 230.
[233] ILO. 2008. *Promoting Equity: Gender-Neutral Job Evaluation for Equal Pay. A Step-by-Step Guide.* Geneva.
[234] M. Oelz, S. Olney, and M. Tomei. 2013. *Equal Pay: An Introductory Guide.* International Labour Organization. Geneva.

Examples of Good Laws

Four examples of good laws are provided here: (i) Maldives, (ii) the Philippines, (iii) South Sudan, and (iv) Jordan.

Example 1: Maldives	
Maldives Gender Equality Act, 2016	
This is a simply expressed good law section which requires that where women and men perform work that is "adequately equal in value and weight," they are to receive equal wages. This formulation indicates that the work does not have to be exactly the same value and weight. Furthermore, women are to receive not only equal wages, but equal "overtime compensation, benefits, and allowances." These are frequently overlooked in laws.	**Article 20**: Employers in public and private sectors shall ensure the following rights... c) Men and women at the same place of employment with work adequately equal in value and weight shall be given equal wages, overtime compensation, benefits, and allowances.

Example 2: The Philippines	
Philippines Labor Code, 1989	
The combination of these two articles is a good law example because it recognizes that failure to provide women with equal remuneration is a form of discrimination. It refers to work of "equal value" and extends the protection of women beyond wages to "other form(s) of remuneration and fringe benefits." In addition, a clause specifically recognizes that male employees should not be favored over female employees in respect of other benefits. Finally, the law renders a breach unlawful, employers can be penalized, and it does not prevent an employee from seeking civil relief.	**Article 135**: Discrimination prohibited. It shall be unlawful for any employer to discriminate against any woman employee with respect to terms and conditions of employment solely on account of her sex. The following are acts of discrimination: (i) Payment of a lesser compensation, including wage, salary, or other form of remuneration and fringe benefits, to a female employee as against a male employee, for work of equal value; and (ii) Favoring a male employee over a female employee with respect to promotion, assignment, training opportunities, study and scholarship grants, solely on account of their sexes. Criminal liability for the willful commission of any unlawful act as provided in this article...shall be penalized...[but] shall not bar the aggrieved employee from filing an entirely separate and distinct action for money claims, which may include claims for damages and other affirmative relief..." **Article 137**: Prohibited acts. a. It shall be unlawful for any employer: (1) To deny any woman employee the benefits provided for in this Chapter or to discharge any woman employed by him for the purpose of preventing her from enjoying any of the benefits provided under this Code. [Additional penalties apply including fines and imprisonment and they do not bar a civil claim by a female employee for salaries or benefits.]

Example 3: South Sudan

South Sudan Labour Act, 2017

This is a good law example because in addition to requiring "equal remuneration for work of equal value," the law requires the employer to take positive steps to "guarantee" that for all employees. In addition, **Article 8(3)** goes some way to expressing some of the objective indicia to be addressed when assessing equal value, which effectively conveys that an assessment is to compare not simply qualifications, but also "work experience," "acquired experience," responsibilities, and both physical and intellectual efforts. Too often, men are given a higher value for physical effort in comparison with women who are not as frequently engaged in such work.

The law also renders unilateral agreements made by employers to be null and void and expressly gives a right to employees to recover underpayments. Another matter of interest is that **Article 8** is expressed in a gender-neutral form and allows all employees to claim equal remuneration whether it is inequality between men and men, women and women, or women and men.

Article 8 needs also to be viewed in the context of **Article 6** of the Act that addresses Nondiscrimination. If there is unequal remuneration between women and men in respect of work of equal value, it may also amount to an act of discrimination against women on the basis of sex.

Article 8: Equal Remuneration for Work of Equal Value

(1) Every employee shall be entitled to equal remuneration for work of equal value.
(2) Every employer shall take steps to guarantee equal remuneration for every employee for work of equal value.
(3) Work of equal value is work, which requires of workers a comparable amount of knowledge attested to by a qualification, or work experience, capacities derived from acquired experience, responsibilities and physical or intellectual effort.
(4) Any unilateral decision by an employer or group of employers and any provisions of any agreement of whatever nature, which contravenes the provisions of this section shall be deemed null and void.
(5) The rate of remuneration of employees who have been prejudiced by any discriminatory decision or agreement shall be replaced by the rate of remuneration attributed by virtue of that decision or agreement to the other employees.
(6) An employee who has been paid remuneration at less than the rate to which such employee is entitled in keeping with the equal pay rule, shall have the right to recover from the employer the amount by which such employee has been underpaid.
(7) The Ministry of Labour, Public Service and Human Resources Development has the right to apply this section without prejudice to subsection (6) above.

Example 4: Jordan

Jordan Labour Code, 2020

This is a good law example of penalizing employers for breaches. It has similar provisions to those in the Philippines Labor Code, 1989 Articles 135 and 137. It also provides for a doubling of the penalty for repeated violations.

Article 53: states that employers shall be punished by a fine of not less than five hundred dinars and not exceeding one thousand dinars for each case in which they pay a worker a wage less than the minimum wage or for any wage discrimination between the sexes for work of equal value, in addition to the ruling for the worker with the difference in the wage. The penalty is doubled whenever the violation is repeated.

Minimum Wage Setting

Context

There is an interrelationship between setting and applying national minimum wages, and reducing wage and remuneration inequality between women and men. A minimum wage sets a wage floor that influences wage levels generally and women tend to be at the bottom end.[235] A minimum wage floor can be general, or it can be applied to specific categories of work, in particular work in which women tend to be disproportionately represented, such as agricultural workers and domestic workers. They have also been used effectively in garment factories to raise women's pay and conditions. A well-designed and effective minimum wage system can contribute to achieving equality. As described by the ILO, it can help to ensure "a just and equitable share of the fruits of progress to all" [236] and "a minimum living wage to all employed and in need of such protection."[237] In contrast, poorly designed minimum wage systems, can put the well-being of workers at risk, undermine effective implementation, and risk encouraging informality (footnote 236).

The recent coronavirus disease (COVID-19) pandemic provides a good example of the ways in which women are particularly vulnerable in times of crisis. The ILO *Global Wage Report 2020–2021: Wages and Minimum Wages in the Time of COVID 19* has much to offer.[238] It documents how the impacts of the pandemic have fallen differently on men and women, with women being disproportionately affected in many ways which could widen gender gaps in the labor market. It reveals that women, young workers, workers with lower education, rural workers, and workers with dependent children are all overrepresented as minimum wage and subminimum wage earners. These are also the groups most vulnerable to a labor market crisis arising from the COVID-19 pandemic. The report concludes that minimum wages play a vital role in enabling these groups to weather such difficult times. The report

Notes for Lawmakers

- Further assistance for lawmakers in Southeast Asian countries can be found in a comprehensive report on the Lao PDR by Pong-Sul Ahn published in 2015.[a] The report traced the impact of minimum wage processes and the impact of minimum wages on the living standards of working people and their families. Its findings include that although civil servants are not legally eligible for the minimum wage, the minimum wage was used as an important barometer for adjusting their salary scales.

- The Report recommendations include:
  - Establishing a statutory minimum wage-fixing institution with a public budget to provide administrative services (including the collection of supporting data); and the organization of tripartite forums and the monitoring of minimum wage implementation in their workplaces.
  - A single survey on cost of living to be conducted by a competent research institution, to improve transparency in the collection of data, and analysis of living costs for workers. The results would assist tripartite partners in amicably reaching an agreement on minimum wage increases.

- In addition to those referred to above, lawmakers need to:
  - ensure that there is a well-designed and effective minimum wage system that can contribute to achieving wage equality between women and men;
  - take account of crises that can have a disproportionate on the wages of women and men in the labor market;
  - ensure a wage setting process that is evidence based, transparent, and applies objective criteria and addresses gender inequality;
  - provide for a council, panel, body, or tribunal to set or recommend the minimum wages; and
  - note the many different approaches available as indicated in the good law examples.

[a] P. Ahn, ILO Decent Work Technical Support Team (DWT) for East and South-East Asia and the Pacific and Bureau for Workers' Activities. 2015. *Minimum Wage and Its Relevance to Socioeconomic Progress in the Lao People's Democratic Republic: A Workers' Perspective.* Bangkok: International Labour Organization.

[235] J. Romeyn, S. Archer ,and E. Leung. 2011. *Research Report 5/2011. Review of Equal Remuneration Principles.* Fair Work Australia. Canberra.
[236] ILO. 2016. *Minimum Wage Policy Guide.* Geneva. p. 2.
[237] ILO. 2008. ILO Declaration on Social Justice for a Fair Globalization. Geneva. p. 10.
[238] ILO. 2020. *Global Wage Report 2020–2021 Wages and Minimum Wages in the Time of COVID-19.* Geneva.

demonstrates that well-designed and well-applied minimum wages can effectively protect workers from unduly low wages and reduce inequality.

There are two major forms of setting minimum wages: (i) government laws that set national or regional minimum wages, and (ii) collective bargaining processes between employers and workers. Sometimes there is a combination of both. A common approach is for national legislation to establish minimum wage councils or bodies which can either recommend or determine general minimum wages or sector minimum wage setting. In this regard, the ILO C100 Article 3 indicates that bodies responsible for determining applicable national minimum wage levels should do so in accordance with C100, which requires "objective appraisal of jobs on the basis of work to be performed" without gender bias.

International Norms

  (i)   ILO Convention 131 (1970) on Minimum Wage Fixing, with special reference to developing countries
  (ii)   ILO Recommendation 135 (1970) on Minimum Wage Fixing

The ILO has also undertaken several reviews on minimum wage setting practices.[239] It published a comprehensive *Minimum Wage Policy Guide* in 2016.[240] Rather than promote a single model for all countries, the ILO emphasizes key principles of good practice and provides country examples. The Guide also provides that minimum wages should afford adequate protection to all workers in an employment relationship, including women, youth, and migrant workers, regardless of their contractual arrangements.[241] There are also other groups frequently excluded, including domestic workers, workers in the informal economy, workers in nonstandard forms of employment, home-based workers, workers in agriculture, and public sector employees. The ILO Convention 189 (2011) on Domestic Workers Article 11 requires that: "Each Member shall take measures to ensure that domestic workers enjoy minimum wage coverage, where such coverage exists, and that remuneration is established without discrimination based on sex." These good practices are reflected in the key elements below.

Key Elements of Good Laws

Key Elements of Good Law on Minimum Wage Setting

- National legislation which provides for a council, panel, body, or tribunal to set national minimum wages or other minimum sector wages as required.
- Legislation or regulation which specifies the functions, powers, and processes to be followed.
- The body to consist of independent, skilled, and experienced persons preferably to include tripartite interests of workers, employers, and government, and include women.
- The wage setting process should be evidence-based, independent, transparent, and apply objective criteria that addresses inequality.
- Empower the body should accept information from experts, or have access to research and sex-disaggregated data as requested by the body.
- Include minimum wages for sectors, persons with disability, apprentices, trainees, and persons in informal and vulnerable sectors such as domestic workers, home-based workers, or workers in agriculture.
- Provide reasons for the determinations, that are made publicly available.
- Require monitoring at regular intervals.

---

[239] ILO. 2014. *Minimum Wage Systems*. General Survey of the Reports on the Minimum Wage Fixing Convention, 1970 (No. 131) and the Minimum Wage Fixing Recommendation, 1970 (No 135). Geneva; ILO. 2016. *Minimum Wage Policy Guide*. Geneva.
[240] Footnote 236.
[241] Footnote 236, p. 28.

Examples of Good Laws

The country law examples provided below, summarize an overall approach in the law, rather than setting out the individual sections of the Acts. Four different examples of wage setting have been included from four countries: (i) the Republic of Korea, (ii) Malaysia, (iii) Australia, and (iv) South Africa.

Example 1: Republic of Korea

Republic of Korea Minimum Wage Act, 1986 (revised 2012).

This is an example of government delegation.

Under this Act, the Minister of Employment and Labor requests the Minimum Wage Council to deliberate, decide, and submit a proposal. The Minister determines the wage accordingly unless:

(i)   a representative of workers or employers has an objection to the proposal and the Minister deems the objection to be reasonable; or
(ii) the Minister deems it difficult to accept the proposal.

In either case, the Minister can resubmit the proposal to the Council and request it to redeliberate indicating the reasons for the objection or request. The Council then submits the result of the redeliberation to the Minister.

Importantly, if the Council decides either to change the proposal or to reaffirm the original proposal, the Minister determines the minimum wage according to the proposal of the Council.

The Council consists of nine worker representatives, nine employer representatives, and nine public interest members. The Chair and Vice Chair are elected from among the public interest members. In addition, there can be three special members who are public officials.

The functions of the Council include conducting research and hearing the opinions of workers, employers, or persons concerned with the wage-setting process. The Council may also appoint technical committees from among its members.

This is a good law example because the Minimum Wage Council is a broad-based tripartite body with flexibility to appoint technical committees. Ultimately, it is the Council that sets the minimum wages for the country because, in practice, the government delegates that responsibility to the Council. The Minimum Wage Council can also conduct research and obtain opinions from the social partners and the community.

Example 2: Malaysia

Malaysia National Wages Consultative Council Act, 2011

This is a government advisory example.

Overall, the process set up under this act is a good example of working in partnership, taking account of public consultation processes and evidence-based information from technical experts.

Section 5: sets up a tripartite advisory body, called the National Wages Consultative Council, which has an independent Chairperson, Deputy Chairperson, and a public officer acting as the Secretary and includes technical experts.

Section 17: allows the Council to establish committees.

Section 21: provides for consultation with the public and includes collection and analysis of data and information.

Section 22: sets out the process for the Council to make recommendations with which the government may agree or disagree or request a fresh recommendation. If the government after that process agrees, then a determination is made, if not, the government then makes its determination.[a]

A negative aspect of the Law is that it excludes domestic workers from being covered by the national wage.

[a]   Government of Malaysia, Ministry of Human Resources. Minimum Wage Portal.

Example 3: Australia

Australia Expert Panel for Annual Wage Reviews under the Australia Fair Work Act, 2009 (revised 2012)

This is an example of a determination process independent of government.

The strong feature of this wage setting process is that an Expert Panel undertakes an annual review and sets minimum wages. The Panel is independent and its work is transparent.

The Expert Panel comprises three full-time members and three part-time members. The full-time members of the panel are chosen by the President of the Fair Work Commission and they are quasi-judicial members. The part-time members are appointed by the government and are obliged to have knowledge of or experience in one or more of the fields of: workplace relations; economics; social policy; or business, industry, or commerce.

The annual wage review requires consideration of written submissions from interested organizations and individuals, as well as consultations and, importantly, research commissioned by the Panel. All submissions and research outcomes are published. The research is undertaken or commissioned by the Modern Awards, Economics and Research Branch of the Fair Work Commission and is endorsed by a Minimum Wage Research group. The research group itself is tripartite membership including government, workers, and employers.

The Panel sets minimum wages nationally (save those who are governed by collective agreements that are unable to give lesser than the minimum wage) and has separate minimum wages for workers with disability, junior employees, apprentices, and trainees.

This is a good law example as it is entirely independent, evidence-based, requires monitoring on an annual basis, and includes categories of workers that require special consideration. Furthermore, it is decisive on the minimum wages.

Example 4: South Africa

South Africa Act to provide for a national minimum wage; to establish the National Minimum Wage Commission (and others), 2018

This is an example of a modified government advisory, with minimum wages for special categories.

This is one of the best examples of a good law and system for establishing a national minimum wage and a commission, including its composition and functions.

Section 2: The purpose of the Act is set out clearly and includes advancing economic development and social justice by improving the wages of lowest paid workers in protecting workers from unreasonably low wages.

Section 3(1): The Act applies to all workers and their employers, except members of the defence force intelligence agency and secret service and it does not apply to volunteers (**Section 3 (2)**).

Sections 4(4) and (5): The Act provides for a legal entitlement to workers in the legal obligation on employers. It requires a National Minimum Wage Commission to be established under the Act to review the national minimum wage annually and make recommendations to the Minister.

Section 6: If the Minister does not agree, the Minister may refer the report and recommendations back to the commission to clarify and reconsider its recommendation (**Section 6 (4)**) and then the Minister is required to determine the adjustment (Section 6 (5)).

Section 6(2): An important feature to increase transparency is that the review report by the commission to the Minister "must reflect any alternative views, including those of the public, in respect of any recommendations made."

Section 7: Provides detail on what a Commission is required to have regard to when conducting an annual review and recommending adjustments that is quite detailed. The commission itself consists of a chairperson appointed by the Minister, as well as three independent experts knowledgeable about the labor market and conditions of employment.

Section 9: The other nine members of the committee include: three nominated by organized business, three nominated by organized community, and three nominated by organized labor.

Section 10(5)(c): Each of the members of the Commission is required to act impartially when performing any functions of the commission.

Finally, the **schedule** sets out the National Minimum Wage and has specific minimum wages for farmworkers, domestic workers, workers employed on expanded public works programs, and workers who have concluded learnership agreements. "Domestic worker" is also defined and includes those employed or supplied by employment services.

This is a good law example and fulfills all of the key elements. Also, as of 2019, there was a good cross-section of expertise on the National Minimum Wage Commission, including women and youth.

Monitoring Decent Work Conditions

Context

Good laws within a country often lack effectiveness because of complex complaints systems, inadequate investigation, and ineffective enforcement. Together, this results in a failure to: (i) bring offenders to account for the breaches of law and (ii) provide remedies to women. Labor inspectorate systems can be one mechanism to address those issues and improve women's rights to decent work and employment. Addressing these barriers will strengthen women's resilience in changing work environments due to disasters and climate change, including their engagement in green jobs.

Monitoring and enforcement mechanisms in countries vary depending on their economic and development situations, as well as the nature of the work. They often include specialized equality or nondiscrimination bodies, industrial bodies, the courts, and also labor inspectorates. Monitoring decent work should include a range of aspects such as: sex discrimination and harassment, failure to pay correct wages, failure to pay minimum wages, as well as occupational health and safety conditions. An effective means of doing so is though labor inspections systems. Their main functions are to: secure enforcement of legal provisions relating to conditions of work, protect workers while engaged in their work (including wages, safety, and health and welfare), supplying technical information and advice to employers and workers concerning effective ways of complying with legal provisions; and to bring to the notice of the competent authority any defects or abuses.[242] Effective monitoring and enforcement mechanisms on conditions of work include: ensuring that women are not subjected to discrimination and unequal treatment in their work, and that they receive appropriate remedies and compensation for breaches.

Supervising the enforcement of legal provisions requires the use of different instruments and administrative measures to ensure efficient and rapid enforcement at all stages of labor inspection interventions. This includes

> **Notes for Lawmakers**
>
> - Labor inspectorate systems can be an important mechanism to monitor discrimination and inequality issues and strengthen women's rights to decent work and employment and work conditions.
>
> - Lawmakers should use data collection, both quantitative and qualitative, to determine the topics which should be the subject of labor inspection.
>
> - Labor inspection is more than being "factory police." As has been demonstrated in relation to the COVID-19 pandemic, they have important roles that can be performed in conveying information and training. Laws and duties of labor inspectors can be adapted to address climate change and disaster situations.
>
> - The decentralized and local presence of labor inspectors make them ideally placed to provide gender-sensitive information, training, and responses as required with a centralized system of reporting.

---

242 ILO. 2010. *Labour Inspection: What It Is and What It Does. A Guide for Workers.* Geneva. p. 11.

inspection visits, but also preventive, awareness-raising, and educational activities and campaigns, and training as part of a holistic and integrated approach to enforcement. A wide range of actions should also be available to inspectors to enforce compliance, from penalty procedures to stoppage orders, as well as other different measures and actions to carry out their duties.[243]

Labor inspection systems play a key role in the world of work and should be able to effectively remedy a wide range of labor problems (footnote 243). This has most recently been demonstrated by the immediate and innovative responses taken by labor inspectors during the current COVID-19 pandemic. In 2020, the ILO shared innovative ways in which labor inspectorate systems can assist in crises.[244] Their decentralized and local presence means that labor inspectors are ideally placed to provide information, training, and responses as required, with a centralized system of reporting. Their training also enables them to address concerns about gender and sex discrimination and harassment. These approaches could equally apply to situations arising from climate change and disasters.

International Norms

(i)   ILO Convention 81 (1947) on Labour Inspection (ILO C81)
(ii)   ILO Convention 129 (1969) on Labour Inspection (Agriculture) (ILO C129)
(iii)   ILO Protocol 81 (1995) to the Labour Inspection Convention, 1947
(iv)   ILO Recommendation 82 (1947) on Labour Inspection (Mining and Transport)
(v)   ILO Recommendation 133 (1969) on Labour Inspection (Agriculture)

ILO C81 and ILO C129 are the most relevant and have served as models for most national laws and regulations creating modern inspection systems. ILO C81 has become one of the most widely ratified of all ILO conventions (141 countries out of 187). Together, they define the functions, duties, and responsibilities of labor inspection systems, their enforcement powers, obligations, and reporting activities and are both included in the four Governance (priority) Conventions of the ILO.

National laws differ between countries according to: the extent and nature of laws covering the powers conferred on labor inspectors, changes in working environments, and the differing sectors of economy within a state or territory. The tasks of national inspection services can be restricted or vary wide depending on the country context.[245] The general importance of labor inspectors is illustrated by the regular meetings held by the Association of Southeast Asian Nations (ASEAN) on the topic of labor inspectorates to improve their impact for the mutual benefit of all ASEAN countries.

---

[243] J. Barbero, A.F. Rodríguez, and C. Zhu. 2020. *Guide on Labour Inspection and Social Security.* ILO. Geneva. pp. 18.
[244] International Association of Labour Inspection; ILO News. 2020. Labour Inspectors Across Asia And The Pacific Share COVID Experiences. *International Labour Organization.* 29 September.
[245] Footnote 242, p. 11.

Key Elements of Good Laws

Key Elements of Good Law on Sexual Harassment in the Workplace

- Labor inspection systems at the workplace should be implemented in all workplaces based on legislation and be carried out by labor inspectors.
- Labor inspection functions should:
  - Guarantee law enforcement on work conditions and workers' protection and regulation concerning working hours, wages, safety, health and welfare, child labor and youth, and other related issues.
  - Provide information on technical issues to the employers and workers on effective ways to obey laws and regulations.
  - Inform the government on violations or misuse that are not specifically regulated in the prevailing laws.
- The labor inspection should be under the supervision and control of the central government.
- The central government should stipulate regulations in order to increase:
  - the effective cooperation between the inspection unit and the government and private institutions that are handling the activity; and
  - cooperation between the labor inspector, the entrepreneur, and workers.
- Labor inspectors should be Civil Government Officials whose employment and tasks are regulated to guarantee the implementation of an independent labor inspection.
- Both men and women should be eligible for appointment to the inspection staff, and special duties may be assigned to men and women inspectors, respectively.
- Qualifications should be stipulated in national laws and inspectors must:
  - be recruited according to position requirements, and
  - undertake appropriate training.
- The salary and professional qualifications of inspectors must be adequate to guarantee implementation of effective inspection work.
- The authorized official is under an obligation to:
  - provide labor inspectors with a local office, facilities, and adequate transportation in accordance with their work requirements; and
  - refund their work-related traveling costs.
- Adequate funding should be provided to establish and maintain an efficient and comprehensive labor inspection system.
- Labor inspectors or the local inspection office should provide periodic reports to the central inspection office.
- ILO member states that have ratified the applicable conventions should report on the measures taken to implement them.
- The range of topics that labor inspectors may investigate should include:
  - promotion of occupational safety and health;
  - checking wage/salary records and overtime payments;
  - sick and maternity leave;
  - sex discrimination and harassment;
  - promotion of fundamental labor rights (e.g., combating forced labor);
  - promoting equality and antidiscrimination measures;
  - employment of women, children and young persons, and other workers.

A combination of ILO conventions themselves and several ILO publications[246] provide guidance on these key elements of good laws. In this regard, it is noted that:

(i)   Laws provide the necessary backbone for an effective and efficient labor inspection system.
(ii)   The scope of labor inspection is defined in general legislation such as labor codes, general labor acts, conditions of work legislation, and industrial relations law.
(iii)   The determining factor for inclusion in the scope of labor inspection, at least in law, is often the existence of an employment or apprenticeship relationship.

The ILO CEACR General Survey Labour Inspection (2006) Report IB provides both the key topics and the detail that should be covered.[247]

Additional resources on labor inspections systems can be found in the following publications:

(i)   ILO. 2012. Good Practices in Labour Inspection: The rural sector with special attention to agriculture,[248]
(ii)   International Association of Labour Inspection (IALI). 2014. International Common Principles for Labour Inspection,[249] and
(iii)   ILO. 2020. A Study on Labour Inspectors' Careers addresses managers of labor inspection systems and a human resources policy.[250]

Examples of Good Laws

Two country examples of overall good law are provided: (i) Viet Nam and (ii) Indonesia.

Example 1: Viet Nam

Viet Nam Labour Code, 2012 and Law on Inspection (No. 56/2010/QH12)

These laws are under the responsibility of the Ministry of Labour, Invalids and Social Affairs (MOLISA). With the assistance of the ILO, MOLISA has reformed the country's labor inspectorates under a master plan extending to 2020.

It is an integrated approach with trained inspectors undergoing extensive training at the Government Inspector Training School. The inspectors carry out integrated inspections covering hygiene, safety, and conditions of work in a single visit. It also includes a focus on prevention.

In 2019, the government added a regulated self-inspection of labor law compliance by enterprises (Circular 17/2018/TT—BLDTBXH referred to as Circular 17).[a] Under this regulation, self-inspection must be performed annually and is supervised through a website.

Also, in 2019, MOLISA launched a labor inspection campaign in the woodwork industry to promote labor law compliance for the sustainable development of the country's woodwork industry.[b] Each year, there is a different labor inspection campaign in a different industry.

These laws are good examples because of the systematic integrated approach and its potential to be applied to particular industries. This could include, for example, a sector in which women are overrepresented. In considering the conditions of work, it could include issues relating to discrimination and equality for women.

a   Viet Nam Circular No.17/2018/TT-BLDTBXH providing for Self Inspection of Compliance with the Labour Law Performed by Enterprises, 2018.
b   ILO News. 2019. Viet Nam Launches Labour Inspection Campaign to Promote Sustainable Woodwork Industry Development. *International Labour Organization*. 27 March.

---

246   ILO. 2006. *CEACR General Survey Labour Inspection*. Report IB, International Labour Conference 95th Session 2006. Geneva; ILO. 2010. *Labour Inspection: What It Is and What It Does. A Guide for Workers*. Geneva; ILO. 2020. *Guide on Labour Inspection and Social Security*. Geneva.
247   ILO. 2006. *CEACR General Survey Labour Inspection*. Report IB, International Labour Conference 95th Session 2006. Geneva.
248   ILO. 2012. *Good Practices In Labour Inspection: The Rural Sector with Special Attention to Agriculture*. Geneva.
249   IALI. 2014. *International Common Principles for Labour Inspection*. Geneva.
250   ILO. 2020. *A Study on Labour Inspectors' Careers*. Geneva.

Example 2: Indonesia

Multiple Laws (see below)

(i)   Law No. 21 of 2003 concerning ratification of ILO Convention C81a
(ii)   Presidential Decree No. 21 of 2010 concerning and implementation of ILO Convention C81a
(iii) Regulation of Minister of Manpower and Transmigration No. 2 of 2011 concerning regulations on ILO C81a
(iv)   Manpower Ministerial Decree No. 257 of 2014 to respond to shortage of labor inspectors
(v)   Manpower Ministerial Decree No. 33 of 2016 concerning Labour Inspection Procedures

These laws, decrees, and regulations together provide a comprehensive approach on all aspects of labor inspection in Indonesia and in combination, fulfill the key elements. They form the platform on which programs are built. For example, Indonesia has developed a Labour Compliance Program (PROKEP) to: improve compliance; reduce workloads and shortages of labor inspectors; and to promote safe working conditions in particular for women, migrants, and those in precarious employment.[b] Additionally, in the province of Bali, Indonesia has implemented an integrated labor inspection involving key stakeholders to ensure decent work for all aspects of the fishing works, including labor rights of fishers.[c] Indonesia is also piloting an integrated labor inspection system in the fishing sector in North Sulawesi.[d]

However, the labor inspection systems and the number of labor inspectors required, places a strain on funding. This is a constant challenge for all countries.

[a]   Minister of Manpower and Transmigration Indonesia and ILO. 2011. *Laws and Regulations on Labour Inspection in Indonesia*. Jakarta.
[b]   Kemnaker (KNK) and ILO. 2017. Fact Sheet on Labour Inspection in Indonesia. Jakarta.
[c]   ILO News. 2019. Securing Decent Work for Fishers through an Integrated Labour Inspection System in Bali. *International Labour Organization*. 25 July.
[d]   ILO News. 2019. Piloting An Integrated Labour Inspection System in the Fishing Sector in North Sulawesi. *International Labour Organization*. 22 July.

Good Laws to Improve Women's Rights to Assets and Resources

Legal rights to assets and resources are essential for strengthening women's economic opportunities and thereby increasing resilience to climate and disaster impacts. The World Bank Group's annual publication on *Women, Business and the Law*, includes "assets of women" as one of the eight indicators monitored.[251] Based on data gathered from 190 economies, the report examines gender differences in property and inheritance law as prime sources of women's earnings and employment. It assesses five aspects on whether:

(i)   women and men have equal ownership rights to immovable property (including marital property),
(ii)   daughters and sons have equal rights to inherit assets from their parents,
(iii) female and male surviving spouses have equal rights to inherit assets,
(iv)   the law grants spouses equal administrative authority over assets during marriage, and
(v)   the law provides for the valuation of nonmonetary contributions.

Without control of land or housing, women are deprived of direct economic benefits. Assets are a means for women to earn income and obtain credit to further their ability to earn income and to develop micro, small, and medium-sized enterprises (MSMEs) to improve economic capacity for themselves and their families. These are rights that are relevant in normal times, but as Chapters 1 explores, come into sharp focus in times when land, housing, and livelihoods are under threat from disasters and adverse climate change impacts. For example, women often face difficulties proving their land and property ownership, and accessing disaster risk financing and reconstruction loans for their businesses.

---

[251] Footnote 202.

The World Bank's *Women, Business and the Law* index includes questions on the legal framework for women's entrepreneurship, with key questions on whether the law prohibits discrimination in access to credit based on gender, and whether women can sign contracts, register businesses, and open bank accounts in the same way as men. Other important questions relate to women's freedom of movement in the public sphere. Law reform on entrepreneurship and assets indicators has been the slowest area of reform in recent years, with laws prohibiting gender-based discrimination in access to financial services still not in place in 115 economies.[252]

However, laws alone are insufficient to bring about change and there is no "global blueprint" for effectively guaranteeing women's property rights and supporting women's entrepreneurship. Rather, there is a need to combine aspects of law, policy, advocacy, and enforcement to achieve gender equality of ownership and land reform[253] (see the example of Uganda in section 5.3.1.4), and ensure women's access to profitable and resilient business ownership.

This section focuses on good laws with regard to land, inheritance, and housing and briefly refers to the valuation of nonmonetary contributions made by women. It also includes good laws to support women in MSMEs.

Land

Context

Land tenure is a critical issue for women, especially in relation to their coping with disasters and adverse climate change impacts. Security of land tenure provides greater certainty of access to land in the event of disaster and enables people to return to their livelihoods, food production and rebuilding activities.[254] It also enables women to access finance, technology, and training to more sustainably manage their land, bringing co-benefits for climate change adaptation and food security, as explored in Part 2. It enables women to produce food for themselves, their families, and communities, and support sustainable rural development.[255]

Several detailed Food and Agriculture Organization of the United Nations (FAO) Land Tenure Manuals[256] summarize the various land administration system

> ### Notes for Lawmakers
>
> It is recommended that lawmakers ensure that land rights for women are guaranteed by law, preferably in the Constitution, regardless of whether they are recognized by customary or religious systems, by family members, or by communities or their leaders.
>
> - The State has an obligation to guarantee to protect women's rights to equality in plural legal systems. They must take all appropriate measures to eliminate discriminatory social, cultural or religious beliefs, and practices that diminish their enjoyment of land rights.
>
> - This is also an example of a topic where an overall legal framework requires not only laws, but a policy to ensure the protection of women.

requirements and the various types of disasters, including both rapid and slow-onset disasters such as drought which may be related to climate change.[257] The complexity of land tenure is "a web of intersecting interests that include overriding sovereign interests, overlapping rights to the same parcel of land, and complementary interests where more than one person shares the same interest in a parcel of land. Property rights to land may be held by private parties (e.g., an individual or a family), communal groups or the state, or they may be

---

[252] Footnote 202, pp. 3, 15.
[253] N. Berg, H. Horan, and D. Patel. 2010. *Women's Inheritance and Property Rights: A Vehicle to Accelerate Progress towards the Achievement of The Millennium Development Goals.* International Development Law Organization. Rome.
[254] D. Mitchell. 2011. *Assessing and Responding to Land Tenure Issues in Disaster Risk Management. Training Manual.* FAO. Rome. p. 2.
[255] Global Initiative for Economic, Social and Cultural Rights. 2012. *A Practical Guide.* Duluth, United States; Asian NGO Coalition for Agrarian Reform and Rural Development (ANGOC) and Land Watch Asia. 2015. *Women's Land Rights in Asia Issue Brief.* Quezon City, Philippines.
[256] FAO. Land Tenure Manuals.
[257] Footnote 254, pp. 37–38.

part of open—access regimes where specific rights are not assigned to individuals, but rather to a group."[258] It also includes customary land which concerns indigenous persons or a person who belongs to an indigenous group. Additionally, many peoples have traditionally adapted to seasonally variable climate and conditions by migrating to other less affected areas. Therefore, land tenure systems must also accommodate collective ownership with flexibility to recognize traditional patterns of mobility between seasons where collective ownership arrangements have broken down, and there must be a process for resolving disputes.[259]

As countries develop more formal legal systems of land tenure, rights to land are typically managed on a land policy framework, supported by a comprehensive set of land laws and regulations. Responsibility for implementing the policies and legal frameworks is mostly decentralized with the national government providing oversight. Provincial land authorities may maintain maps and records of land ownership, issue land titles or deeds, which form a "cadastre" and resolve disputes over land. The cadastre may be converted into paper records and later to digital records.[260]

International Norms

(i)   UDHR, Articles 2 and 17
(ii)   ICCPR, Articles 2 and 26
(iii)   ICESCR, Articles 2 and 3
(iv)   CEDAW, Articles 1, 2, 14 (rural women), Article 15 (legal capacity/dispute resolution), and Article 16 (family relations)
(v)   CEDAW Committee General Recommendation 34 on the Rights of Rural Women, para. [54]
(vi)   United Nations Declaration on the Rights of Indigenous Peoples (2007), Articles 21 and 22 (1)
(vii) ILO Convention 169 (1989) on Indigenous and Tribal Peoples, Articles 2, 4, 8, 13–19
(viii) Commission on the Status of Women Resolution 42/1, "Human Rights and Land Rights Discrimination" (Adopted by the Commission on the Status of Women, 1989, E/CN.6/1998/12)

In addition to these international sources of good laws, there are two primary sources on best legislation to secure women's rights to land. One published by the FAO, developed a Legal Assessment Tool (LAT) for gender equitable land tenure[261] together with a Gender and Land Rights Database (GRLD) that collects data on a number of topics such as land and water.[262] It commenced in 2016 and LAT assessments are made on various countries as time progresses and there are 30 legal indicators used (some are indirect and also refer to inheritance, which is discussed in the next section).

Another source of a different nature is in connection with women's rights to community forests. In 2017 the Rights and Resources Initiative published a report on a comprehensive survey and analysis entitled *Power and Potential. A Comparative Analysis of National Laws and Regulations Concerning Women's Rights to Community Forests*.[263] The report analyzed over 400 national laws and regulations across 39 low- and middle-income countries from Africa, Asia, and Latin America. It has a primary focus on forest land with particular relevance to community-based tenure rights of Indigenous and rural women. Eight legal elements are summarized in a table and are amplified throughout the publication.[264]

---

[258] Footnote 254, p. 4.
[259] Footnote 254, p. 38.
[260] Footnote 254, pp. 23–24.
[261] FAO. Legal Assessment Tool (LAT) For Gender Equitable Land Tenure (accessed 30 May 2021).
[262] FAO. GRLD (accessed 30 May 2021).
[263] Rights and Resources Initiative. 2017. *Power and Potential. A Comparative Analysis of National Laws and Regulations Concerning Women's Rights to Community Forests*. Washington, DC.
[264] Footnote 263, p. 20.

Detailed elements on women's rights to customary land can also be found in the abovementioned report (footnote 263). Two overarching recommendations in that publication are: (i) that genuine consultation procedures should be developed with indigenous and tribal peoples whenever legislative or administrative measures about land tenure are being considered, including representative institutions and indigenous and tribal women; and (ii) that laws should guarantee that indigenous women have the right to vote or take equivalent binding action in community general assemblies or equivalent community decision-making bodies, with a named quorum of women voters to be present. The key elements of good laws set out below have used these sources and adapted them to suit the context of this report.

Key Elements of Good Laws

Key Elements of Good Law on Sexual Harassment in the Workplace

- Prohibit gender discrimination.
- Recognize customary law, practices, and rights, but legally provide that such practices are superseded by the principle of nondiscrimination in the Constitution.
- Recognize religious law, but ensure that gender-based discrimination in religious law is superseded by the principal of nondiscrimination in the Constitution.
- Promote the adoption of special measures for the advancement of women generally.
- Provide that women and men are able to conclude contracts under the same basic conditions, rights, and obligations.
- Special measures to guarantee women's equal rights to land ownership and control.
- Recognize gender equality in the right to own or control property, regardless of the type of marriage.
- Guarantee equal access to judicial systems and statutory or customary dispute resolution mechanisms to resolve disputes over land tenure rights.

Most of these key elements should be expressed within the Constitution, but here, good law examples cover both the constitution and national laws as well as a legal framework on land tenure.

Examples of Good Laws

Three country examples are provided here: (i) Kenya, (ii) Uganda, and (iii) Nepal.

Example 1: Kenya
Kenya is an example of modern legislation. In relation to the protection of land rights for women, there is a legal framework that combines the **Constitution 2010**, the **Land Registration Act 2012**, and the **Community Land Act 2016**, to provide a comprehensive and harmonized system of land management with guarantees for women. It also includes a National Land Commission set up under the Constitution with functions set out under the Constitution under Section 60. Collectively, they cover each of the key elements of good law.
Kenya Constitution, 2010
Article 1(4): Any law, including customary law, that is inconsistent with this Constitution is void to the extent of the inconsistency, and any act or omission in contravention of this Constitution is invalid."
Article 27: This article comprehensively expresses equality before the law; the equal protection and benefit for women and men to rights and fundamental freedoms; equal opportunities; prohibition of discrimination on the basis of sex (and other grounds), both direct and indirect; and affirmative action laws measures and programs to redress past discrimination and any such measure have no more than two-thirds of the members of elective or appointive bodies being of the same gender.

Example 1: Kenya

Article 60(1): Land in Kenya shall be held, used, and managed in a Principles of land manner that is equitable, efficient, productive, and sustainable, and in policy accordance with the following principles—

- (i)   equitable access to land;
- (ii) elimination of gender discrimination in law, customs, and practices related to land and property in land; and
- (iii) encouragement of communities to settle land disputes through recognized local community initiatives consistent with this Constitution.

Article 63(1): Community land shall vest in and be held by communities identified on the basis of ethnicity, culture, or similar community of interest [...].

Article 63(3): Any unregistered community land shall be held in trust by county governments on behalf of the communities for which it is held.

Article 63(4): Community land shall not be disposed of or otherwise used, except in terms of legislation specifying the nature and extent of the rights of members of each community individually and collectively.

Article 63(5): Parliament shall "enact legislation to give effect to this."

Article 67: Establishes the National Land Commission that has functions of managing, recommending, advising, conducting research, and [...].

- (i) to initiate investigations, on its own initiative or on a complaint, into present or historical land injustices, and recommend appropriate redress;
- (ii) to encourage the application of traditional dispute resolution mechanisms in land conflicts;..."

Kenya Land Registration Act, 2012

Article 93: addresses spouses obtaining land for co-ownership and use by both. The article provides that there shall be a presumption that the spouses shall own land as joint tenants, with some exceptions. Where land is held in the name of one spouse only, but another spouse contributes their labor, productivity, upkeep, or improvement, both can be recognized as being registered. It also provides for land registered in the name of one spouse only and requires consent be obtained by both in situations of disposition through a charge on land or a transfer of land.

Although this article is expressed in gender neutral language, it is a good law because the content of it would have its greatest impact on protecting women's right to land. It recognizes that women spouses are often not registered on the title of land, that they often work on and improve the land, and that the land may otherwise be sold without their knowledge.

Kenya Community Land Act, 2016

This article is a good law example because of its specific and express protection of women across broad forms of potential intersector discrimination.

Article 30:

- (1) Every member of the community has the right to equal benefit from community land.
- (2) Equality includes full and equal enjoyment of rights of use and access.
- (3) Women, men, youth, minority, persons with disabilities, and marginalized groups have the right to equal treatment in all dealings in community land.
- (4) A registered community shall not directly or indirectly discriminate against any member of the community on any ground including race, gender, marital status, ethnic or social origin, color, age, disability, religion, or culture.
- (5) For the avoidance of doubt, every man or woman married to a member of the community shall gain automatic membership of the community and such membership shall subsist until the spouses legally divorce and the woman remarries, or the woman remarries after the death of a spouse.
- (6) Subject to Article 159 of the Constitution, the culture of each community shall be recognized in accordance with Article 11(1) of the Constitution in the exercise of community land rights."

Example 2: Uganda

More than 80% of the land in Uganda was undocumented customary law. Many tribes' customary rules recognized women's land rights, but they had been eroded and required action. The combination of amendments to two laws, the **Constitution of 2005** and the **Land Act of 2013**, improved the situation of customary land in relation to women and children. These two laws enabled customary land to be registered, prevented discrimination against women, and required a minimum number of women to be involved in the decision-making positions within community associations and on District Land Boards.

While on the face of it, these are good laws that give women rights, the reality in practice was very different.[a]

In recognition of this, the **Uganda National Policy on Land 2013** acknowledged that having good laws on land tenure was not enough and that further measures, as set out in the policy, are required to make them an actuality for women.

Uganda Constitution, 2005

The provisions in the Constitution provide for equality and protection, nondiscrimination, and land tenure. They are powerful provisions in relation to women, children, and persons with disability, particularly related to customary land.

Article 21: Provides equality and protection in all spheres of political, economic, social, and cultural life and prohibition against discrimination, including on the grounds of sex. It also permits laws, implementing policies and programs to redress social, economic, educational, or other imbalances in society.

Article 32: Provides for affirmative action and redress in favor of marginalized groups on the basis of gender, disability, or other reasons due to history, tradition, or custom. Furthermore, it expresses that laws, cultures, customs, and traditions, which are against the dignity, welfare, or interest of women or any other marginalized group, are prohibited under the Constitution.

Article 33: Directly concerns the rights of women. It provides that women be accorded full dignity and equality with men, with opportunities to enhance their welfare and realize their full potential and advancement. It expressly grants women the right to affirmative action to redress imbalances as expressed in Article 32.

Article 237: Refers to land ownership and provides relation to women and children.

Article 237(3): Land in Uganda shall be owned in accordance with the following land tenure systems—customary, freehold, mailo, and leasehold.

Article 237(4): On the coming into force of this Constitution—all Uganda citizens owning land under customary tenure may acquire certificates of ownership in a manner prescribed by Parliament; and land under customary tenure may be converted to freehold land ownership by registration [...].

These articles are to be read in conjunction with the reinforcing provisions of the **Uganda Land Act, 1998**.

Uganda Land Act, 1998

Article 4(1): Provides that any person, family, or community holding land under customary tenure on former public land may acquire a certificate of customary ownership in respect of that land under the Act.

Articles 15 and 16: Concern communal land associations and their formation. A communal land association may be formed by any group of persons whether under customary law or otherwise. A meeting to determine whether to form an association and then elect a managing committee, requires not less than 60% of the group determine to incorporate themselves, and elect between 3–9 persons to be the officers of the association, of whom at least one-third shall be women.

Article 27: Addresses rights of women, children, and persons with a disability regarding customary land. It provides that any decision taken shall be in accordance with the customs, traditions, and practices of the community concerned, except if a decision denies them access to ownership, occupation, or use of any land or imposes conditions which violate articles 33, 34, and 35 of the Constitution. If there is violation, any ownership, occupation, or use of any land shall be null and void.

Example 2: Uganda

Article 47: Provides that membership of the Uganda Land Commission, consisting of a chair and four persons and at least one shall be a woman.

Article 57: Provides that membership of a District Land Board requires at least one-third to be women.

These are good laws for the protection of women, children, and persons with disability regarding community land and also goes some way to ensuring that women are given a voice in all decision-making.

Uganda National Land Policy, 2013

Collectively the Acts and this Policy work together as a legislative framework within Uganda to address the rights of women, that is responsive to the situation in that country.

Part 4.10: Land Rights of Women and Children

Article 63: This paragraph recognizes that in Uganda, women are generally unable to own or inherit land due to the restrictive practices under customary land tenure or are not economically endowed to purchase land rights in the market. It also expresses that customary practices in some areas of the country continue to override statutory law and undermine recognition and enforcement of women's land rights. It also acknowledges that the provisions in the Constitution and the Land Act have been insufficient, particularly regarding land rights of widows, divorcees, and children.

Article 68: This paragraph expresses that that women should be fully integrated in all decision-making structures and processes regarding access to, and use of, land. The government will take special measures to mainstream gender into development planning so as to improve the status of women, with further details given.

ᵃ M. Nakirunda. 2011. *Decentralised Land Administration and Women's Land Rights in Uganda: An Analysis of the Legal Regime, State Institutional Arrangements, and Practice.* Kampala.

Example 3: Nepal

Nepal is an interesting example of good laws which have largely arisen as a consequence of major earthquakes in 2015. The disaster situation revealed gross deficiencies in the ability to identify, verify, and record land held by persons including squatters and other informal tenure holders. Land was rarely held by women. Subsequently, a combination of new laws and policies were put in place including the Constitution of 2015, numerous amendments to the **Land Act of 1964** and a **National Land Policy of 2018**. This has led to significant improvements in land ownership and gender equality.

Nepal Constitution, 2015

These provisions are simply expressed, but they contain basic provisions in the Constitution that are relevant and important to women and property.

Article 18: Provides for the right to equality for all, with no discrimination on the basis of, among others, sex, matrimonial status, and pregnancy. It also grants special legal provisions by law for protection, empowerment, and advancement of many groups including women who are behind socially and culturally, and includes sexual minorities and others.

Article 25(1): Every citizen shall, subject to laws, have the right to acquire, enjoy, own, sell, have professional gains, and otherwise utilize or dispose of property. For the purpose of this Article, "property" means all type of movable and immovable property and the word also includes intellectual property."

Article 38(4): Women shall have the right to access and participate in all state structures and bodies on the basis of the principle of proportional inclusion.

Article 38(5): Women shall have the right to special opportunity in the spheres of education, health, employment, and social security on the basis of positive discrimination.

Article 38(6): Both the spouses shall have equal rights in property and family affairs.

Example 3: Nepal
Nepal Land Act, 2019

This Act was amended in 2018 and 2019, the latter came into force on 11 February 2020. It works in tandem with the recent **National Land Policy 2019**. Unfortunately, none of these are available in English, but a brief description of the provisions and their effect is summarized by the Global Land Tool Network facilitated by the United Nations Human Settlements Programme (UN HABITAT).[a]

The National Land Policy commits to securing tenure and land ownership, protection of land rights, rehabilitation of the landless, squatters, and informal tenure-holders for improved housing, equitable access to land for all, including women and vulnerable groups.

The Land Act amendments provide a legislative framework to achieve key land policy goals including a pro-poor, gender-responsive, participatory, and affordable land information system. This applies to informal tenure holders residing on government land for more than 10 years and who also have registered land in the Social Tenure Domain Model. This concern has been considered a technically sound method for generating the information required to implement the new Land Act.

This is an example of a where a national policy has given rise to new laws, and not the other way around. It also appears to be a good example of an overall integrative approach to land tenure and the need for housing.

[a]   Global Land Tool Network (GLTN). n.d. New Land Legislation Guarantees Tenure Security and Access to Land for All Nepali.

Inheritance and Housing

Context

Inheritance refers to the transmission of the right to property such as land, and housing on land, upon death of the property owner. Inheritance can happen two ways: by will or testament (a written document with formal requirements) or inheritance by law (where there is no will or an invalid will, called intestacy). This report refers primarily to inheritance by law. Almost all countries have other formal laws or informal rules concerning inheritance.

Inheritance law and practice are sources of serious discrimination against women. They may require women to receive a smaller share of the husband's or father's property at his death than would widowers and sons.[265] In some instances, the rights of women are limited to receiving only income rather than assets, such as a house, from the deceased's property. Often inheritance rights for widows do

> **Notes for Lawmakers**
>
> - There can be many legal obstacles to the realization of women's inheritance rights:
>   - The laws themselves may be discriminatory, or sometimes the law permits customary or religious laws to prevail over the statutory requirements.
>   - Sometimes, customary or cultural practices are applied to deny women rights or religion and culture and/or are misinterpreted in a way that benefits patriarchal ideals.
>   - Sometimes, the protective law is there, but it is not implemented in practice.
> - It is suggested that when lawmakers seek to address these complicated issues, the best start is to gain a comprehensive understanding of the current practice of inheritance through good data collection, both quantitative and qualitative, and then develop a combination of constitutional protections and national laws, supported by policy to ensure effective implementation.

not reflect the principles of equal ownership of property acquired by marriage (footnote 265). Furthermore, legal provisions on intestacy may require a widow to be cared for by the relatives of her deceased husband. In some cases, they may require that inheritance passes to the widow's children, making her a dependent of her children.[266] This can include the house that she formerly regarded as her own.

[265] Global Initiative for Economic, Social and Cultural Rights. 2012. *Using CEDAW to Secure Women's Land and Property Rights. A Practical Guide.* Duluth, United States.
[266] Footnote 253, pp. 3–4.

In 2018, *Women Business and the Law* and the *Global Findex Databases* analyzed the laws of 189 economies and found that almost one-quarter did not grant widows the same inheritance rights as widowers.[267] Daughters were also prevented from inheriting in the same way as sons (footnote 267). The publication *Women, Business and the Law 2019* recorded that "Managing Assets" (which includes inheritance law and ownership rights to property by women) had the slowest pace of reform between 2009 and 2018 as compared to the other eight elements evaluated.[268]

Inequality of inheritance denies women decision-making power and self-determination. Inheritance rights and housing are vital for women and are inextricably linked to their economic autonomy. Such inequalities increase their likelihood of experiencing homelessness and poverty. Inheritance rights are important for widows, who may depend on inheritance for financial security, and also female children, who may become more economically independent with greater educational opportunities if they are allowed the equal inheritance rights of sons (footnote 268). A study in India found that improved inheritance rights led to a greater likelihood of women having bank accounts.[269]

These rights are, therefore, essential for strengthening women's economic resilience to disasters and the adverse effects of climate change.

International Norms

(i)   UDHR, Article 25(1)
(ii)   ICESCR, Article 11(1) (protects the right to housing)
(iii) ICCPR, Article 17 (protects against unlawful interference in the home)
(iv)   ICCPR General Comment No. 28, Article 3 (The Equality of Rights Between Men and Women) Adopted at the Sixty-eighth session of the Human Rights Committee, on 29 March 2000 CCPR/C/21/ Revised 1/Add.10, General Comment No. 28. (General Comments) (includes rights to inheritance)
(v)   CEDAW, Article 14 (h)(2) (provides for housing), Article 15 (equality), Articles 16(1)(c) and (h) (equality in property during and after marriage)
(vi)   Convention on the Rights of the Child (1989), Article 27 (recognizes the right of every child to adequate housing)
(vii) Beijing Declaration and Platform for Action 2000, para. 65(b) (provides for equal inheritance rights)
(viii) Habitat II Agenda and Platform for Action, paras. 25(a) and 26 (reaffirms the right to adequate housing), para. 27 (ensures equal access to housing, land and inheritance), para. 40 (provides legal security of tenure), and para. 46 (integrating gender in human settlements)
(ix)   UN Declaration on the Elimination of Discrimination against Women, Article 69
(x)   Commission on Human Rights Resolution 2003/22 "Women's equal ownership of and access to and control over land and the equal rights to own property and to adequate housing" (adopted by the Commission on Human Rights, 22 April 2003, E/CN.4/2003/22)

Further guidance for the key elements for good laws has been adapted from: *Fact Sheet Two Women's Inheritance Rights*, Centre on Housing Rights and Evictions (COHRE); *Women and Housing Rights Programme (WHRP)*[270] which makes recommendations for model legislation on inheritance; and FAO LAT assessment tools devised by the GRLD, which has six elements for gender equality in inheritance. There are common features and key elements for good practice that are generally applicable.

---

[267] World Bank. 2018. *Women, Business and the Law 2018*. Washington, DC. p. 32.
[268] World Bank. 2019. *Women, Business and the Law 2019: A Decade of Reform*. Washington, DC.
[269] K. Deininger et al. 2014. *Inheritance Law Reform, Empowerment, and Human Capital Accumulation: Second-Generation Effects from India.* Policy Research Working Paper 7086. World Bank Group. Washington, DC.
[270] The Centre on Housing Rights and Evictions (COHRE). 2009. *Fact Sheet Two—Women's Inheritance Rights*. Accra, Ghana. p. 4.

Key Elements for Good Laws

> ### Key Elements of Good Law on Sexual Harassment in the Workplace
>
> - Develop a combination of constitutional and national laws to provide for equal protection for gender equitable inheritance in relation to intestate inheritance (rights of daughters, widows, and women in consensual unions).
> - The surviving spouse should be granted user rights to the matrimonial house for life.
> - Under the law of succession, the surviving spouse should be entitled to a minimum share of the matrimonial property.
> - The law should allow for partners living in consensual union to inherit from each other.
> - The protection of inheritance rights, including equality and nondiscrimination, should apply to all marriages, whether entered into under customary and/or religious rights and/or civil or common law.
> - Women married under customary and/or religious systems should not be unduly prejudiced.
> - All children, whether female or male children regardless of age, should be treated equally in all inheritance matters.
> - The writing of wills should be encouraged and a proper system for validating wills should be established and regulated by civil law.

Examples of Good Laws

Four examples are included here: (i) the Lao People's Democratic Republic (Lao PDR), (ii) Australia, (iii) Nigeria, and (iv) Brazil.

Example 1: Lao PDR

The Lao PDR has an overarching legislative framework that combines provisions from the Constitution 2015, the Law on Inheritance 2008, Family Law 1990, and the Law on Gender Equality 2020. This is a good example of simply expressed laws which, when applied together, provide for gender-equitable inheritance for women.

Lao PDR Constitution, 2015

Article 17: Provides that the State protects property rights including inheritance in accordance with laws. In effect, this means that the rights in laws discussed below on property and inheritance become enforceable as though they were in the Constitution.

Lao PDR Law on Inheritance, 2008

The Law on Inheritance is a simply expressed comprehensive law that covers two separate forms of passing property upon the death of a person, (i) according to a written will that expresses the intention of the person before they die; and (ii) property that passes by law, where there is either no will, or it is defective (called intestacy). The focus below is on intestacy.

Article 10 describes the heirs: (i) children (offspring, adopted children, stepchildren) of the deceased; (ii) the surviving spouse of the owner of the inheritance; (iii) relatives of direct lineage: parents or paternal grandparents and maternal grandparents or great grandparents; (iv) relatives of indirect lineage: older and younger brothers and sisters, or paternal uncles and aunts, and maternal uncles and aunts, or nephews and nieces; and (v) the State, or legal entities, and other individuals as specified in this law.

Article 11 describes the order of inheritance. The closest relatives to the owner of the heritage are entitled to receive their share first. Relatives of the next lower order will only receive a distribution when there remain are no closer relatives of the owner of the heritage.

Example 1: Lao PDR

Article 12 specifies the distribution of inheritance or heritage among the surviving spouse and children. In the event a spouse dies leaving the other spouse and children behind, the children have the right to inherit the three-quarters of the "original assets"[a] of the deceased; the remaining quarter shall pass to the surviving spouse. The "matrimonial property"[b] shall be divided in half, namely the first half shall pass to the surviving spouse and the other half to be divided into equal parts among the children. The surviving spouse shall have the right to administer the assets passed to the children who have not reached the age of maturity.

Article 15 specifies the distribution of inheritance among the children of the deceased and provides that:

(i) If the deceased only has offspring, the total matrimonial property and original assets shall pass to them and be divided equally;

(ii) If the deceased has offspring, adopted children, and stepchildren, the matrimonial property of the deceased shall be divided equally;

(iii) Adopted children are entitled to receive the original assets of the deceased in the same manner as offspring. Stepchildren have no right to the original assets of their deceased stepparents; and

(iv) Adopted children will have no right to inherit from their original parents, unless a Will and Testament of the original parents states as such. Offspring, adopted children, and stepchildren who took care of their parents until death and handled the funeral rites, shall be entitled to an allocation of the inheritance of the deceased at a greater portion than other heirs.

Article 16: This article provides that unborn children are entitled to their share of inheritance of the deceased and that the mother shall manage the inheritance.

Article 20: This article expresses that if spouses have separated, but have not yet legally divorced, they still have the right to inherit from each other.

The combination of these provisions positively address the key elements of good laws. However, it should be noted that key element 5 regarding the protection of inheritance rights in marriage is not expressed in law and remains an issue, as traditional succession practices may still adversely affect women. An additional good legal provision under this Act is that it also includes the rights of unborn children.

Lao PDR Family Law, 1990

Article 2: Women and men have equal rights in all aspects pertaining to family relationships.

Article 26 distinguishes "initial assets" owned by a spouse before marriage or required after marriage by inheritance or a grant. "Matrimonial property" is acquired by the married couple is common during the marriage (except personal or low value property).

Article 28 addresses the topic of the division of property between a married couple. Initial assets remain the property of the owner, whether a husband or a wife. Matrimonial property is to be equally divided between the married couple, unless the husband or wife is responsible for the break-up of the matrimonial relationship or for damage to the matrimonial property. In this case, the wrongdoer receives one-third of the matrimonial property, but in the event that minor children remain with one parent, that parent may receive a bigger share according to the court's decision.

These provisions are examples of good law because they are simply expressed and give clarity to the division and ownership of property between spouses that provides for equality for women and men.

Lao PDR Law on Gender Equality, 2020

Article 17: The Family Law provisions above are repeated here in a summary form.

---

[a] Meaning those assets brought into the marriage by a spouse.

[b] Matrimonial property is defined in Article 3 as "property gained and acquired by the married couple during married life, except for assets for personal use with low value."

Example 2: Australia

New South Wales Succession Act, 2009

This Act is not a national Act of Australia, but a state Act from New South Wales. It is used, however, as a good example of law when there is intestacy of an Indigenous person.

Articles 133, 134, and 135: together permit "the personal representative of an indigenous intestate, or a person claiming to be entitled to share in an intestate estate under the laws, customs, traditions, and practices of the indigenous community or group to which an indigenous intestate belonged, to apply to the Court for an order for distribution of the intestate estate."

The application "must be accompanied by a scheme for distribution of the estate in accordance with the laws, customs, traditions, and practices of the community or group to which the intestate belonged" and will require the assistance of elders of the clan to which the deceased belonged.

This is a good example of a law recognizing the legitimacy of property passing in accordance with indigenous laws, customs, traditions, and practices.

The following two country examples are illustrations of a good law being interpreted by courts to enforce the rights of women in inheritance.

Example 3: Nigeria

Nigeria Constitution, 1999

Section 42(1): A Citizen of Nigeria of a particular community, ethnic group, place of origin, sex, religion or political opinion shall not, by reason only that he is such a person;

   (i) be subjected either expressly by, or in the practical application of, any law in force in Nigeria or any executive or administrative action of the government, to disabilities or restrictions to which citizens of Nigeria of other communities, ethnic groups, places of origin, sex, religious or political opinions are not made subject; or

   (ii) be accorded either expressly by, or in the practical application of, any law in force in Nigeria or any such executive or administrative action, any privilege or advantage that is not accorded to citizens of Nigeria of other communities, ethnic groups, places of origin, sex, religious or political opinions.

Section 42(2): No Citizen of Nigeria shall be subjected to any disability or deprivation merely by reason of the circumstances of his birth...

In April 2014, the Nigerian Supreme Court unanimously found an Igbo customary law of succession unconstitutional because it excluded female offspring from eligibility to inherit the property of their fathers. The Supreme Court decision concluded "...no matter the circumstances of the birth of a female child, such child is entitled to an inheritance from her later father's estate. Consequently, the Igbo Customary Law which disentitles a female child from partaking in the sharing of her deceased father's estate is in breach of Section 42 (1) and (2) of the Constitution, a fundamental rights provision."[a]

This decision is important for three reasons. First, it highlights the need for fundamental rights to be set out in the Constitution of the country. Second, it confirms the jurisdiction of a Supreme Court to declare a law unconstitutional if it offends fundamental human rights and the Constitution. Third, it accepts the application of nondiscrimination to a female child in inheritance granted by customary law.

---

[a] H. Goitom. 2014. Global Legal Monitor. Nigeria: Supreme Court Invalidates Igbo Customary Law Denying Female Descendants the Right to Inherit. *Library of Congress*—Law. 6 May.

Example 4: Brazil
Brazil Civil Code, 2002
Article 1,723: recognizes a family entity as a "stable union between a man and a woman that is configured in a public, continuous and lasting relationship for the purpose of forming a family."
On 10 May 2017, the Brazilian Federal Supreme Court concluded that for the purpose of inheritance rights, a "stable union" and marriages have the same legal value, providing partners in stable unions the same rights as those of married persons. In a related ruling, the Court further determined that, for the purposes of inheritance rights, the equivalence of partners in a stable union and married persons also includes homosexual couples. Furthermore, the Court considered stable unions and marriages on the same legal footing. In doing so, it also declared Article 1,790 of the Civil Code unconstitutional, as it applied different rules for inheritance in the case of stable unions.[a] The Civil Code, in combination with the court ruling, is a good example and important for three reasons. First, it adopts an expansive description of a "stable union" which would embrace many different types of relationships. Second, it demonstrates the important supervisory role of the Supreme Court in interpreting laws, including the Constitution. Finally, it underscores the benefits of having inheritance equality protected by the Constitution.

[a] E. Soares. 2017. Brazil: Federal Supreme Court Rules All Couples Have the Same Inheritance Rights. *Library of Congress—Law*. 17 May.

Good Laws to Support Women in Micro, Small, and Medium-Sized Enterprises

Notes for Lawmakers

All countries have a specific regulatory framework that establishes the enabling environment for doing business, and many also have specific laws to underpin MSME development. When these frameworks are being reviewed or drafted for the first time, lawmakers can make them more inclusive and gender-sensitive by including key stakeholders in law development, and ensuring policy measures are based on good data, backed by adequate mandates and resources to address the gender gap in MSME ownership and profitability.

In preparing new laws and amendments lawmakers should:

- Engage with the key ministries responsible for women's equality, education, and training, as well as on climate change and DRM, to access the full range of expertise and policy experience in gender-inclusion for MSME resilience.
- Establish formal policy and planning structures that include nongovernment stakeholders with expertise on gender and entrepreneurship, especially women's civil society and business organizations.
- Review laws on companies, insurance, and financial services to ensure that all discriminatory laws have been revised and that there is a clear legal prohibition against sex discrimination (direct and indirect) in access to business and financial services.
- Commission expert gender analysis of any proposed reforms to the regulatory environment for doing business to understand direct and indirect impacts or gaps that may differentially impact women.
- Consult widely and request submissions on positive measures that are likely to work in practice to support women's entrepreneurship and existing women-owned MSMEs.
- Ensure that any positive measures introduced have an implementation mechanism, sufficient mandates, adequate budget, clear targets and indicators, and monitoring and evaluation based on gender-disaggregated data.

Context

Globally, large numbers of women are engaged in MSMEs, but generally, they are less involved as business owners than men, and are in smaller and less profitable enterprises,[271] including in developed economies.[272] In Asia and the Pacific, where the agrarian economy remains important, women-led enterprises are also more likely to be micro or small, and less likely to be formalized through business registration. Yet, MSMEs are the backbone of the national economies in Asia and the Pacific and account for a high proportion of employment.[273] As a key source of wage employment and self-employment for women in the region, the extent and profitability of women's engagement in MSMEs has a significant impact on their socioeconomic resilience in the face of disasters and climate change.

Some of the reasons identified for women's lower participation as owners and lower profits from MSMEs in Southeast Asia,[274] South Asia,[275] the Pacific,[276] and globally[277] include:

(i) **Gender stereotypes.** Social expectations and encouragement about who should go into business, what type of business, and which sector affects women's choices and others' responses to their business ventures.

(ii) **Business skills.** Girls' education levels are lower in some countries, and even where there are high participation rates for girls in university education, their education is generally less oriented to science, technology, and business skills.

(iii) **Domestic work and childcare.** Women remain the primary carers of children and dependent adults and continue to undertake a disproportionate share of other domestic work in the home, as explored in Part 1, which often reduces their available time, energy, and the scale and type of enterprise they can undertake. Availability of childcare services and more equal work distribution between men and women in the home are important for women's greater engagement as business owners.

(iv) **Capital and financial services.** Women on average have lower incomes and fewer assets than men, meaning less personal capital to start a business and fewer assets as collateral for business loans. They also face direct and indirect sex discrimination in access to services from financial institutions, especially capital investment and risk financing (including disaster insurance and recovery loans).

(v) **Entry barriers to formalization.** Administrative burdens, taxation, and other costs of doing business are barriers to formalization for low-income-earning micro and small enterprises, where women are concentrated in some sectors, in some countries.

(vi) **Access to markets.** Women-owned micro and small enterprises often have limited access to markets, especially for agricultural enterprises in remote rural areas or small islands in the Pacific island states.

(vii) **Access to business networks.** Business organizations are predominantly male networks because more men are business owners of larger businesses. These may not cater well for women in MSMEs due to organizational culture, time commitment, hours, locations of meetings, and other factors.

---

[271] C. Plantin. 2017. *Strengthening Women's Entrepreneurship in ASEAN*. OECD and ASEAN. Paris. p. 28.

[272] For example, the European Union countries. OECD and European Union. 2017. *Policy Brief on Women's Entrepreneurship*. Luxembourg. pp. 2–4.

[273] ADPC and M. Picard. 2017. *Strengthening Disaster and Climate Resilience of Small and Medium Enterprises in Asia*. Regional Synthesis Report: Indonesia, Philippines, Thailand, Viet Nam. Bangkok. p. 1.

[274] Footnote 271, pp. 28–30.

[275] C.G Goodrich et al. 2018. *Reflections on Policies for Women Small and Medium Entrepreneurs: Status, Challenges and Opportunities in Hindu Kush Himalayas and the SAARC Region South Asian Women Development Forum*. SAWDF—South Asian Women Development Forum. Kathmandu. pp. 6–7.

[276] ADB, K. Francis, and V. Nagarajan. 2018. *Emerging Lessons on Women's Entrepreneurship in Asia and the Pacific: Case Studies from the Asian Development Bank and The Asia Foundation*. Mandaluyong City, Philippines. pp. 5–14.

[277] International Council for Small Business (ICSB). 2019. *Annual Global Micro, Small and Medium-Sized Enterprises Report*. Washington, DC.

(viii) **Access to business development support.** Increasingly, governments have introduced programs to develop MSMEs as part of national development strategies. Unless these schemes include positive measures to encourage and support women-owned enterprises, they do not improve the numbers for MSMEs' ownership or profitability for women.

While many of these barriers to women's participation as MSMEs' owners require cultural, administrative, and policy responses, law has an important role to play in establishing the enabling environment. It should also be recognized that there is a real element of personal choice. Women and men often have different motivations in becoming entrepreneurs or running businesses. Law and policy need to focus on the gender gap that arises from gender-based barriers, rather than on removing all the differences.[278] However, the economies that support women's entrepreneurship through greater access to resources, funding, training, and development do increase business opportunities for women.[279]

A national framework approach points to the need to reduce broader forms of gender bias and discrimination, including educational disadvantage and gender role barriers to workforce participation such as domestic work burden, and lack of child care, as well as supporting women's equal rights to land assets, property, credit access, and control over economic resources.[280] More specifically on the business environment, relevant laws are those that create the enabling framework for doing business, including business registration and taxation, financing and insurance, and special laws on MSME development. Ideally these should also interact with the laws and institutions on DRM and action on climate change to support MSME business continuity through climate change adaptation, disaster risk reduction (DRR), preparedness, response, and recovery. This is the focus of networks such as the multicountry, multistakeholder Asian Preparedness Partnership,[281] and research by the Asian Disaster Preparedness Center on the national enabling environments for MSME disaster resilience in Asia.[282]

> The CEDAW Committee General Recommendation 37 highlights the nexus between women, MSMEs, and the opportunities that may arise from climate change adaptation and green development, recommending that states should:
>
> **Para. 51(b).** Encourage entrepreneurship among women and create incentives for women to engage in businesses involved in sustainable development and climate-resilient livelihood activities in areas such as the clean energy sector and agroecological food systems. Businesses working in those areas should also be encouraged to increase the number of women whom they employ, in particular, in leadership positions.

An OECD 12-point checklist on a small and medium-sized enterprises (SMEs)-friendly legal, regulatory, and administrative environment, developed in 2004 and used in a 2018 report, surprisingly lists as a positive criterion that "Legislation and regulations are gender-blind, applying equally to men and women."[283] Assuming the intent was to state that the laws do not discriminate unlawfully against either men or women, this is, nevertheless, an outdated approach. The best legal frameworks for MSMEs combine positive measures for development and resilience, and the removal of barriers to doing business. These measures benefit men and women in MSMEs. In addition, it is increasingly recognized that positive measures are needed to reduce the gender gap in MSMEs' ownership and profitability, as illustrated in the Viet Nam case study in section 5.4.4 below.

---

[278] OECD and European Union. 2017. *Policy Brief on Women's Entrepreneurship.* Luxembourg, p. 11.
[279] ICSB. 2019. *Annual Global Micro, Small and Medium-Sized Enterprises Report.* Washington, DC. p. 67 (citing Index of Women Entrepreneurship Worldwide—MIWE).
[280] Footnote 271, pp. 27–81.
[281] Asian Preparedness Partnership (APP).
[282] ADPC et al. 2017. *Strengthening Disaster and Climate Resilience of Small and Medium Enterprises in Asia: Enabling Environment and Opportunities: Viet Nam.* Bangkok.
[283] OECD and Economic Research Institute for ASEAN and East Asia (ERIA). 2018. *SME Policy Index: ASEAN 2018: Boosting Competitiveness and Inclusive Growth.* Paris, France and Jakarta, Indonesia. p. 154.

Given that laws on MSMEs' development are now commonplace in Asia and the Pacific, key elements of them need to be positive measures to increase (i) the number and proportion of women-owned MSMEs; and (ii) their profitability and capacity for business continuity in the face of economic stress, including from disasters and climate change. Ten elements of the above OECD checklist are useful in conceptualizing the elements of good MSME laws that benefit men as well as women. These are:

(i)   "Property rights are clearly recognized.

(ii)   Contracts are easily enforced.

(iii)   A simple and transparent tax system with low compliance costs is operational and perceived as fair.

(iv)   Businesses are able to register with the authorities through a simple and inexpensive system, preferably via the internet.

(v)   Business licensing requirements are minimized, and when enforced they aim to safeguard the health and safety of consumers and labor rather than to serve as a source of revenue for local and/or central government.

(vi)   Labor regulations are balanced and flexible, protecting the rights of labor and the firm equally.

(vii)   SMEs interact with a streamlined customs administration that is efficient, simple, and transparent.

(viii)   Financial sector regulations (banking, insurance, leasing) recognize SME constraints and include legal and regulatory instruments that enable commonly available SME assets to be used as collateral.

(ix)   SMEs can easily set up and join membership organizations.

(x)   Bankruptcy legislation does not impose unduly high penalties on entrepreneurs or SMEs" (footnote 283).

These general provisions for MSME support require supplementation with positive measures for women. A recent study of ASEAN countries' support for women's entrepreneurship development, identified 12 essential policy reforms which are also relevant to other contexts in Asia and the Pacific.[284] Most of these are purely policy-based, such as: making strategic plans for MSME development gender-inclusive; integrating MSME policies and measures with the national gender strategy and establish closer links with the women's ministry; commissioning and acting on studies on the challenges women entrepreneurs face in starting, managing, and growing a business; establishing ministerial focal points; creating women's business networks; and encouraging chambers of commerce and SME associations to establish businesswomen committees or women entrepreneur working groups (done in Cambodia, Malaysia, and Viet Nam). Other suggested reforms require a regulatory base, including:

(i)   requiring comprehensive reporting and analysis of sex-disaggregated data on MSME ownership in national census data (done in Cambodia for the 2011 economic census);

(ii)   appointing an interministerial committee, with private sector representation, to oversee the production of a national women's entrepreneurship development strategy;

(iii)   establishing a Women's Business Council or similar to advise the government on appropriate policy directions; and

(iv)   establishing "formal mechanisms for conducting policy dialogue with women entrepreneurs and their representative organizations and mainstreaming their concerns and issues; ensure that women entrepreneurs are represented in public private policy dialogue fora and consulted on legislative and policy reforms."[285]

These last points combine good gender mainstreaming in lawmaking processes and legal empowerment of women in policy making and governance, highlighted throughout this report as fundamental to supporting women's equality and resilience.

---

[284] Footnote 271.
[285] Footnote 271, pp. 83–84.

Promotion and development of women-owned MSMEs through specific legislation needs to be part of a national framework to promote gender equality, prohibit direct and indirect discrimination, and empower women in the public and private spheres. It is a central part of women's socioeconomic resilience to disasters and climate change, along with access to assets and land. MSMEs themselves also need to be made resilient to shocks and stress from disasters and climate change through participation in and implementation of DRR and climate change adaptation as part of business continuity management.

International Norms

There are no specific treaties relating to MSME development or gender equality in opportunities for entrepreneurship, but they are underpinned by the core human rights treaties and post-2015 international agreements on sustainable development, DRR, and climate change.

(i)   ICESCR, Articles 2 and 3
(ii)   CEDAW, Articles 1-3 (general prohibitions on discrimination and special measures), Article 10 (education and vocations), Article 11 (employment and remuneration), Article 13 (bank loans, mortgages, and other forms of financial credit), Article 14 (rural women (legal capacity and dispute resolution)
(iii) CEDAW Committee General Recommendation 34 on the Rights of Rural Women, para. [54]
(iv)   CEDAW Committee General Recommendation 36 on the Right of girls and women to education, paras. [24, 63, 81]
(v)   CEDAW Committee General Recommendation 16 on Unpaid women workers in rural and urban family enterprises
(vi)   CEDAW Committee General Recommendation 37, para. [51]
(vii) SDG5: Achieve gender equality and empower all women and girls

Key Elements of Good Laws

The key elements of good laws to support the establishment, development, and profitability of women-owned MSMEs are addressed to the broader regulatory framework for doing business as well as specific laws that support MSMEs' development, access to financial services, and resilience to disaster and climate change shocks and stresses. It requires the establishment of cross-sector institutional frameworks to develop and/or advise the government on women's entrepreneurship, including the women's ministry and women's organizations in the governance institutions on the basis of gender parity.

Key Elements of Good Laws to Support Women in MSMEs

- Provide for the establishment of programs for business skills education for women and girls.
- Remove barriers to women's labor market participation, such as providing access to childcare.
- Prohibit direct and indirect gender discrimination in access to financial and business services and monitor compliance.
- Ensure that the national census and other key data-gathering, analyses, and reports on all economic data with gender-disaggregated analysis to underpin an MSMEs policy.
- Create a general enabling environment for MSMEs' development, such as national laws, secondary or subordinate legislation, that:
  - Streamlines registration and business administration for micro and small enterprises to encourage formalization.
  - Provides tax incentives to register and operate MSMEs.
  - Provides access to transport and facilities for supply chains, especially for rural women.
  - Provides for the establishment of business incubation support, start-up grants, and access to training.

Examples of Good Laws

The following good law examples focus on laws made specially to support MSMEs' development: (i) gender-inclusive laws on MSMEs' development: Viet Nam, Angola, India, and Dominican Republic; and (ii) laws that promote MSMEs' development and financing that women can access: Mexico and Gabon.

Example of Type 1: Gender-Inclusive Laws on MSMEs' Development
Viet Nam Law for the Provision of Assistance for Small and Medium-Sized Enterprises, 2017 (SME Law)
This law aims to support SMEs to develop and grow through: • access to credit supported by a state credit guarantee fund for SMEs; • a lower tax rate for a start-up period; • simpler tax and accounting regimes for microenterprises; • release of land and establishment of industrial precincts with rent subsidies for SMEs engaged in processing of primary produce; • access to technology, technical support, advice, and start-up incubation premises; • remissions from taxes, fees, land rental, land levies, and other financial obligations; and • direct grants. It provides the regulations on principles, contents, and resources of assistance and the various responsibilities related to the provision of assistance for SMEs.

Sources of funding for assisting SMEs include loans subsidized and guaranteed by the State, direct state budget funding, remissions from taxes, fees, land rental, land levies, and other financial obligations (Article 6). The SME law includes a definition of women-owned SMEs and provides that, all other things being equal, in competition for assistance, a women-owned SME or the SME that employs the most women, will receive priority.	**Article 3(1):** For the purpose of this Law… "women-owned SME" means an SME having one or more women owns at least 51% of its charter capital and at least a woman is the executive director of this enterprise. **Article 5(5):**…If more than one SME satisfy the conditions for the assistance in accordance with regulations of this Law, the women-owned SME and the SME using more women employees will be given priority.

Example of Type 1: Gender-Inclusive Laws on MSMEs' Development	
It also incorporates the international treaties to which Viet Nam has assented, which includes the CEDAW and the other core human rights treaties.[a]	**Article 5(1)**: Provision of assistance for SMEs shall comply with market rules and international treaties to which the Socialist Republic of Viet Nam is a signatory. **Article 13(3)**: Microenterprises and small enterprises will be given priority during contractor selection in accordance with regulations of law on bidding.

The SME Law is also supported by other national policy and secondary legislation, including:

- the Five-Year SME Development Plan (2016–2020), with specific targets for the development of the SME sector;
- Decision No. 601/QD-TTg (17 April 2013) establishing the SME Development Fund to support SMEs having feasible business plans and projects in prioritized sectors; and
- Circular 04/2014/TTLT-BKH-BTC (13 August 2014) on training support for SMEs.[b]

This is an example of a good law because it:

- provides general support to SMEs to help them become established and resilient,
- includes positive measures to support women-owned SMEs or SMEs that employ more women in access to assistance, and
- imports international treaty obligations into the laws' governing principles, which include the CEDAW.

Angola Law on Micro, Small and Medium Enterprises, 2011

The Angola MSMEs Law[c] is a good law example because it mentions the types of programs required as incentives, including tax and financial.	**Article 1**: This establishes the rules regarding the differential treatment of MSMEs, as well as the conditions of access to their incentives and facilities **Article 2**: This law and the regulations arising from it shall apply to MSMEs, incorporated and registered in the national territory, as instruments to promote national private entrepreneurship and formalize the economy, promote employment, competitiveness, and reduce poverty, under the terms defined below. **Article 11**: (Incentive Programs) 1. The policy of support to MSMEs integrates fiscal and financial incentive programs, organizational, skills creation, innovation, and technological capacity building, created by the Executive, formulated through the consultation of business associations, and/or recognized national professionals. 2. The Executive shall structure *specific tax, financial and organizational incentive programs for women and young people, including training courses and/ or professional overcoming with the involvement of recognized national business associations and/or professionals.*

Example of Type 1: Gender-Inclusive Laws on MSMEs' Development	
India Micro, Small and Medium Enterprises Development Act, 2006	
The India MSME law ensures a minimum representation of both women's enterprises and microenterprises in the National Board for Micro, Small and Medium Enterprises. This is a good law provision because it ensures that women-led MSMEs have a voice in the national policy body.	**Section 3**: Establishment of Board. (i) With effect from such date as the Central Government may, by notification, appoint, there shall be established, for the purposes of this Act, a Board to be known as the National Board for Micro, Small and Medium Enterprises... (ii) The Board shall consist of the following members, namely: twenty persons to represent the associations of micro, small and medium enterprises, including not less than three persons representing associations of women's enterprises and not less than three persons representing associations of micro enterprises, to be appointed by the Central Government.
Dominican Republic Law Establishing a Regulatory Regime for the Development and Competitiveness of Micro, Small and Medium-Sized Enterprises (MSMEs), 2008	
The Dominican Republic MSMEs Law[d] takes a step further than most MSME development laws by imposing quotas for government procurement. This is a good law example because it has quantifiable quotas to support the policy objective.	**Article 25**: Purchasing of goods and services. State institutions, at the time of purchasing goods and services, must make 15% of the same to micro, small, and medium-sized enterprises (MSMEs), provided that the goods and services demanded by these institutions are offered by MSMEs. **Article 26**: MSMEs run by women. In the case of *micro, small and medium-sized enterprises run by women with more than 50% of their share capital*, state institutions must purchase 20% of the goods and services from them, provided that the goods and services demanded by those institutions are offered by them.

[a] OHCHR. United Nations Human Rights OHCHR—Viet Nam Homepage.
[b] World Bank. 2020. *Women, Business and the Law 2020*. Washington, DC. p. 10.
[c] *Lei No. 30/11 Lei das Micro, Pequenas e Médias Empresas* (informal translation).
[d] *Ley No. 488-08, establece un Régimen Regulatorio para el Desarrollo y Competitivdad de las Micro, Pequenas y Medianas Empresas* (MIPYMES) [Law No. 488-08, establishing a Regulatory Regime for the Development and Competitiveness of Micro, Small and Medium Enterprises (MSMEs)]. 30 December 2008. (informal translation).

Example of Type 2: Laws That Promote MSMEs' Development and Financing that Women Can Access

Mexico Law for the Development of the Competitiveness of Micro, Small and Medium Enterprises, 2002

The Mexico MSME Law[a] guarantees equal opportunities rather than making special measures for women, and its sets out a relatively comprehensive range of support services for MSMEs.

Additionally, the Secretariat will promote schemes to facilitate access to public financing and private to MSMEs, with *equal opportunities for women and men*, putting special emphasis on ensuring access to such funding for women.

This is a set of good law provisions because it guarantees equal opportunities for women and men and is very proactive on MSMEs' development in general.

Article 7: The Secretariat will design, encourage, and promote the creation of guarantee instruments and mechanisms, as well as other schemes to facilitate access to financing for MSMEs, *with equal opportunities for women and men...*

Article 10: The planning and implementation of policies and actions to promote competitiveness of MSMEs should meet the following criteria:..

III. Focus efforts in accordance with regional, state, and municipal needs, potential and vocations, *taking into account the gender perspective and promoting equality between women and men* at all times...

Article 11: For the execution of the policies and actions contained in the previous article, the following Programs shall be considered:

(i)   Business training and education, as well as advisory and consultancy services for MSMEs;
(ii)   Promotion of the creation of business incubators and training of entrepreneurs;
(iii) Training, integration, and support to Production Chains, Business Groups, and local and regional economic development opportunities;
(iv)   Promoting a technological culture in MSMEs; modernization, innovation, and development technology;
(v)   Development of suppliers and distributors with MSMEs;
(vi)   Consolidation of exportable supply;
(vii) General information on economic matters in accordance with the needs of MSMEs; and
(viii) Promotion of sustainable development within the framework of applicable ecological regulations.

Gabon Law on the Promotion of Small and Medium Enterprises and Small and Medium Industries, 2005

The Gabon MSME Law[b] does not have specific gender provisions, but it is a good example of the types of support that enable MSMEs' development and benefit both women and men.

This is a good law example of the scope of an MSMEs law, although it is not specific to gender.

Article 9. The following advantages are open to SMEs–SMIs approved in accordance with the provisions of this law:

(i)   access to public funding agencies of small and medium-sized businesses;
(ii)   priority access to public procurement;
(iii) exemption for 5 years from taxes on profits and customs taxes on inputs, in accordance with the texts in force;
(iv)   the preferential pricing of petroleum products and the costs of transporting materials;
(v)   equipment and miscellaneous products;
(vi)   preferential pricing of fees of assistance from any approved public body; and
(vii) interest rate subsidies by the State.

[a] *Ley Para el Desarrollo de la Competitividad De La Micro, Pequeña y Mediana Empresa*, 30 de diciembre de 2002—Última reforma publicada DOF 13-08-2019 (informal translation).
[b] *Promotion des PME—PMI* (informal translation).

Part 6
Concluding Observations

The research for this report has revealed that legislation is a key ingredient to overcome the gender inequalities that increase women's risk to disasters and climate change, and promote women's participation in climate action and resilience-building. Laws play a foundational role in guaranteeing women's rights, including their right to participate equally in governance and to have their specific needs met. In addition to gender mainstreaming laws on climate change and disaster risk management, laws must also address the underpinning factors that lead to women's inequality. This is influenced by the socioeconomic circumstances in which women live their normal lives and require proactive laws.

Each country needs to ensure that the main legal pylons to promote equality and prohibit discrimination against women are developed and implemented to strengthen women's resilience to climate and disaster risk. It requires a holistic approach, as identified by CEDAW Committee GR37.

This report and the legislative framework provide the foundation to ensure that women's human rights are upheld in the context of disasters and climate change impacts. This entails making disaster risk management and climate change adaptation measures gender-sensitive and protecting women from sex- and gender-based discrimination and violence. Crucially, while many laws and policies on climate change and disasters focus on women as a vulnerable group, there is an overarching need to address the underlying inequalities between men and women and the need for women's empowerment. This report has outlined the importance of preventing violence and sexual harassment in all contexts and implementing positive measures based on women's human rights to equality and freedom from direct and indirect discrimination. It has also emphasized the importance of strengthening women's economic resilience and ensuring substantive equality across access to inheritance, land and assets, decent employment, and business opportunities. The report and the legislative framework provide ways forward to support women as key stakeholders and active participants in creating and implementing disaster risk management and climate change solutions.

Appendix: Terminology

Climate change adaptation: "Adjustment in natural or human systems in response to actual or expected climatic stimuli or their effects, which moderates harm or exploits beneficial opportunities."

Source: United Nations Framework Convention on Climate Change (UNFCCC) Terminology.

Climate change mitigation: In the context of climate change, a human intervention to reduce the sources or enhance the sinks of greenhouse gases. Examples include using fossil fuels more efficiently for industrial processes or electricity generation, switching to solar energy or wind power, improving the insulation of buildings, and expanding forests and other "sinks" to remove greater amounts of carbon dioxide from the atmosphere.

Source: UNFCCC Terminology.

Committee on the Elimination of Discrimination against Women (CEDAW): The body of independent experts that monitors implementation of the CEDAW Convention. It is composed of 23 experts from all regions of the world, nominated by their governments and elected by the States Parties to the Convention. Its mandate includes to receive State Parties' mandatory reports and review their individual progress under the Convention, as well as to make general recommendations on interpretation and implementation of the Convention (Articles 17–30 of the Convention). CEDAW is also mandated to consider individual and group complaints submitted to it about violations of the Convention by a State that has ratified the Optional Protocol to the Convention.

Source: CEDAW Convention and United Nations Human Rights, Office of the High Commissioner, 2020.

Convention on the Elimination of All Forms of Discrimination against Women (CEDAW): A binding international treaty that commenced in 1981. With 189 State Parties, it is has near-universal application and is a highly authoritative treaty. Fiji has agreed to be bound by the CEDAW Convention without any current reservations.

Sources: United Nations Treaty Collection; and United Nations Human Rights, Office of the High Commissioner, 2020.

Disaster risk management: The application of disaster risk reduction policies and strategies to prevent new disaster risk, reduce existing disaster risk, and manage residual risk, contributing to the strengthening of resilience and reduction of disaster losses.

Source: United Nations Office for Disaster Risk Reduction (UNDRR) Terminology 2017.

Disaster risk reduction: Disaster risk reduction is aimed at preventing new and reducing existing disaster risk and managing residual risk, all of which contribute to strengthening resilience and therefore to the achievement of sustainable development.

Source: UNDRR Terminology 2017.

Discrimination: Any distinction, exclusion, or preference made on the basis of status such as race, color, sex, age, disability, ethnicity, language, religion, political or other opinion, national or social origin, property, birth, sexual orientation, indigenous, refugee, or other status, which has the effect of nullifying or impairing the recognition and enjoyment or exercise on an equal basis with others, of any of the human rights and fundamental freedoms in the political, economic, social, cultural. or civil or any other field.

Sources: International Covenant on Civil and Political Rights (ICCPR) Article 26; International Convention on the Elimination of All Forms of Racial Discrimination (CERD) Preamble and Article 1; CEDAW Article 1 and Convention on the Rights of Persons with Disabilities (CRPD) Preamble and Article 2.

Discrimination against women: Any distinction, exclusion, or restriction made on the basis of sex which has the effect or purpose of impairing or nullifying the recognition, enjoyment, or exercise by women irrespective of their marital status, on the basis of equality of all men and women, of human rights and fundamental freedoms in the political, economic, social, cultural, civil or any other field. The definition includes not just **direct discrimination** (or intentional discrimination), but any act that has the effect of creating or perpetuating inequality between men and women which may be indirect discrimination.

Source: CEDAW Article 1; UN Women Gender Equality Glossary (accessed 2020).

Multiple discrimination: Where a person can experience discrimination on two or several grounds, in the sense that discrimination is compounded or aggravated.

Source: Meghan Campbell. 2015. CEDAW and Women's Intersecting Identities. A Pioneering New Approach to Intersectional Discrimination. Rev. direito GV 11(2) Jul–Dec. https://doi.org/10.1590/1808-2432201521.

Intersectional discrimination: Where several grounds operate and interact with each other at the same time in such a way that they are inseparable.

Sources: CEDAW Committee General recommendation 25; CRPD General comment No. 3 (2016) Article 6 Women and girls with disabilities.

Empowerment: Refers to increasing the personal, political, social, or economic strength of individuals and communities, both women and men. Empowerment of all women and girls' concerns gaining power and control over their own lives. It involves awareness-raising, building self-confidence, expansion of choices, increased access to and control over resources and actions to transform the structures and institutions which reinforce and perpetuate gender discrimination and inequality. The core of empowerment lies in the ability of a person to control their own destiny. This implies that to be empowered, all women and girls must not only have equal capabilities (such as education and health) and equal access to resources and opportunities (such as land and employment), but they must also have the agency to use these rights, capabilities, resources, and opportunities to make strategic choices and decisions (such as is provided through leadership opportunities and participation in political institutions).

Source: United Nations Children's Fund (UNICEF), Gender Equality: Glossary of Terms and Concepts, 2017.

Gender: Refers to the roles, behaviors, activities, and attributes that a given society at a given time considers appropriate for men and women. In addition to the social attributes and opportunities associated with being male and female and the relationships between women and men and girls and boys, gender also refers to the relations between women and those between men. These attributes, opportunities, and relationships are socially constructed and are learned through socialization processes. They are context and/or time-specific and changeable. Gender determines what is expected, allowed, and valued in a woman or a man in a given context. In most societies there are differences and inequalities between women and men in responsibilities assigned, activities undertaken, access to and control over resources, as well as decision-making opportunities. Gender is part of the broader sociocultural context, as are other important criteria for sociocultural analysis including class, race, poverty level, ethnic group, sexual orientation, age, and others (see discrimination above).

Sources: UN Women Gender Equality Glossary (accessed 2020); UN Women Office of the Special Adviser to the Secretary-General on Gender Issues and Advancement of Women (OSAGI) Gender Mainstreaming—Concepts and definitions.

Gender analysis: A critical examination of how differences in gender roles, activities, needs, opportunities, and rights or entitlements affect men, women, girls, and boys in certain situations or contexts. Gender analysis examines the relationships between females and males and their access to and control of resources and the constraints they face relative to each other. A gender analysis should be integrated into all sector assessments or situational analyses to ensure that gender-based injustices and inequalities are not exacerbated by interventions, and that, where possible, greater equality and justice in gender relations are promoted.

Sources: UNICEF, United Nations Population Fund (UNFPA), United Nations Development Programme (UNDP), UN Women. Gender Equality, UN Coherence and You, UN Women Gender Equality Glossary (accessed 2020).

Gender-based violence (GBV) or violence against women (VAW): These are overall terms to refer to any harmful act that is perpetrated against a person's will and that is based on socially ascribed (gender) differences between females and males. The nature and extent of specific types of GBV vary across cultures, countries, and regions and can occur either in public or in private life. Examples include sexual violence, including sexual exploitation and abuse and forced prostitution; domestic violence including physical, verbal, and socioeconomic violence as well as threats; trafficking; forced or early marriage; harmful traditional practices such as female genital mutilation; honor killings; and widow inheritance. As these acts are mostly done against women they are also described as VAW.

Sources: Adapted from UNICEF, UNFPA, UNDP, UN Women Gender Equality Glossary (accessed 2020).

Gender equality: Refers to the equal rights, responsibilities, and opportunities of women and men, and girls and boys. Equality does not mean that women and men will become the same, but that all women's and men's rights, responsibilities, and opportunities will not depend on whether they are born male or female. Gender equality implies that the interests, needs, and priorities of both women and men are taken into consideration, recognizing the diversity of different groups of women and men. Gender equality is not only a women's issue, but should concern and fully engage men as well as women. Equality between all women and men is seen both as a human rights issue and as a precondition for, and indicator of, sustainable people-centered development.

Sources: UN Women, OSAGI Gender Mainstreaming—Concepts and definitions; UN Women Gender Equality Glossary (accessed 2020).

Gender equality includes not only **formal equality** (de jure equality—treating men and women the same), but also includes **substantive equality** (de facto equality—equality of outcome in fact for both women and men).

Source: CEDAW and General Recommendation No. 25.

Gender gap: Refers to any disparity between women and men's condition or position in society. It is often used to refer to a difference in average earnings between women and men, e.g., "gender pay gap." However, gender gaps can be found in many areas, such as the four pillars that the World Economic Forum uses to calculate its Gender Gap Index: economic participation and opportunity, educational attainment, health and survival, and political empowerment.

Sources: Hausmann, R., L. D. Tyson, S. Zahidi, eds. 2012. The Global Gender Gap Report 2012. World Economic Forum, Geneva, Switzerland; UN Women Gender Equality Glossary (accessed 2020).

Gender mainstreaming: The chosen approach of the United Nations system and international community toward realizing progress on women's and girl's rights, as a subset of human rights to which the United Nations dedicates itself. It is not a goal or objective on its own. It is a strategy for implementing greater equality for women and girls in relation to men and boys. Mainstreaming a gender perspective is the process of assessing the implications for women and men of any planned action, including legislation, policies, or programs, in all areas and at all levels. It is a way to make women's as well as men's concerns and experiences an integral dimension of the design, implementation, monitoring, and evaluation of policies and programs in all political, economic, and societal spheres so that women and men benefit equally and inequality is not perpetuated. The ultimate goal is to achieve gender equality.

Source: UN Women. 2017. Gender Equality Glossary.

Gender neutral: Refers to where a law, policy, project, or program does not affect gender norms and roles of women and men and they are not worsened or improved.

Source: UN Women Gender Equality Glossary (accessed 2020).

Gender parity: Another term for equal representation of all women and men in a given area, for example, gender parity in organizational leadership or higher education. Working toward gender parity (equal representation) is a key part of achieving gender equality, and one of the twin strategies, alongside gender mainstreaming.

Source: UN Women Gender Equality Glossary (accessed 2020).

Gender perspective: A way of seeing or analyzing, which looks at the impact of gender on people's opportunities, social roles, and interactions. This way of seeing is what enables one to carry out gender analysis and, subsequently, to mainstream a gender perspective into any proposed program, policy, or organization.

Source: UN Women Gender Equality Glossary (accessed 2020).

Gender positive or gender transformative: Refers to where a law, policy, project, or program not only considers, but addresses gender norms and roles, with a view to transforming or changing them to achieve positive development outcomes and transform unequal gender relations to promote shared power, control of resources, decision-making, and support for all women's empowerment.

Source. Adapted from UN Women Gender Equality Glossary (accessed 2020).

Gender-responsive: Pays attention to specific needs of women and men and intentionally uses gender considerations to affect the design, implementation, and results of legislation, policies, and programs.

Source: UNICEF 2017 Gender Equality Glossary of Terms and Concepts.

Gender-responsive budgeting: A method of determining the extent to which government expenditure has detracted from or come nearer to the goal of gender equality. A gender-responsive budget is not a separate budget for women, but rather a tool that analyzes budget allocations, public spending, and taxation from a gender perspective and can be subsequently used to advocate for reallocation of budget line items to better respond to all women's priorities as well as men's, making them, as the name suggests, gender-responsive.

Source: Adapted UN Women Asia and the Pacific (accessed 2020).

Gender-sensitive: Considers gender norms, roles, and relations taking into account sociocultural factors, but does not actively address gender inequalities.

Source: World Health Organization. 2012. *Mainstreaming Gender in Health Adaptation to Climate Change Programmes.*

International Labour Organization (ILO): The ILO is a unique United Nations body composed of three groups—governments/States, employers organizations, and workers organizations. This is referred to as a "tripartite" structure, and the employers organizations and workers organizations are referred to as the "social partners." There are 187 member States. Its primary function is to develop and supervise the application of international labor standards for work in ILO Conventions that now number 190. The work of the ILO includes the function of the Committee of Experts of the Application of Conventions and Recommendations.

Source: ILO Website, "About the ILO": https://www.ilo.org.

ILO Committee of Experts of the Application of Conventions and Recommendations (CEACR): The ILO CEACR, often called the ILO Committee of Experts, is an independent body of the ILO consisting of some 20 judges, academics, and lawyers drawn from countries that are geographically, culturally, and linguistically distinct, with differing legal systems. The CEACR is responsible for conducting an examination of laws and practices of member States to assess their compliance with the provisions of ratified ILO Conventions. Their assessments are published annually, together with a General Survey on a particular topic(s) of conventions across all member States. General Observations are also made when there are common issues of noncompliance to assist and guide all member States. In the process of assessing compliance, there is necessarily interpretation of the meaning of Conventions, that is regarded as authoritative.

Source: ILO Website, "Committee of Experts on the Application of Conventions and Recommendations": https://www.ilo.org.

Women's rights to land: A phrase that must be understood holistically and in a manner, which is grounded in the international human rights framework. These rights entail the ability of all women to own, use, access, control, transfer, inherit, and otherwise take decisions about land and related resources. They also encompass all women's rights to secure land tenure and to meaningfully participate at all stages of land law, policy, and program development, from assessment and analysis; program planning and design; budgeting and financing; implementation; to monitoring and evaluation. Women's land rights must also be understood in the context of intersecting forms of discrimination.

Source: Office of the High Commissioner for Human Rights (OHCHR) and UN Women. *Realizing Women's Rights to Land and Other Productive Resources 2013.* p. 1.

www.ingramcontent.com/pod-product-compliance
Lightning Source LLC
Chambersburg PA
CBHW061235270326
41929CB00031B/3497